Globalization and its Critics

International Political Economy Series

General Editor: **Timothy M. Shaw**, Professor of Political Science and International Development Studies, and Director of the Centre for Foreign Policy Studies, Dalhousie University, Halifax, Nova Scotia

Titles include:

Francis Adams, Satya Dev Gupta and Kidane Mengisteab (*editor*)
GLOBALIZATION AND THE DILEMMAS OF THE STATE IN THE SOUTH

Edward A. Comor (*editor*)
THE GLOBAL POLITICAL ECONOMY OF COMMUNICATION

Barry K. Gills (*editor*)
GLOBALIZATION AND THE POLITICS OF RESISTANCE

Stephen D. McDowell
GLOBALIZATION, LIBERALIZATION AND POLICY CHANGE
A Political Economy of India's Communications Sector

Ronaldo Munck and Peter Waterman (*editors*)
LABOUR WORLDWIDE IN THE ERA OF GLOBALIZATION
Alternative Union Models in the New World Order

Ted Schrecker (*editor*)
SURVIVING GLOBALISM
The Social and Environmental Challenges

Caroline Thomas and Peter Wilkin (*editors*)
GLOBALIZATION AND THE SOUTH

Kenneth P. Thomas
CAPITAL BEYOND BORDERS
States and Firms in the Auto Industry, 1960–94

Geoffrey R. D. Underhill (*editor*)
THE NEW WORLD ORDER IN INTERNATIONAL FINANCE

Amy Verdun
EUROPEAN RESPONSES TO GLOBALIZATION AND FINANCIAL MARKET INTEGRATION
Perceptions of Economic and Monetary Union in Britain, France and Germany

International Political Economy Series
Series Standing Order ISBN 0–333–71708–2 hardcover
Series Standing Order ISBN 0–333–71110–6 paperback
(*outside North America only*)

You can receive future titles in this series as they are published by placing a standing order. Please contact your bookseller or, in case of difficulty, write to us at the address below with your name and address, the title of the series and one of the ISBNs quoted above.

Customer Services Department, Macmillan Distribution Ltd, Houndmills, Basingstoke, Hampshire RG21 6XS, England

Globalization and its Critics

Perspectives from Political Economy

Edited by

Randall D. Germain
Senior Lecturer in Politics
University of Newcastle upon Tyne

Foreword by Anthony Payne

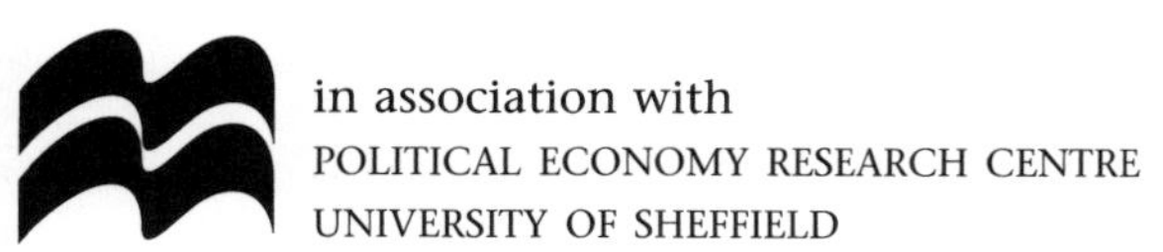

First published in Great Britain 2000 by
MACMILLAN PRESS LTD
Houndmills, Basingstoke, Hampshire RG21 6XS and London
Companies and representatives throughout the world

A catalogue record for this book is available from the British Library.

ISBN 0–333–68211–4 hardcover
ISBN 0–333–68212–2 paperback

First published in the United States of America 2000 by
ST. MARTIN'S PRESS, INC.,
Scholarly and Reference Division,
175 Fifth Avenue, New York, N.Y. 10010

ISBN 0–312–22414–1

Library of Congress Cataloging-in-Publication Data
Globalization and its critics : perspectives from political economy /
edited by Randall D. Germain.
p. cm. — (International political economy series)
Includes bibliographical references and index.
ISBN 0–312–22414–1 (cloth)
1. International economic relations. I. Germain, Randall D.,
1961– . II. Series.
HF1359.G5828 1999
337—dc21 99–18535
CIP

This book is printed on paper suitable for recycling and made from fully managed and sustained forest sources.

10 9 8 7 6 5 4 3 2 1
09 08 07 06 05 04 03 02 01 00

Printed and bound in Great Britain by
Antony Rowe Ltd, Chippenham, Wiltshire

Contents

List of Figures and Tables

Figures

Tables

Foreword

This book is the latest of a number of books produced by research groups convened under the auspices of the Political Economy Research Centre (PERC) of the University of Sheffield. PERC itself was created in late 1993 in the belief that the perspectives of the past cannot address the problems posed by the world-wide economic and political transformation of the last decade or so. Its mission has thus been to explore the new issues in political economy from an interdisciplinary standpoint. For a new research centre committed to such an intellectual project, the very concept of globalization itself was manifestly ripe for critical interrogation for, as is well known, the term has quickly generated as many critics as advocates. Randall Germain, as PERC's first Assistant Director, saw the need to both contextualize and problematize the concept of globalization from a political economy perspective, and accordingly organized the workshop from which this book subsequently emerged. For all that 'globalization studies' has now become a markedly crowded, and somewhat disorganized, field of study, this book contributes significantly to the debate, not least by setting out its main contours in signally clear fashion. It also stands as a tangible reflection of the much wider contribution which Randall, better known to us of course as Randy, made to the work of PERC in its first few years of existence.

ANTHONY PAYNE
Director of PERC

Acknowledgements

This volume has been a long time in the making. It was originally conceived during the summer of 1995, when I was Assistant Director of (PERC) at the University of Sheffield. After the initial preparations were completed a workshop was organized by PERC and convened at the University of Sheffield in June 1996. Funding for that event, for which most of these contributions were first written, came from a number of sources associated with PERC. In particular, I wish to thank the following people for their encouragement and financial support: David Marquand (then the Director of PERC), Tony Payne (Head of the Politics Department at the University of Sheffield), John Bird (Head of the Law Department at the University of Sheffield) and Antony Fretwell-Downing (then Head of the Management School at the University of Sheffield). Sylvia McColm organized the workshop with her characteristic efficiency and charm and Susanne Presland acted as rapporteur. Although they did not contribute written chapters to this project, Ankie Hoogvelt and Hugo Radice certainly enriched the workshop discussions with their usual energy and insight. The authors are grateful for the hard work, support and encouragement offered by all of the above. Tim Shaw has shown remarkable support for the time and effort required to produce this collection of essays for his series. At the University of Newcastle upon Tyne, where the task of editing the chapters has been undertaken, I would like to thank Tim Gray for providing the resources to compile the references and index, and Bertrem Welker and Guy Scuffham for efficiently carrying out those tasks.

RANDALL D. GERMAIN

The editor and publishers would like to thank the following for permission to reprint copyright material: Table 8.1 (*Levels of world economic performance, 1500–1992*), reprinted by permission of the OECD; Table 8.2 (*Per capita levels of industrialization*), reprinted by permission of the Banca di Roma; and Table 8.3 (*Geographic location of large firms' patenting, 1981–88*), reprinted by permission of Taylor & Francis Books Ltd.

Notes on the Contributors

Philip G. Cerny is Professor of International Political Economy at the University of Leeds. His work has been published in journals such as the *Review of International Political Economy, Policy Sciences, Government and Opposition, Millennium* and *International Organization*. He has edited *Finance and World Politics* (Edward Elgar), and is the author of *The Politics of Grandeur: Ideological Aspects of de Gaulle's Foreign Policy* (Cambridge University Press) and *The Changing Architecture of Politics* (Sage).

Randall D. Germain is Senior Lecturer in Politics at the University of Newcastle upon Tyne. His work has been published in journals such as *New Political Economy*, the *Review of International Studies* and the *European Journal of International Relations*. He is the author of *The International Organization of Credit: States and Global Finance in the World-Economy* (Cambridge University Press).

R.J. Barry Jones is Professor and Head of the Department of Politics at the University of Reading. He has published widely on interdependence and international political economy, most recently in the journal *New Political Economy*, and is the author of *Globalisation and Interdependence in the International Political Economy: Rhetoric and Reality* (Pinter).

John MacLean is Senior Lecturer in International Relations at the School of Social Sciences, University of Sussex. His work has been published in *Millennium*, and his latest publication is 'The Ideology of the End of Marxism/End of Socialism Thesis', in Kaldor and Einhorn (eds), *Citizenship and Democracy in Contemporary Europe* (Edward Elgar).

Ronen Palan is Lecturer in International Relations at the School of Social Sciences, University of Sussex. He is one of the founding editors of the *Review of International Political Economy*, and has co-edited (with Barry Gills) *Transcending the State-Global Divide: A Neo-structuralist Agenda in International Relations* (Lynne Rienner). His work has been published in journals such as the *Review of International Studies, Political Geography* and *International Studies Quarterly*, and he is most recently the co-author (with Jason Abbott) of *State Strategies in the Global Political Economy* (Cassell).

Jonathan Perraton is Baring Fellow in Political Economy at the Political Economy Research Centre and a Lecturer in the Economics Department at the University of Sheffield. His work has been published in *New Political Economy*, and he is co-author (with David Goldblatt, David Held and Anthony McGrew) of *Global Transformations: Politics, Economics, Culture* (Polity Press).

Timothy J. Sinclair is Lecturer in International Political Economy in the Department of Politics and International Studies at the University of Warwick. His work has been published in the journals *Review of International Political Economy* and *Policy Sciences*. His publications include, with Robert W. Cox, *Approaches to World Order* (Cambridge University Press), *Approaches to Global Governance Theory* (co-edited with Martin Hewson: forthcoming, State University of New York Press) and *Structure and Agency in International Capital Mobility* (co-edited with Kenneth P. Thomas: forthcoming, Macmillan/St Martin's Press).

Nick Stevenson is Lecturer in the Department of Sociological Studies, University of Sheffield. His work has been published in journals such as *Citizenship Studies, The European Journal of Cultural Policy* and *The Sociological Quarterly*. He is the author of *Understanding Media Cultures: Social Theory and Mass Communication* (Sage).

Ngai-Ling Sum is Simon Research Fellow at the University of Manchester. She was previously Alec Horsley Research Fellow at the Political Economy Research Centre, University of Sheffield. She has published in the journals *Economy and Society* and *New Political Economy*. She is also the author of various book chapters on 'Greater China' and East Asian regionalisms and is currently working on a manuscript entitled *New Regionalisms and Identity Politics in East Asia*.

Michael Talalay has taught in the UK and Canada, and is currently a Senior Consultant for Cambridge Technology Partners. He and Chris Farrands edit the book series 'Technology and the Global Political Economy' published by Routledge. His work has appeared in the journal *Competition and Change*, and he has co-edited, with Chris Farrands and Roger Tooze, *Technology, Culture and Competitiveness: Change in the World Political Economy* (Routledge).

List of Abbreviations

APEC	Asia Pacific Economic Community
ASEAN	Association of South East Asian Nations
ERM	exchange rate mechanism (Europe)
EU	European Union
FDI	foreign direct investment
GATT	General Agreement on Tariffs and Trade
GDP	gross domestic product
IMF	International Monetary Fund
IPE	international political economy
IR	international relations
ISP	Internet Service Provider
IT	information technology
IWS	industrial welfare state
JICA	Japan International Co-operation Agency
LDC	less-developed country
MNC	multinational corporation
NAFTA	North American Free Trade Agreement
NIC	newly industrializing country
OECD	Organization for Economic Cooperation and Development
ODA	official development assistance
R&D	research and development
TISA	technology-based international strategic alliance
TNB	transnational bank
TNC	transnational corporation
WTO	World Trade Organization

Introduction: Globalization and its Critics

Randall D. Germain

The term globalization, we are told, did not enter the vocabulary of everyday life until about 1960 (Waters, 1995: 2). If that is accurate, then it has made astonishing progress over the past 40 years. There are few terms in current use which can claim such a dominant hold over our imagination. The familiarity of this term, however, belies its decidedly Janus-faced quality. The popular press cannot decide on balance whether globalization has a liberating or a pernicious effect on society, while those who are paid to evaluate the strategies of businesses and others active in the global market place cannot decide whether institutions should adapt to a globalized world or make that world work for them. Some argue that a global world has come into being lock, stock and barrel, while others point to the inherent unevenness of globalization in the face of many natural and social obstacles. Perhaps the only certainty here is that globalization is as inherently contested as a 'reality' as it is as a concept or a representation of that 'reality'. Acknowledging this conceptual and material ambiguity is the starting point for the contributors to this volume, who hope to take current debates on globalization beyond increasingly standardized and well-ploughed intellectual paths.

In order to evaluate properly the contribution which the authors of this volume make, however, it is necessary to be clear about which paths in these debates they refuse to follow. One such path is to define globalization in narrowly circumscribed terms, whether economically, politically, culturally or technologically, and then to examine how globalization thus defined is reshaping certain elements of the social world. Globalization, for example, has often been defined almost purely in financial terms and explored with respect to its impact on markets or states. Although the empirical detail resulting from such studies is indeed valuable, the balance necessary for evaluating the place of globalization as articulated throughout the broader constitution of social life becomes compromised. For these studies, globalization is viewed as defining social life rather than as being one dimension within its broader parameters. Such a narrow, circumscribed view of the meaning of globalization is refused by the authors of this volume.

We also refuse to take the path of assuming globalization to be a process imbued with a set of exogenous determinants. It is neither a reality whose dynamics are established 'out there' (beyond the reach of organized political, economic and social agents) nor a process whose meaning is straightforward and unproblematic. In line with other recent critical inquiries into globalization (e.g., Ruigrok and van Tulder, 1995; Boyer and Drache, 1996; Hirst and Thompson, 1996; Mittelman, 1996), the authors of this volume consider one of their central intellectual tasks as being to provide an account of the experience which we have come to identify as globalization, and to place this experience into some kind of broad historical and intellectual context. In other words, the contributors to this volume do not simply criticize globalization for its pernicious effects (as important as these may be in their own right), but they explore both the social practices which make globalization possible in the first place and the shared intellectual and ideational frameworks of thought that allow globalization to colonize our way of thinking about the social world. They attempt to provide ways of thinking about globalization that bring it back into the domain of normal, everyday praxis.

Themes

This volume strengthens and deepens recent critiques of globalization which accept the proposition that it is an endogenous social phenomenon. It seeks to situate our understanding of globalization within the parameters of a critical social inquiry, and enlists three broad themes to accomplish this. First, this volume tries to match the multifaceted nature of the social relations of globalization with an approach to the subject which alternately spans and fuses the many disciplines that guide our inquiry. The sub-title of the volume, *Perspectives from Political Economy,* was chosen precisely to convey the need to bring together different analytical traditions and tools in order to provide the critical foundations for an approach to understanding globalization. Political economy, it should be emphasized here, is interpreted more broadly than a simple cross between political science and economics. This volume includes chapters from scholars whose principal disciplinary homes range from political science to economics, international relations, sociology and political theory. Their interaction speaks to the utility of conceptualizing globalization, to follow John MacLean's lead in Chapter 1, in strictly 'anti-disciplinary' terms.

The second theme is concerned with problematizing the relationship between social relations, discourse and practice within the context of the institutionalization of social relations. Most definitions of globalization follow Malcolm Waters's (1996: 3) account of it as 'a social process in which the constraints of geography on social and cultural arrangements recede and in which people become increasingly aware that they are receding'. The contributors to this volume question both the notion of globalization as a process (which lies at the heart of much of the literature) and the reliance on geography as the medium through which constraints on social and cultural arrangements are represented. While there is much of value in Waters's quintessentially sociological definition of globalization, it misses out some of the most dynamic ways in which social practices are linked to particular kinds of discourses and refracted through highly fluid sets of institutionalized social relations.

Here a focus on the changing contexts of institutions in terms of social relations, discourse and practice helps to broaden our conception of globalization and ground it very carefully in the manifold interests of actual human agents. Although difficult to accomplish in terms of concrete historical analysis, most of the contributors to this volume strive to balance their understanding of globalization between the intellectual non-starters of structural determinism and individual voluntarism. They also attempt to delineate the competing dynamics that lie at the heart of the struggle between those individual and collective agents who are at the forefront of globalizing practices and those agents whose motivations derive from different concerns. By acknowledging the different motivational sources of social agents and their embeddedness in broader structural constraints, the contributors to this volume push the debate on globalization beyond the binary oppositions of universal and particular, global and local, inside and outside. As a complex phenomenon globalization is rife with ambiguities, and these contributors work with rather than against the grain of such complexities.

Finally, the third theme can be succinctly stated as 'ideas matter'. Globalization is as much an ideational set of claims as it is a material set of practices, and the focus on the part of several contributors to this volume on the complex place of ideas or modes of thought within the dynamic of globalization represents a belief that globalization cannot be comprehended adequately without considering the ideational dimension of social life. Globalization in part exists because of the very categories of thought we use to give meaning to the social world; it is not simply that we react ideationally to an expanding world, but rather that we construct the terrain of globalization as much by particular forms of thought as by the achievements of our will. Especially significant here are the ways in which the ideational pillars of the modern sovereign state are in the throes of change. Many of the contributors to this volume are therefore keen to ask what makes globalization possible within the frameworks of academic investigation, as well as the more familiar set of social actors that usually inhabits investigations into 'globalization'.

Organization of the book

Globalization and its Critics is organized into three substantive sections. Part I is concerned to contextualize how we think about globalization. In Chapter 1, John MacLean explores one of the key philosophical issues lying behind the question of globalization from the point of view of the discipline of international relations, namely the extent to which we are using a transhistorical analytical framework to comprehend a deeply historicized development. He argues that the philosophical roots of international relations are deeply flawed, and demonstrates how they in fact reproduce rather than challenge the orthodoxy which is responsible for the intellectual possibility of an exploitative globalizing world. In order to move beyond the misrecognition of globalization which current international relations theory produces, MacLean argues that we must forge ahead with a new set of philosophical categories, a new route to understanding, if we are to introduce an emancipating and critical set of postulates capable of understanding (and indeed refashioning) the contemporary world.

In Chapter 2 Randall Germain issues a caution to those who would assume that the meaning of globalization is homogeneous both through time and across the hierarchies of social life. He employs an analytical framework adapted from the work of the French historian Fernand Braudel to argue that what we call globalization today – namely a set of specific globalizing social practices – has in fact a long history. Moreover, in the contemporary period the degree to which globalization has led to a compression or a shrinking of time must be carefully delineated. Germain approaches globalization from a historical perspective which suggests that time and space continue to refuse an unproblematized compression, and that history and the historical record exhibit far more complexity (and ambiguity) than many globalization theorists allow.

Chapter 3 closes Part I, and here Nick Stevenson considers globalization through the lens of cultural political economy. Stevenson argues that globalization has a much more complex configuration in the cultural realm than the usual binary distinctions between homogeneity and difference suggest. He frames his analysis with reference to the complexity and unevenness of the cultural practices of globalization, and argues that we should position the debates over these practices within the broader terrain of an ongoing struggle between modernity and an as-yet-to-be-articulated post-modernity. This theoretical position refuses to consider the cultural complexity of the contemporary era in terms of a reductionist link between economy and culture. Instead, Stevenson reaches for an approach informed by cultural political economy in order to place the reflexivity and fluidity of cultural relations into what he identifies as an open hermeneutic circle, where culture is neither completely structured by the 'hard' dimensions of modernity nor wholly undetermined by the 'softer' and more subtle axes ushered in by the post-modern condition.

Part II explores globalization by looking closely at what are commonly believed to be its central political and economic practices. In Chapter 4 Philip Cerny moves beyond his earlier work to explore the impact of the 'competition state' on the bonds of solidarity and community which have characterized social relations within the state since the middle years of the twentieth century. In the face of the growing pressures of economic globalization, the 'competition state' is paradoxically driving political globalization to new heights, and in the process is increasing the pace of economic, social and cultural change throughout a range of institutional settings. Like other contributors to this volume, Cerny sees no single set of consequences arising out of the contradictory and complex practices of globalization; rather we are entering into a fluid and open-ended era in which the state is both the engine room and the steering mechanism of what is at heart an agent-driven process.

In the following chapter Ronen Palan argues that political authority is being recast today as differently situated agents contest the changing parameters of governance. Globalization, he contends, is characterized by a new principle of territorial rationalization which is distinct from the nineteenth-century principle of nationality. The new principle of governance is competition, and it results in a form of state which Philip Cerny has called the 'competition state'. Although Palan broadly follows Cerny in this characterization of state authority today, he extends the argument to embrace other political dynamics such as regionalism and what he calls the new political geography. Here 'offshore' tax havens are the archetypal embodiment of how political authority is realized in an era of globalization. He concludes that a new concept of governance is required to apprehend adequately the current heterogeneity of state forms.

Jonathan Perraton shifts the focus of analysis in Chapter 6 towards markets, and asks how we can assume markets are global without considering them as social institutions for whose construction and maintenance human agency is required. Perraton argues that the way markets are constituted significantly affects the nature of economic processes, thus problematizing global markets by considering them in social terms. Here he builds upon and extends the insights of the transaction costs and new institutionalist literature in economics, which sees markets as only one way of organizing trade, and one moreover which is declining in importance as globalization alters the costs of organizing trade hierarchically (i.e., through trade networks and strategic alliances). According to Perraton, over the post-war period global markets have been constructed increasingly by large firms establishing export networks, thereby linking domestic markets through chains of institutionalized relationships that stretch across borders. Rather than being an exogenous creation, such markets are actively built and maintained by specific agents at significant cost to themselves.

Part III problematizes the practices of knowledge and technology as two of the most critical but as yet underexplored foundations of globalization. Timothy Sinclair uses Chapter 7 to unpack what he terms the 'deficit discourse', showing how this discourse is less an objective consideration of an unpalatable fact than a powerful rhetorical tool in the hands of specific social forces intent on pursuing a determined political strategy. He argues that we should view the deficit discourse as a mechanism of social and political hegemony conducive to entrenching certain modes of thought associated with globalizing elites. Drawing in part on Stephen Gill's notion of the 'new constitutionalism' and Robert Cox's emphasis on the diachronic rather than the synchronic, Sinclair argues that the deficit discourse makes certain unwarranted assumptions about the constitution and exercise of power in a neoliberal era. Although this discourse reinforces the global spread of

American norms, it also provides an intellectual space for the articulation of alternative mental frameworks precisely by situating a part of the new constitutionalist debate on political terrain. These debates, Sinclair reminds us, are always inherently political, and as such always contestable.

In Chapter 8 Michael Talalay considers the way in which technology and globalization shape one another. As an enabling factor, technology facilitates the practices lying at the heart of globalization. The more technology allows a fuller range of transportation and communication possibilities to flourish, the more it erodes the so-called tyranny of distance, that bundle of ideational and material constraints that have kept our social practices provincial in scope and scale for so long. This is the fulcrum upon which technology pivots as one of the key dimensions of globalization. It is one of the conditions which make for a global world, yet at the same time Talalay acknowledges that it is not a world in which all share equally. As he insists, a world which depends upon technology will be at the same time a world where rewards will increasingly go to those best able to exploit it.

In Chapter 9, Ngai-Ling Sum considers the changing shape of technological competitiveness in east Asia and its implications for the region's 'geo-governance'. She challenges understandings of globalization which seek to consider it either in 'placeless' terms which elide national and regional differences or in 'place-based' terms which are dependent upon traditional notions of sovereignty and territoriality for their meaning. Instead she develops a perspective which can accommodate variable relations between time and space in terms of how they interact with globalization to both reinforce and resist it. This perspective leads her to question the binary opposition of regionalization and globalization which infuses so many popular debates. She deploys the concept of 'geo-governance' as a suitable way of capturing the multilayered complexity of social re-ordering under way today. Sum explores how new identities are being forged in east Asia, arguing that these new 'techno-identities' are being driven by the changing constellation of technological imperatives now unfolding in the region. It is her contention that the complex interplay of these 'techno-identities', interests and strategies is shaping the contemporary contours of globalization in east Asia.

In the concluding chapter, R. J. Barry Jones adopts an agent-centred conception of globalization to explore the purposes and practices that various agents have brought to the debate on globalization. He concurs with Susan Strange (1986: ch. 2) in the importance of certain non-decisions as key causal determinants in the progressive liberalization and privatization of the global financial system, and on the impact which these developments have had for the increased practices of globalization more generally. Jones relates the purposes lying behind these non-decisions to the practices which emerged as a consequence, in order to stress the uneven nature of globalization today. While financial integration remains relatively high, many other indices are much more ambiguous. For Jones, both the purposes and practices of globalization remain contested, leading him to predict that debates over globalization will continue to excite our interest far into the future.

If this volume should leave one impression on readers, it is that the material and ideational 'reality' of globalization is far from settled. It is not simply, as many recent studies have argued, that globalization is uneven and ambiguous in its grip on the world; rather, it is that the entire ideational infrastructure of globalization is rent with motivational and ideological fissures which are replicated in the multiple ways we apprehend the meaning and representation of globalization to ourselves and others. Before we can identify the positive and negative aspects of globalization, we must more clearly and forcefully acknowledge the analytical and conceptual pitfalls that need to be overcome before we can fashion adequate mental maps to guide our understanding and awareness of globalization in the first place.

In various ways, and to varying extents, the chapters in this volume speak to that problem, to what must be done before we can proceed to evaluate honestly the place of globalization within our world. It is fundamentally a recognition that we know less about the social world than we often claim, and that we must work on improving our conceptual clarity and analytical rigour before significant advances in our understanding of globalization can be achieved. It is a call, in other words, to be as critical of ourselves as we are of the subjects which we investigate.

Part I

Contextualizing Globalization: Philosophy, History, Culture

1
Philosophical Roots of Globalization and Philosophical Routes to Globalization[1]

John MacLean

At first sight, the title of this chapter might imply, at least to those familiar with such things, that what follows is a contribution to the debate about 'globalization' situated firmly in the arena of unbounded post-modern linguistic playfulness. This is not the case, although I will aim to give due weight to the ways in which the complex structure of language – including its potential forms – can both reflect and hide the complexity of concrete substantive circumstances in the world, without at the same time reducing complex social practices simply to their linguistic forms. What the title does attempt at the outset is first, to capture a deep ambiguity in the notion of the 'philosophical roots' of globalization, and second, to assert an important (albeit densely problematic) space for philosophy as already embedded within the concept and practices of globalization.

With regard to the first of these, I will aim to interrogate that conception wherein 'philosophical roots' is understood as the appropriate intellectual tradition of the International Relations discipline,[2] established and reproduced in particular through classical Western political theory and in terms of which globalization is endowed with a long history. Most often, this is constructed as an evolutionary history, part of which – that is, up to Grotius – appears to predate the modern states system, and part of which then reproduces and legitimates the states-system up to the late-modern period in what is assumed to be a more-or-less constant form. Although this view has not gone unchallenged, in my view it has not yet been displaced as a central aspect of the dominant orthodoxy within the discipline.

This view of the dominant orthodoxy holds that the 'philosophical roots' of the discipline, understood as a historically established tradition located primarily in a set of texts, can help us to understand or explain contemporary phenomena in international relations, including globalization. However, this is in the simple, derivative sense of some or all of what are minimally claimed to have transhistorical status, and maximally claimed to have ahistorical status, such as similar questions to be asked, relevant concepts to the gleaned, timeless truths to be reasserted and/or reconfirmed, or applicable analytical frameworks to be borrowed. [3]

The ambiguity I want to identify within this dominant conception of 'philosophical roots' is quite stark. On the one hand, it is argued that classical Western political theory presents itself as a treasure house of experiences, ideas and concepts which are in general directly relevant still to current (and by implication any future) issues, problems or developments within international relations, and therefore directly relevant in particular to the problematic of globalization. A recent text, which is itself self-consciously a part of the apparent regeneration (which I would prefer to call a reassertion) of classical political theory, exemplifies this derivative view very clearly (Williams, Wright and Evans, 1993). In the introduction to their book, *International Relations and Political Theory,* the editors argue that one of the main reasons why the publication of this reader is 'particularly appropriate at the present time' is that the 1980s was a decade which 'witnessed revolutionary changes in the real world at both the national and international levels', which have rekindled some political questions which had, in their view, remained unasked for almost 50 years. The central point here is in the editors' connected assertions, first that the most important of all these rediscovered questions 'are questions to do with sovereignty and self-determination' and second (more importantly so far as my argument is concerned), that 'such questions have always been at the heart of political theory' (Williams, Wright and Evans, 1993: 5–7).

On the other hand, this tradition of classical Western political theory within International Relations theory, in order to be constructed as continuously relevant across time, has had to declare itself as timeless or ahistorical. This in turn implies that political theory, socially reproduced through its long tradition as a branch of philosophy, has come to construct itself, like other branches of philosophy, as also separate from, or other than, the rules, institutions and practices of government, politics and citizenship it seeks to specify, clarify, develop, analyse or prescribe: that is, philosophy becomes seen, and sees itself, as occupying a specific and unique meta-theoretical domain, as a privileged department of inquiry governed by radically different principles from those of and in social practice (Meszaros, 1986: 14; MacLean, 1988b). I will argue later that the 'philosophical roots' of International Relations, taken for the moment as synonymous with the discipline's established intellectual tradition, and expressed either explicitly[4] or implicitly,[5] rather than offering a secure basis for understanding and explaining globalization, instead operates as a disciplining device within the discipline – a hegemony within theory – which polices, generally in a quiet way, what might be said or thought about globalization and leads to a severe misrecognition of it. However, this is not an argument of despair, and neither is it only concerned with critique, even though the range of literature referred to above might seem to most to be surprisingly, or even unsustainably, comprehensive. Four points are important to note here.

First, I am not claiming that there are *no* substantial differences between the analyses referred to so far, but rather that together they occupy a terrain of debate and engagement which transforms what is really a deep ontological and epistemological orthodoxy into the form of heterodoxy. Here it appears as though the different approaches, substantive foci and methodologies, as shown for example in the notorious classical versus behaviourist debate (Bull, 1966; Kaplan, 1966) or with the more general and influential posing of the three core paradigms of the discipline by Michael Banks (1985), constitute a basis for real alternative conceptualizations and practices in the sense of fundamental opposition about how we come to have knowledge of the world, how we might best evaluate knowledge claims about the world, what kind of things can be properly said to exist in the world, and finally, what opportunities there might be for bringing about change in the world.

Second, my assertion earlier that this body of work is likely to misrecognize globalization does not entail that it cannot generate anything useful about the modern problem of globalization, and either does it depend upon reference only to those analyses which take the issue of globalization as their specific and explicit object of inquiry. What it does claim is that approaches to international relations located somewhere within the terrain of disciplinary orthodoxy, engendered and sustained regularly through the International Relations tradition, can only develop partial or inadequate conceptualizations of globalization, because they are able only to deal with the form or appearance of globalization. The reasons for this rather large claim I will set out in the next section of the chapter. There, I will also extend the argument to include a further proposition: although accounts of globalization developed from within the orthodoxy of the International Relations tradition can, and do, tell us something about this complex problematic, at the same time they are a necessary part of the social reproduction of globalization, where the latter is seen as the realization of an historically specific set of social practices, or social relations.

I am not saying here that this process of the social reproduction of globalization through conceptualization on the part of International Relations scholars is an intentional one, but rather that it is a necessary consequence of the way International Relations scholars generally go about their business. Neither am I supposing here that this constitutive relation between International Relations theory and globalization is the defining or sufficient element in the process of globalization. What I am asserting is the existence of a mediated relationship of reciprocal causality between the dominant orthodoxy of realism and neo-realism in its various forms, including (as I will argue later) the so-called 'new normative approaches' (Brown, 1992; S. Smith, 1992), and the conditions, institutions, content and 'causal powers' (Sayer, 1992: 104–5) of globalization as a relation, rather than a 'thing'.

Notwithstanding these few disclaimers, my connected propositions (about the misrecognition and simultaneous reproduction of globalization) are contentious. They hinge upon a central general assumption, namely that International Relations theory is not outside or external to international practice, but is constitutive of it. This relation is very rarely apparent; indeed it is regularly and consistently (but not consciously) obscured. It is this quality of relative invisibility that in my view makes this dimension of globalization of great, but not determining significance, and explains why the focus of this chapter is from the start upon 'the philosophical roots', or intellectual tradition of the discipline.

So far the argument may appear to be excessively or unnecessarily abstract or philosophical, at least insofar as philosophical abstraction is usually understood. However, such a view depends upon the security of the claim that philosophical speculation, meta-theory and theory about social relations is indeed categorically separate from, and other than, social practice. I asserted earlier that this conception of philosophy and meta-theory, although powerful in its consequences, is unsustainable. In order to substantiate this, it will be necessary for me to show not only how it is that the traditional 'philosophical roots' of the discipline both constrains analysis of globalization *and* enables these very social practices to continue, but also how a reconstructed conception of the philosophical and meta-theoretical elements of globalization might help us to explain globalization better, and consequently contribute to changing the large-scale inequalities of gender, race, space, property and violence which in my view are systematically realized within the practices of globalization in the late-modern world. The first part of this task is therefore necessarily a critique, while the second part is the articulation of a constructive alternative, and I will aim to set these out in subsequent sections of the chapter.

Third, to claim as I have that most attempts to explain globalization (in the discipline of International Relations and related disciplines which have in part concerned themselves with the issue of globalization, such as sociology, international business studies, economics and political science), have fundamentally misrecognized it, does not entail either that I have some privileged access to an already developed and known to be correct view of what globalization is, or that there is a single correct view on the matter. Such a criticism might seem plausible, and indeed it is worth noting that responses of this kind have long operated to constrain and marginalize critical theory in the discipline of International Relations, as elsewhere. A good example of this policing is Chris Brown's response to post-modernism, captured in his claim that, in terms of evaluating its contribution, 'one distinction that is useful is between programmatic articles about what postmodernist work might look like, or should look like, and actual attempts to deliver the goods' (Brown, 1994: 60). This echoes, although in different terms, the earlier attempt by Keohane to discipline both critical theorists and post-modernists to develop a research programme of their own (Keohane, 1989). I have no desire to defend or extend post-modernism here. However, my own analysis is based upon a meta-methodology derived from the assumptions and project of what, within the International Relations discipline, I would now have to describe oddly as traditional critical theory.[6] Consequently, I have a definite interest in all the motifs of the discipline's internal disciplinary techniques and devices of exclusion as well as those of reward and inclusion.

The attack generally upon 'critique' is couched in plausible terms, mostly because the discipline is already receptive to it. But is mistaken, and quite dramatically so, for the following reason. It is quite consistent logically (although not always the case) to deny that something constitutes the correct explanation of an event, or phenomenon – for example, that arms races cause wars, or liberal political economies cause peace or, for that matter, that capitalism as a global political economy causes inequality – without knowing in advance what does cause war, or peace, or international inequality. To go further, if this was a requirement, it would necessitate that everything was already explained, and this would remove the requirement for explanation in the first place. This is clearly logically absurd. What this shows, however, is that part of the process of disciplining within disciplines, and the reproduction of tradition it embodies, although often articulated through the discourse of formal, symbolic logic (i.e., a concern with consistency, with deduction and induction, with entailment, with contradiction and so on; more generally, a concern with the logical relations between statements), is actually less about logic as such than it is about hegemony and hierarchies within theory and methodology.

This concern gives us a clue that the grounds for inclusion and exclusion within the International Relations discipline, as within international relations practices, might be found to be more concerned with maintaining the authority of the traditional orthodoxy than with developing genuine and autonomous academic inquiry. Having said all this, a much weaker sense of this criticism, which is the idea of advancing competing explanations of international activity, and offering them for evaluation and critical assessment in a spirit of dialogic co-operation, is possible, and I think must be conceded, for it would be equally absurd (although not logically so) to ever *only* construct critiques. In defence briefly of the line of argument in this chapter, my method is that of critical theory, and the starting point always for this is to interrogate both the item in question – in this case globalization – *and* existing conceptualizations of it together; that is to say, to problematize it.

Fourth, the extensive scope of literature I referred to earlier, as either explicitly or implicitly basing itself within 'the philosophical roots', meaning the intellectual tradition of the discipline, might be taken to imply a view that everything ever written about international relations, except this chapter, has succumbed to the discrete charms and promises of the dominant orthodoxy. This is not the case. There has been a continuous production of radical, critical work in International Relations that has sought reflexively to comprehend its own relationship, both with the discipline and with international relations practices, especially since about 1980,[7] and I will refer to some of this work more fully later in the chapter. For the moment, it can be said that such attempts have constituted a very small minority of published work, and consequently have not been widely available, especially to students and younger scholars. Furthermore, when published, they have most often been explicitly or tacitly marginalized, and sometimes characterized as representing either an adolescent urge, or a trendy, (and thus insubstantial) temporary fad within the discipline (see especially James, 1989; Jones, 1994). Some implications of this exclusion will be considered later in the chapter.

With regard to the second implication of the chapter title, namely 'philosophical routes' to globalization, I will aim to show that the ambiguity I have exposed within the notion of the 'philosophical roots' of the discipline, when developed and substantiated further, can be positively re-established as the basis for a critical alternative conceptualization of the social relations of globalization. Here, the central plank of the argument is an assertion that in the process of exposing the elements of misrecognition embedded in and reproduced by the notion of 'philosophical roots', understood as a particular intellectual tradition, the initial basis for a critical reconstruction of the real content of globalization may be developed. Furthermore, although this reconstruction of globalization will be an alternative one, it will not be arbitrary in the philosophically idealistic sense. Rather, it will be worked up out of the conditions which are inscribed already within globalization, and its historical development.

To put all this more briefly now, the starting claim is that attempts to account for globalization, in terms of its conceptualization and concrete historical analysis, by means of reference (explicitly or implicitly) to its philosophical roots, understood as the intellectual tradition of the discipline, necessarily leads to various related forms of misrecognition. However, by taking the deep ambiguity involved in the long history of the International Relations tradition as a central part of what initially needs to be taken into account, the possibility is opened up of reconstituting 'philosophical roots' as more positive and alternative 'philosophical *routes*' to explaining globalization. In this process, it will be argued that philosophy is not outside globalization, but a central element within it.

This is not a reference simply to the variety of substantive forms of philosophy that can be said to exist in the world, such as linguistic-analytical philosophy, continental European philosophy, Indian philosophy, American pragmatic philosophy and so on. It is more concerned to demonstrate, first, that all attempts (actual or potential) to explain globalization have a necessary philosophical or for the moment meta-theoretical content within them, usually embedded, unacknowledged, unrecognized and taken for granted. Second, that concrete, observable social practices have meta-theoretical content embedded in them over and above the usual, often analysed sets of values and beliefs that underpin purposive behaviour. And third, in order to develop a coherent account of globalization as a set of social relations rather than as a thing in itself, it is necessary to construct an analytical framework which is, at least in part, explicitly philosophical.

In the next section, I will aim to show how it is that 'the philosophical roots' tradition in the discipline disables and constrains attempts to conceptualize globalization, resulting in a general misrecognition of it, while simultaneously contributing to – that is, reproducing – the very practices of hegemony and inequality which, I will argue, globalization realises in complex new forms. On the basis of this critique, I will develop in the second section of the chapter a coherent analytical framework, or meta-methodology, for conceptualizing globalization. Although not offered at all as the true, or correct, or only possible account, it seeks to regenerate the historically powerful constitutive relationship between philosophy and society: that is, the meta-theory/theory-practice relationship.

Disrupting the 'philosophical roots' discourse

Before developing a critical analysis of the philosophical roots of the discipline in relation specifically to the issue of globalization, it is necessary to set out four important contextual postulates about the idea of 'philosophical roots' itself, in order to understand the deep structural power of the intellectual tradition within the discipline of International Relations. The reason for this is that there is an important intellectual and practical problem involved in the causal weight I have placed upon the idea of the 'philosophical roots' of the discipline. I have asserted two closely connected claims, each of which is contentious: first, that the philosophical roots are a central aspect of the dominant orthodoxy within the discipline, not yet displaced; and second, that the philosophical roots, rather than offering a secure basis for explaining globalization, instead operate as a disciplining device, policing what might be said or thought about globalization, albeit generally in a quiet way.

It could be plausibly objected here that I have given a grossly exaggerated significance to the philosophical roots, or the intellectual tradition of the discipline on grounds such as the following. Although it may well be the case that in the early days of the discipline, say from 1919 to the early 1940s, explicit reference back to classical political philosophy texts such as Thucydides, Aquinas, Grotius, and especially Machiavelli, Hobbes and Clauswitz represented a prominent motif in academic International Relations, especially that of the so-called 'English School' (Jackson, 1996: 211–13), this is simply no longer the case. Furthermore, this objection might run, even though from time to time since the 1940s, texts referring to (or explicitly located within) the classical political theory discourse have emerged in International Relations,[8] they are no longer at the centre of the International Relations discourse. This is so, the objection might continue (still plausibly) because since 1919, there have been three 'Great Debates' in the discipline. The first debate concerned the idealist/realist schism of the 1930s and 1940s, which effectively foreclosed the discipline of International Relations as a largely normative project. The second debate was the traditionalist/scientific debate of the 1960s, which effectively foreclosed classical realism and established empiricist epistemology at the center of the discipline. The third and last so-called positivist/post-positivist debate began in the late 1980s and still continues. Although this last debate is yet to be resolved, it is seen by many to represent nothing more than a fashionable, albeit temporary, confusion (e.g., James, 1989; Jones, 1994; Jackson, 1996).

Taken together, these debates show that the International Relations discipline is characterized not so much by a tradition of orthodoxy, but more a tradition of healthy heterodoxy, wherein the 'philosophical roots' of the discipline, understood as classical political theory, continues to play a useful role in its long history. Robert Jackson (1996: 208) puts it like this:

> To sum up thus far it may be worth emphasising this last point: an adequate theoretical understanding of international relations cannot be achieved by any one tradition alone: it can only be achieved by all traditions taken together, and thus by an analysis of the debates they jointly provoke.

In response to this layered objection, I will take the Jackson view first. In spite of the apparent openness of the above assertion, Jackson himself disarmingly reveals how difficult it is to sustain such claims of openness and debate convincingly. Towards the end of the same paper, definite and explicit limits emerge and it is worth quoting Jackson (1996: 215–16, emphasis added) in full here:

> Whether any of the new theories discussed in this book become important additions to international theory – or turn out merely to be temporary fashions – only time will tell. Here, I merely suggest that *the history of international political theory, like any other intellectual history, is open to new ideas* most of which will prove to have little historical staying power but a few of which are *perhaps destined for a permanent place in the pantheon of classical international theories alongside enduring theoretical voices of the past. In that way the classical approach is continually renewed and enriched.*[9]
>
> *However, this thesis should not be pressed too far. There are limits to the accommodation of new international theories by the classical tradition.* I suppose the basic limit is determined by the intelligibility of a theory and its communication with other classical theories. When I try to read some of the most self-consciously scientific theories of contemporary international relations I feel rather like a visitor to another planet: as if I had entered a remote place whose inhabitants speak an arcane language and seem preoccupied with theoretical concerns entirely unconnected with those of history or ordinary human experience. That same feeling also occurs when I try to make sense of post-modern theories of an anti-foundational kind which deny the possibility of universal human reason and an historical conversation among human beings. *In short, I cannot see how the classical approach could possibly accommodate theories which explicitly repudiate the classical tradition itself.*

At this point, I propose to leave Jackson's claims to speak for themselves, although I will have more to say about them, and the classical tradition in general, later in this section. So far as the other lines of my imagined but plausible objection are concerned, I will briefly set out why I think such an objection is internally coherent (and also true in parts) but nevertheless unconvincing. This is because a number of core assumptions upon which it rests are insecure. The first of these is the assumption that the three 'Great Debates' really have been fundamental debates, representing real antagonisms and capable of leading to distinct qualitative shifts in the tradition. I will show later that they have not yet done so. The second assumption is that evidence for the existence of debates is in and of itself sufficient to establish heterodoxy and that heterodoxy stands in categorical opposition to orthodoxy. I will also show later that neither of these assumptions hold. The third is that an intellectual tradition resides only within the texts to which it claims allegiance, and that the concept of 'philosophical roots' is meaningful only in a literal sense. I will argue later in this section that such a view is too narrow, and obscures the persuasive and embedded nature of the philosophical tradition. Furthermore, in the second section, I will aim to show that not only do the philosophical roots in International Relations extend far beyond explicit classic political theory texts within the discipline, but also that observable everyday practices in the late-modern world, structured and reproduced through the 'causal powers or liabilities' (Sayer, 1992: 104–17) of globalization, have a deep philosophical content to them as part of what they actually are.

In the rest of this section, I will first set out my four contextual postulates. Then, I will show how it is that the philosophical roots/ intellectual tradition of the discipline establishes an obscured but powerful orthodoxy which, following Bourdieu (1977: 159–71), I shall characterize as a doxy-doxa relationship. Next, I will relocate the orthodoxy in its representation as heterodoxy, and show how the main structure in the discipline which mediates this relationship is that of realism and neo-realism. However, I will aim to show here that neo-realism has a deeper, wider and more extensive content than that which it is generally assumed to encompass. Finally in this section, I will set out more precisely what in my view are the major elements of the philosophical roots of the discipline, which together explain the comprehensive failure of the International Relations discipline so far to develop a convincing concrete analysis of the concept of globalization.

Disciplinary references

My first postulate then, as implied in the distinction I made in the introduction between explicit and implicit forms of the intellectual tradition, is that the detailed content of this tradition – which I have called its 'philosophical roots' – is neither confined to, nor restricted in, its relevance, disciplining authority and importance only to, those conceptualizations and writings which make *direct* reference to the texts, concepts, arguments and substantive concerns of classical political philosophy.[10] Here, some reference back to the classical canon – be it via Thucydides, or Aquinas, or Machiavelli, or Grotius, or Hobbes, or more recently Kant – is taken as the core and necessary signifier for what counts as the tradition and for being safely located within it. I prefer to call such direct, explicit representations the 'strong version' of the intellectual tradition within international theory, for reasons I will come to in a moment. In passing, it is also worth noting that the tradition, in both its strong and weak versions, is just as much exclusive as it is inclusive. Indeed, in opposition to Jackson's claim, quoted earlier, that 'the history of international political theory, like any other intellectual history is open to new ideas', (1996: 215) my view is that this simultaneous inclusive/exclusive quality is one of the defining characteristics of intellectual traditions in general, the exposure of which allows us to establish them as constituting orthodoxies when they appear to represent heterodoxies. That is to say, they are disciplining devices – a form of hegemony within theory (which I shall argue later is causally connected to hegemony within international practice) – which set boundaries for what is to be properly included as relevant substantive content; what are seen as the discipline's central concepts and problematics; what count as appropriate and inappropriate methodologies; what criteria must be met to establish coherence and validity and, underpinning all this, what is seen as worthy of dissemination in the discipline by means of peer review and publication.

In the International Relations discipline notable exclusions from the mainstream of debate include issues of racism, of migration and refugees, of labour and employment, of health poverty and land tenure, of gender subordination and of imperialism and neo-imperialism. Putting this more generally now, issues connected to and indicative of gross and systematic inequality in the world have not been, and are not yet seen, as central problematiques within International Relations: unless of course they are inequalities of military capability, of sovereign territory, or of access to credit and finance. Consequently, theories of racism as a global phenomenon, theories of social welfare, theories of forms of migration, theories about the application of science to society through technology, theories of property and land use, feminist theories and Marxist theories, have at best managed only to establish a tenuous and inhospitable space at the margins of the discipline.

It is not enough to answer here, as Alan James (1989) has done, that such issues as those referred to above, although clearly important, nevertheless remain outside the domain of the International Relations discipline, and need to be explained elsewhere. For, if the classic realist distinction between high politics and low politics can no longer be sustained either on substantive or conceptual grounds, and further, if people's security individually and collectively is increasingly threatened by such social conditions, and, finally, there are prima facie grounds for supposing that the causal mechanisms for such conditions reside (partly at least) within the structures and processes of the global political economy, then the discipline of International Relations could be said to have a clear responsibility to open up its substantive and conceptual boundaries.

One final comment is called for. The intellectual tradition of International Relations not only disciplines the conditions and possibilities for new entrants to 'the Pantheon of classical international theories' (Jackson, 1996) but also disciplines its own internal history. What I mean by this, briefly, is that the intellectual tradition carries with it the possibility of internal marginalization, or marginalization and exclusion at the centre as well as at the boundaries. The reasons for this assertion will become clear when I develop the content of the third contextual postulate below, but I will exemplify it now. A fair number of general texts on the history of political theory (e.g., Sabine, 1973; Wolin, 1960; Germino, 1974), and a small number of general texts on political theory and its relevance to International Relations (that is to say, writings representing the strong version of the intellectual tradition, such as Parkinson 1977; Donelan, 1978; Williams, 1992; Williams, Wright and Evans, 1993; Williams, 1996), do cite, to varying degrees, Hegel or Marx, or often both. Oddly, however, they seem to be included *in* Jackson's now famous 'pantheon', but not quite of it. I will expand upon this later. What is not in doubt, within the dominant Western tradition at least, is that Marx has been marginalized at the centre – consider, for example, this judgement from Sabine (1973: 643, emphasis added) about Marx's theory of dialectical materialism:

> And, since the ideological superstructure merely reflects the internal growth of the underlying metaphysical substance, the problems that appear upon the level of the consciousness will always be soluble with the further unfolding and the progressive realization of the substratum behind them. *Quite obviously, this metaphysical conclusion is not susceptible of any empirical proof.*

Most often, Marx is included in order to demonstrate what constitutes bad political theory. At the same time, later Marxists and neo-Marxists, from Lenin through to Gramsci, and even Gill, Rosenberg and others more recently within the International Relations discipline, have been marginalized at the margins of the discipline as has been noted more fully by Thorndike (1978), MacLean (1981a, 1981b, 1988b) and H. Smith (1996).

Strong and weak versions

My second contextual postulate, a corollary of the first and therefore strongly implicated in what I have argued so far, is that a 'weak version' of the philosophical roots/intellectual tradition also exists within international theory wherein the relationship with classical political theory is not at all as clear or explicit as it is in the 'strong version'. In the weak version the need for reference to the texts and ideas of those writers generally included in the canon of Western political theory is muted.[11] What is maintained across both strong and weak versions, however, is a set of categorical separations: the political from the economic but also from other important spheres of social practice such as law, culture, ethics, language, sexual reproduction and so on; the public from the private sphere; the state from society; the international or the global from the national or the domestic and both of these from the regional; the theoretical from the practical; agency from structure, objectivity from subjectivity; and time from space. I will say more about these categorical separations later. A further and important shared view is that establishing and maintaining order in the world is continuously precarious, not just for some, but for all.

Two ironic revelations now emerge from identifying strong and weak versions of the intellectual tradition, the first of which has been implied in what I said earlier about the so-called three 'Great Debates' in the discipline. This is the widespread tendency to construct the 'philosophical roots' as an essentially taxonomic concept, the central purpose of which is to constitute the basis for a categorical distinction between (i) traditional or classical approaches and (ii) scientific or empirical approaches, within international theory. Candidates for category (ii) are defined in terms of their relatively explicit normative aims and content. In particular, they are defined in terms of their explicit rejection of normative propositions, at least so far as methodology is concerned, on the grounds that normative theory is necessarily partial (which it is) and that such propositions contaminate, or at least inhibit, their aim to develop objective – meaning value-free – social knowledge (which they do not develop because scientific knowledge, as I will demonstrate later, is itself necessarily value-laden).

Now, this taxonomic construction of the 'philosophical roots' concept is both confusing and mistaken. It is confusing because it tends to obscure the extent to which the 'philosophical roots' in International Relations extends considerably beyond analyses that depend explicitly upon classical political theory texts. It is mistaken because it presupposes that classical political theory was *only* (and distinctively) normative and therefore non-scientific, and consequently had nothing to do with the long process of the objectification of science as the assumed-to-be maximally reliable form of knowledge construction. This point has acquired a renewed irony and replication within the recent development characterized by Chris Brown and others as 'new normative approaches'. Right at the start of *International Relations Theory*, in relation to the problem of seeing that 'theory is a term which is used in international relations with a bewildering number of different meanings', Brown asserts that 'A primary distinction here might usefully be made between "empirical" and "normative" theory – although, as will be suggested below, the term "normative" is in many ways unsatisfactory' (1992: 1). However, although the categorical separation of traditional theory (as normative) from scientific theory (as non-normative) is mistaken – except in the narrow and disabling context of the symbolic logical distinction between descriptive statements and evaluative statements, within which the distinction is simply analytically true – its significance in respect of maintaining power of the philosophical roots in International Relations has been, and still is, enormous.

Sub-texts and contexts

The second ironic revelation disclosed through identifying strong and weak versions of the philosophical roots introduces the third contextual postulate. What constitutes the philosophical *content* of the philosophical roots is not exhausted by reference to classical political theory alone. This is not to deny that the latter more or less fully represents the appearance of the content of the philosophical roots, but rather that there is more going on philosophically within the philosophical roots than might be assumed at first sight. This is so in at least two respects. First, not all the texts and writers that would be properly included in an encyclopaedic history of the intellectual tradition of International Relations could be said to sit comfortably, if at all, within the conventions of classical political philosophy. I have in mind here writers such as Gentili, Grotius, Vattel or Puffendorf. The central concern of these writers was international law, and although of relevance to such central issues in classical political philosophy as the form of the state and the conduct of war, they cannot be said without substantial external argument to be part of Jackson's pantheon of great theoretical voices of classical political theory. It is interesting to note that, whereas in the Forsyth *et al.* text (1970), extracts from Gentili, Grotius and Vattel, together with commentary upon them, occupy a little over one-third of the whole book, in the Williams, Wright and Evans reader (1993) only Grotius of these three makes any appearance at all.

More importantly for my argument, there is a second, underlying form of philosophy going on within, or being mediated by, the explicit appearance of political philosophy, even though it is the latter alone which is generally taken as defining or situating the philosophical roots of the discipline. A rather simple first step towards explaining what I mean by this is to assert that the texts which together constitute the library of the philosophical roots of the discipline, like all extant texts, have a sub-text and a context. That is to say, what a text is cannot be said to reside only in the literal form of the text as an observable artefact. This assertion does not herald a sudden turn towards post-modern analysis; however, writers who analyse and interpret classical texts from a position of sensitivity to the sub-textual and contextual dimensions of their task do so usually in what is in my view an enlightening but none the less narrow fashion which means that sub-textual elements are normally restricted to items of allegory or allusion to other observable items, or to omissions or inclusions, the relevance of which to the argument in the text is insignificant, but which might reveal aspects of political, religious, despotic or nepotistic pressures upon the author.

Clearly, sub-textual elements such as these lead directly into (because they depend upon) contextual knowledge: for example, about the writer's family, education, employment, political and economic history; about the religious, cultural and social conditions at the time of writing; or about motives and intellectual influences. Knowledge of such conditions can be important in helping the reader to understand why a particular author chose to write about what he/she did (it is usually he, and it is interesting to note that to date no female voices have been sufficiently endowed with historical staying power to achieve a permanent place in Jackson's pantheon of enduring theoretical voices within the intellectual tradition of International Relations) and the manner or form of analysis in which they did so. There are many examples of such contextualizations of the classic political theory texts. Indeed, it is difficult to find a modern reproduction of a classic text which does not have a substantial introduction covering such matters. More rare, especially in International Relations, are studies of classic writers which utilize contextualization as the basis for a continuous analytical framework which serves to structure the interpretation throughout. One important exception to this general rarity is R. J. B. Walker's study of political theory (1993). Outside the International Relations community, however, there are many such excellent texts, attention to which would in my view greatly enrich and inform our reading of our own discipline's intellectual history. Here, I would include Macpherson's (1962) study of Hobbes, Harrington and Locke; Winch's (1978; 1996) studies of Smith, Burke, Malthus and other contemporary British political-economists; Hoffe's (1994) study of Kant; and Skinner's (1996) new study of Hobbes.

However, what I want to develop here is a *philosophical* contextualization of the philosophical roots of the discipline for, as I asserted earlier, I want to be able to show that there is more going on in political philosophy than simply 'the political'. To do so, I have to relocate the idea of context spatially and temporally, by proposing that there is an internal as well as an external context to the texts of the tradition. This binds them together as a long project, over and above the specific concerns focused upon by individual authors. Furthermore, it is this quality which allows for the realization of a doxic power within the tradition, and for orthodoxy to represent itself as though it were its opposite, namely heterodoxy.

This deep structure of philosophy within the philosophical roots can be summarized, following Pocock (1962), as a constant tendency to become philosophy of a particular kind. As my earlier example of Sabine's comment upon Marx reveals, embedded in the philosophical roots – understood as political philosophy – is a transtextual philosophy, which is a philosophy of knowledge itself: that is, an epistemology. And as Pocock demonstrates in respect of the history of political theory, this transtextual embedded philosophy is one which predominantly involves a set of presuppositions which bias the philosophical roots towards the rules of analytic, or linguistic philosophy (compare MacLean 1981b in regard to international theory). In other words, the 'philosophical roots' as a whole system is constructed on the basis of a concern with precise definition, with the formulation of abstract or hypothetical models, with the specification of general rules, with the logical relations between concepts, and with Aristotelian principles of logical consistency, identity, contradiction, universal conditions and so on.

To return to Hobbes briefly, and notwithstanding Skinner's (1996) recent revisionist study, the general consensus is that Hobbes was a central agent, in the long development and movement through the work of Bacon, Locke and Hume, of the English empiricist tradition. Indeed, in his influential study of Hobbes, Macpherson (1962: 11–15) shows that it was not at the time seen as improper or illogical for Hobbes to seek to derive obligation, right and equality from fact, even though the traditional view of his work is that in seeking to deduce moral obligation from empirical postulates of fact, Hobbes committed a grave logical error. Macpherson raises the question of whether or not post-Hobbesian logical canons should be imposed upon Hobbes. He argues that there is a prima facie case for turning to social and historical considerations when confronting the issue of Hobbes's logical consistency.

Additionally, in his articulation of the embedded view of possessive market relations within Hobbes's theory of the polity, Macpherson (1962: 46–78) does not construct this as something which Hobbes so to speak kept quiet about, but as the only model of the *economy* that is consistent with Hobbes's *political* theory. And Macpherson (1962: 78) shows that in exposing this deeper philosophy within *Leviathan*, 'a fundamental connection between this political philosophy and his scientific materialism becomes evident". I have concentrated on Hobbes in this part of the discussion mainly because of the large relevance and continuing importance that his writing is presumed to hold for theorizing international relations past and present. Furthermore, when I set out more fully shortly what I mean by the philosophical roots of the discipline understood as a doxy-doxa relation, I will say more about Hobbes, and why it is that Hobbes is of large significance in the discipline, although I will do so on quite different grounds from those usually offered.

This long development of empiricist epistemology as a hegemonic form of knowledge, by means of the construction of a *particular* intellectual tradition, has come to underpin the political philosophy surface of the philosophical roots of the discipline. This tradition is not reducible to any of the individual texts said to constitute it, and neither can it be identified from an aggregation of all the texts together. Consequently, we have to conclude that inclusion in, and exclusion from the pantheon that makes up the observable form of the philosophical roots cannot be explained simply or only by reference to the texts in their literal form (MacLean, 1981b: 114–15). As Gunnell (1979) has argued, the isolation of classical political theory as a tradition, and the specification of sub-themes such as reason, obligation, equality, justice, power, freedom, property and so on, are really analytical exercises. The tradition can then be seen to be constructed as a historically developed convention of scholarship in general, rather than a convention discovered in and drawn out from the works themselves.

In this way, the establishment of the idea of an intellectual tradition – philosophical roots – in the connected history of political theory and international theory leads to the reification of analytical categories, such that scholarly conventions become a priori assumptions of that history. At the same time, there was something else very important going on in the construction of the philosophical roots of the discipline, at both the surface level of classical political theory, and within the deeper structural philosophy I have just described. This is the long, difficult, complex and conflict-ridden historical development of the dismantling of political economy from about the mid-seventeenth century onwards, and its reconstruction into two apparently separated domains of social relations, namely *the* polity and *the* economy. This separation of politics from economics – in academic, theoretical, and substantive terms – reveals to us (amongst other things) that the binary construction of theory and practice as a categorical opposition cannot be sustained; that linear notions of causality which assume cause must precede effect in time and space (Nicholson, 1996) – although part of the generic concept of causality – do not exhaust what causality means; and that theory and practice are constitutive of each other. The importance of this aspect will become clearer when I analyse in more detail some recent attempts to conceptualize globalization.

Exposing this complex deep structure of the philosophical roots now gives us a clue (indeed it is a necessary condition) about why it is that scholars like Donelan, Forsyth, Williams, Jackson and Buzan can confound ordinary notions of history and time by referring to timeless truths, timeless concepts and timeless wisdom within the classical tradition. In addition, and in my view of greater consequence for the project of this chapter, it establishes in principle coherent grounds upon which I can proceed to substantiate the two claims I made in the introduction that are vital to the overall argument of this chapter. To recapitulate, the first is my claim that the philosophical roots, or intellectual tradition of the discipline, is an orthodoxy which not only disables the capacity of the pantheon of classical political philosophy, or work based upon it, to generate convincing conceptualizations of globalization; it also similarly disables that part of the recent and increasing body of academic work in International Relations concerned with analysing globalization which not only makes no direct reference or linkage to the classical tradition but very often constructs itself explicitly in opposition to it.

The second claim was that philosophy is not external to whatever globalization means, but a central element within it. This is a strong implication of the first claim. But, I extended this claim further, to assert that even though the *established* philosophical roots of the discipline lead to a misrecognition of globalization and the social practices to which it both realizes and defers, nevertheless the articulation of this disciplinary system through the method of ideology critique might allow the possibility of a reconstruction of the philosophical basis of globalization. Consequently, the critique of the philosophical roots of the discipline seen as an orthodoxy is not an attempt to remove philosophy, but to show that philosophy can be relocated from its now taken-for-granted specification as a unique and purely meta-theoretical discourse – that is, as having no direct or indirect causal relation with its object of inquiry – to a specification as a critical analytical concept which is already embedded in everyday social practices. Both of these claims are hugely general in scope, but they are potentially sustainable because they do not depend for their coherence upon an equivalently huge empirical referent. Neither of them is absolute – that is to say, neither takes the form that *if a* then *b* – and neither claim contains or depends upon an essentialist proposition in the sense of a certain (i.e., incorrigible) truth claim. However, nor can either claim be substantiated wholly in the domain of meta-theory.

I will now turn to the matter of showing how the very abstract conception of 'philosophical roots' seen as a doxy-doxa relationship might be made concrete. This does not mean operationalizing the concept, or testing it empirically, for this would be inconsistent with my argument so far that it is the silent transtextual empiricist content of the philosophical roots which is partly accountable for the misrecognition of globalization. Instead, I will aim to approximate that view of concept formation referred to by Cox (which is consistent with, but more simply stated than, Marx's method of political economy, as set out in the *Grundrisse*) as establishing the content of a concept or theoretical term 'through contact with a particular situation it helps to explain – a contact which also develops the meaning of the concept' (Cox, 1983: 162–3).

Orthodox empiricism

The fourth contextual postulate is that Western (and therefore global) social science has developed a contagious generic orthodoxy which might be described as an unspoken epistemological alliance of empiricism, and which manifests itself with varying degrees of rigour and use of measurement. Its purest form is to be found in those disciplines with the highest degrees of orthodoxy, and consequently relatively low levels of disagreement (if any) about what constitutes the boundaries of the discipline; about what its central objects of inquiry are; and about how best to develop explanations of them. Primary examples of such disciplines are economics, social psychology, and business or management studies. It is interesting to note that these are also the disciplines which most often utilize formal statistical and/or mathematical ordering frameworks, and they are also the disciplines that seem most to reflect and consciously adopt a part of the methodology of natural science as the relatively undisputed centre of their orthodoxies. Although such formal examples are rarer in International Relations (e.g., Nicholson, 1989, 1992; or Richardson, 1960), this is not to say that the scientific method, or behaviouralism, has not been important in International Relations. The so-called second Great Debate of the 1960s would be meaningless if this was so, as would claims about the post-Second World War dominance of American academia in the discipline.

Even more obviously than these events, the so-called Third Great Debate, situated around a set of critiques of positivism and characterized by Lapid as a 'discipline-defining debate' (Lapid, 1989: 236), which came to prominence in the late 1980s and which continues unresolved into the present, simply could not have occurred if scientific methodology in its form of empiricist/positivist epistemology had not gained a central position within the International Relations orthodoxy, and simultaneously within dominant social practices. I agree fully with Steve Smith's (1996: 13) evaluation of this post-positivist debate as involving very high stakes first 'because of the links between theory and practice' and second, 'because its [positivist] epistemological assumptions have had enormous ontological consequences' (Smith, 1996: 37). I would add here that this is also the case in International Relations.[12]

What is at first sight puzzling is why the post-positivist – that is, anti-positivist – debate did not emerge in the International Relations discipline until it was fixed into critiques developed out of post-structuralist and post-modernist positions. My quick, but not cursory, answer to this, implicated in my earlier arguments about the comprehensive disciplinary reach of the philosophical roots of the discipline, is that critiques of positivism do not necessarily entail a fundamental disruption of the intellectual tradition. In other words, although a critique of positivism is a necessary condition for the development of radical, emancipatory and non-arbitrary alternative knowledge, it is not a sufficient condition.

Furthermore, I would argue that post-modernist critiques do not provide a secure basis for radical and emancipatory theorization, except in the contradictory sense of therapeutic assistance to the notion of self. Consequently, they remain part of the heterodoxy of International Relations, and thus are capable of entering into debate within it. The detailed basis of this assertion will be developed in the next section, but what it implies is that some critiques of positivism threaten the very deep philosophical basis of the orthodoxy, but some do not, even though all may threaten positivism itself. A very important example of the potential tolerance and generosity of positivism towards *some* of its critics is to be found in the recent paper by John Vasquez (1995) which seeks to reconstruct 'Scientific Enquiry and International Relations Theory After Enlightenment's Fall'. However, not all critiques of positivism/empiricism in the discipline receive such consideration, as Hazel Smith has recently shown. (H. Smith, 1996: 191–212).

Having said all this, the *generic* cross-disciplinary power of empiricist epistemology is not that central to this chapter. What is central are the forms of empiricism developed and reconstructed within the International Relations orthodoxy. The deep paradox implied here, namely the increasing separation of social theory in the twentieth century into apparently discrete disciplines, but coterminous with an increasing convergence of empiricist epistemology across them all, is itself an important reason for the general misrecognition of globalization. It also implies there is a need not so much for an interdisciplinary account of globalization, but more for an anti-disciplinary and holistic account. It is these and other elements of the philosophical roots that I will deal with next.

The structure of orthodoxy

In this section, I will first explain what it means to construct the philosophical roots of International Relations as an orthodoxy by analysing the concept of orthodoxy in terms of its doxy-doxa structure. Then I will show that the core of the orthodoxy is mediated and reproduced as a structure, both in the discipline and in international practice, through classical realism and neo-realism, the latter in a surprising variety of transformations. These include some recent work in International Relations and international political economy (IPE) not normally seen as part of the neo-realist project. Finally, I will summarize what I see as the major elements in the philosophical roots of the discipline which together lead to the misrecognition of globalization. I will conclude here that detailed specification of this enclosure stands as the ground for working up a new, critical analytical framework for conceptualizing globalization. However, this will now be based on a reconstruction of philosophical *roots* into philosophical *routes*, that is, the transformation of philosophy *about* society into philosophy *in* society. Articulation of this framework will be the subject matter of the final section of the chapter.

In the introduction and in the analysis of the contextual postulates, I asserted strongly that the philosophical roots of the discipline represent an orthodoxy. What is central to this orthodoxy in causal terms is the deep generic epistemology of empiricism embedded in (and partly itself developed through) the observable textual forms of classical political philosophy. So far as positions within the discipline are concerned, it seems as though only realism and neo-realism are part of this orthodoxy. Other positions, such as the so-called 'new normative' approaches, post-structuralism and post-modernism, feminism, identity and reflexivity, strict behaviouralism, public choice theory or international political economy, appear to be, and often explicitly see themselves as being, opposed to this orthodoxy. This is so even in recent work which explicitly locates itself within or alongside one of the authors of the political theory tradition, as in Hutchings's (1996: 11) chapter on critical international relations theory, the central thesis of which is that 'the logic of Kantian critique provides an excellent clarification of the patterns of thinking in critical international relations theory'.

I will advance the view that self-declaration of opposition to the orthodoxy is neither necessary nor sufficient to confirm opposition; that a post-positivist dimension is necessary but not sufficient for opposition; and that critical theory in order to be critical, has both to deconstruct and reconstruct the deep meta-theory of philosophy-as-epistemology. This means in part showing the constitutive relationship between the latter, different extant and historical positions in the discipline, and different forms of everyday practices in international relations. It also means showing that evidence of debate is not synonymous with heterodoxy, and that heterodoxy is not necessarily in opposition to orthodoxy. Insofar as my claims about misrecognition are concerned, I do not mean by this misperception, or errors of truth, or illusion, or false consciousness, since all these meanings presuppose and reproduce the assumed categorical separation of theory (as a mental or wholly subjective process) from practice (as an external, objective, wholly material reality).

Instead I will start with the concept of misrecognition developed by Pierre Bourdieu. Here, misrecognition is a reference to the complex ways in which social actors regularly and systematically reproduce established social orders through habitualized practices, in a way that conceals the reality of hierarchical divisions of power and distribution, and access to decision-making within them. They do this by reconstructing conditions which are actually arbitrary and intersubjectively reproduced as though they are the natural, taken-for-granted conditions of social choices and practices; that is to say, as though these conditions constitute the natural limits of reality. Bourdieu (1977: 164) puts it like this:

> Every established order tends to produce (to very different degrees and with very different means) the naturalization of its own arbitrariness ... in the extreme case, that is to say, when there is a quasi-perfect correspondence between the objective order and the subjective principles of organization (as in ancient societies) the natural and social world appears as self-evident. This experience we shall call doxa so as to distinguish it from an orthodox or heterodox belief implying awareness and recognition of the possibility of different or antagonistic beliefs.

A corollary of misrecognition in the sense outlined here is that established orders (social and academic), because they are also subject to change over time – for example, through imperialism and colonization, through war or famine or immigration, through modernization and technological development, through incorporation into the global political economy, or through environmental degradation – have to strive continuously to make that which is initially unintelligible intelligible, and that which is apparently new or different recognizable. This double moment in the academic discipline of International Relations – that is, of inclusion and exclusion within which rendering social items and events recognizable is internal to the complexity of misrecognition – identifies it as a derivative discourse, as part of a larger but heavily mediated totality, which may be described as 'the ensemble of phenomena in and through which the social production of meaning takes place, an ensemble which constitutes society as such' (Laclau, 1980).

This is not just a reference to the language of International Relations, or to the languages within international relations, but also to the material bases of language and the relations between them. Consequently, the historical development of complicated international practices – for example, the construction of free trade as the pure and virtuous form of international trade – or the problem of realizing sovereignty, or deregulation and privatization, and the explanation of them, depends upon the disclosure of orthodoxies within those practices. Orthodoxies are enabled through the articulation of and adherence to efficient normative structures wherein these orthodoxies are represented as 'real' or 'natural', and as constituting external limits to thought about them. Here, the logical distinction between descriptive (or empirical) statements, and evaluative (or normative) statements seems irrelevant, in the sense that normative structures can be seen to be constitutive of, or internally related to, apparently objective conditions in the world such as trade, development, global warming, privatization or humanitarian peace-enforcement. The strict separation of fact from value is mistaken in that it is not itself capable of empirical testing, and therefore only meaningful as an analytical truth, but it is not irrelevant. This is so because this assumed separation, like those of theory from practice and of subjectivity from objectivity, is causally necessary both to the process of constructing social reality as the objective conditions of social practice, and to sustaining relations of power and hegemony within that practice (MacLean, 1988a). In other words, the philosophical roots/intellectual tradition of the discipline, and the possibilities for agency within international relations practice, represent a structure where each element is constitutive of the other.

At the same time, parts of this relationship cannot be directly observed, even in principle, and therefore can only be identified in terms of their consequences (e.g., Bhaskar, 1975, 1989; MacLean, 1981a, 1981b). What is clear is that this structure is one of simultaneous orthodoxy in both thought and practice. This does not imply, and neither is it a requirement for the validity of such an assertion, that a relation of strict identity needs to be established so that orthodoxy *A* in theory matches or corresponds to orthodoxy *A* in practice. This would be to represent exactly the orthodoxy of the separation of theory from practice I argue against.

Rather, the relationship is necessarily indirect, or mediated, and this is what makes it so difficult to deconstruct. This does not deny of course that from time to time specific theoretical orthodoxies are consciously developed and articulated in order to maintain and reproduce specific practical or concrete social orthodoxies. They clearly are, as is demonstrated by the development of 'separate development' in Apartheid South Africa, or the idea of 'dictatorship of the proletariat' in the early days of the former USSR, or the idea of 'stakeholder democracy' in contemporary British politics. But it is not this class of relation, where the connection between explicit theorization and social practice is so explicit and intentional, that I am concerned to deal with here. Large-scale structures generally operate and reproduce themselves where purposive behaviour rather than intention is necessary to, but not the exclusive basis of, social outcomes. Some social outcomes are a strict consequence of purposive behaviour, but only when the purposive behaviour is congruent with a definite intention. For example, a university teacher may well treat male and female students in a seminar differently, and this necessarily involves purposive behaviour. She or he may have no intention here of reproducing gender relations of subordination, but certain possible forms of differential treatment would lead to such subordination, and necessarily so.

In broad terms, these complex social processes can be generally described as social reproduction. I asserted above, following Bourdieu, that the arbitrary nature of established social orders is obscured through a strategy of naturalization. They do not endure automatically, but only so long as people individually or collectively reproduce them. Equally, people do not reproduce them automatically, and rarely do they do so with intention. Underdeveloped political economies, for example, do not engage in world trade in order to reproduce the global capitalist political economy and their subordinated position within it. However, such conditions are partly a necessary if unintended consequence of their activity, as they are simultaneously a necessary condition of the manner of their engagement in world trade in the first place.

These conditions reveal that international activity, like other domains of social practice, are context-dependent, which is to say they are located in sets of acceptable and non-acceptable behaviour, which are invariably rule-governed. Some of these rules are formal and institutionalized, some are informal and a matter of habitualized social practice. The critical element they simultaneously reproduce and obscure is the extent to which a universalized normative structure – which does not mean that the relevant practices (of economy, polity, culture, language, gender, property and so on) are everywhere identical, but that there is an assumed 'natural' standard in terms of which actual and potential forms of practice are evaluated – generally operates in the interests of particular agents, and against the real interests of others. On this view, knowledge in and of international relations is not simply a matter of their direct instruments and artefacts but also a matter at the same time of what is *not* expressed, and *not* disputed, because they are taken as undeniably given, not just by subordinated agents, but by dominant agents too. For Bourdieu (1977: 164), 'The instruments of knowledge of the social world are at the same time political instruments, which contribute to the reproduction of the social world by producing immediate or inevitable adherence to the world, seen as self-evident and undisputed, of which they are actually the product.'He goes on to say that: 'The adherence expressed in the doxic relation to the social world is the absolute form of the recognition of legitimacy through the misrecognition of arbitrariness, since it is unaware of the very question of legitimacy' (Bourdieu, 1977: 168). These complex conditions of social knowledge and social practice are represented figuratively by Bourdieu as shown in Figure 1.1.

Disputes within the doxy, for example between the idealists and the realists, between the traditionalists and the scientists or, recently, between all these and the post-positivists, present the orthodoxy as though it is a domain of continuous debate, or heterodoxy. This tends to conceal the necessary contribution these disputes make to the very

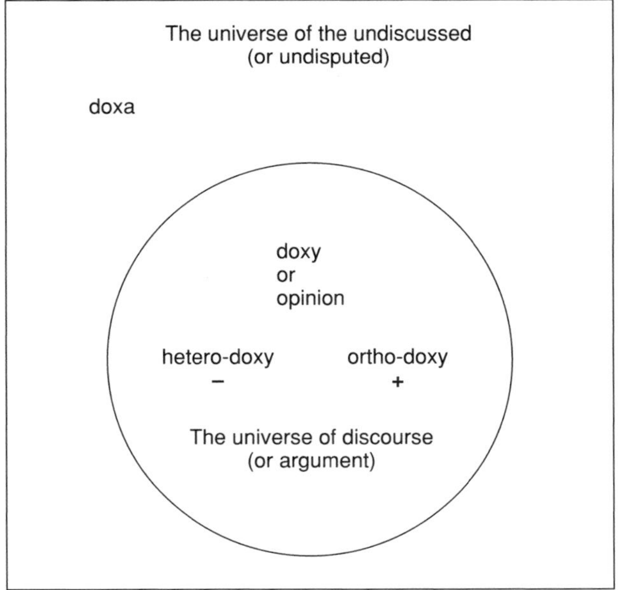

Source: Adapted from Bourdieu (1977: 168).
Figure 1.1 International relations as a totality

confirmation of the boundaries of an issue as given. This is the point when that which constitutes the content of thought and practice in international relations at any given time is located against (and maintained by) that which has been removed from discussion, hidden from history, seen as indisputable or simply not thought. And, no matter how given the givens are, because they are partly located in and reproduced by everyday social practices, they are continuously precarious and capable of disruption. This means that the *boundary* between doxy and doxa is not fixed, or pre-determined, or inevitable, or ahistorical. And although the *relation* between the doxy and the doxa is an internal (that is to say, a necessary) one, its particular form and movements cannot be known in advance and are thus partly contingent.

It is this contingency which provides subordinated groups with an interest 'in pushing back the limits of the doxa and exposing the arbitrariness of the taken-for-granted' (Bourdieu, 1977: 169). Dominant groups, on the other hand, clearly have an interest 'in defending the integrity of doxa, or short of this, of establishing in its place the necessarily imperfect substitute, orthodoxy' (Bourdieu, 1977). Thus, to pin down my first and second postulates, the orthodoxy of the philosophical roots of International Relations exists only in the objective relationship which opposes it to heterodoxy: that is, the range of choices, ideas, policies and practices made possible by the existence of competing and plausible possibilities, but none of which constitute real alternatives in relation to the nature of the boundary between doxy and doxa.

However, the maintenance of the orthodoxy in International Relations is not as mechanical as this might sound. It does represent on its surface, manifest censorship: an official way of speaking, thinking, analysing and practising international relations, with oppositions rejected often as fanciful, fashionable or self-promoting (e.g., James, 1989; Jones, 1994; and Jackson, 1996), or in more serious vein, as 'programmatic' (Brown, 1994: 60) and as likely 'to remain on the margins of the field' unless and until they develop *testable* research programmes of their own (Keohane, 1989: 173). The argument in this section is that this explicit opposition between 'right' and 'wrong' opinions or methods or contents hides what theoretical orthodoxy reproduces, namely the more fundamental, deep opposition between the universe of things that *can* be thought, hence stated and debated, and the universe of that which is taken for granted, not thought, hence not stated and not debated. If all I have said so far is coherent, worth discussion and debate and not simply taken for granted, then reasonable grounds have been established for disclosing the philosophical roots of the discipline as a deeper and more extensive orthodoxy than it seemed at first to be.

The claim that the philosophical roots or intellectual tradition in either its classical realist form or its neo-realist form (both for the moment as in the sense these positions are normally understood) misrecognize globalization is probably fairly uncontentious. Furthermore, showing why this is so is a relatively straightforward matter. The irreducible requirement for conceptualizing globalization, whether as something requiring explanation or as itself an analytical concept, or both – and in my view it is simultaneously both – is to be able to demonstrate initially that globalization refers to a set of qualitatively different practices in international relations than those hitherto; or that globalization offers the possibility of qualitatively different and fuller accounts of international processes than hitherto. If neither of these can be convincingly demonstrated, then the widespread assumption that globalization does refer to something concrete and is not simply 'a buzzword, a term as ambiguous as it is popular' (Scholte, 1996: 45), cannot really be sustained.

To put this another way, attempts in the discipline to articulate globalization which do not pose at the outset the question of what if anything is global about globalization – that is, do not problematize the concept itself – and then provide a distinctive answer to it, are bound to misrecognize globalization for, if the concept only refers to practices and conditions capable of being recognized by the notions of 'international', 'regional' and 'local', then talk of 'the global' in any sense other than an empirically observable, geographical spread of already existing conditions and practices is redundant. Neither is it enough to suppose that answering the core question posed above is satisfied by utilizing taxonomic devices: that is to say, a mode of abstraction articulated through classification, categorization, metricity, separation and difference. The overwhelming tendency in Western/global social science is to enter into analysis by means of a taxonomy, which usually means seeking to define the concept or phenomenon in question in advance.

This pervasive academic practice is one in which items, events, outcomes or agents – generally, that which is to be explained – are first categorized and classified in terms of assumed-to-be discrete and observable characteristics, and then constructed through the form of ahistorical and abstract definition. This leads to classifications of the form: the state is ...; the MNC is ...; international organization is ...;

technology is ...; politics is ...; global society is ...; globalization is ...; and so on. This procedure carries with it an internal, self-generated secondary taxonomy, which allows the procedure to be itself classified as technically prior to (that is, pre-theoretical and wholly separate from) the business of analysis and knowledge construction. In Cox's terminology, this is problem-solving theory, and carries with it all the requirements and implications of taking the world as it appears to us as given and then imposing some order upon it (Cox, 1981: 128–29). Such theorizing makes it possible to generate general statements about regularities or classes of things, (e.g., the 'competition state'), which then appear to have general validity. However, the patterns are generated by the procedure, not by the items in question themselves, because they already presuppose the 'institutional and relational parameters assumed in the problem-solving approach' (Cox, 1981: 129).

Structural-functional, interactive, rationalist, and adaptive theorizations ensue from this starting point. These are not strictly speaking entailments of the taxonomic desire, but they are almost bound to flow from it. Embedded in these technical procedures are many problematic, habitualized and taken-for-granted resolutions of fundamental epistemological and methodological puzzles. Some of these I have referred to already – for example, the theory–practice, subject–object, agency–structure, polity–economy, domestic–international, and time–space relationships – in a variety of internal and external contexts of the discourse of philosophical roots. At the end of this section, I will draw these assumed dichotomies together with each other and with globalization-misunderstood.

For the moment, in relation to globalization and the taxonomic malaise, I will assert the following: if it is the case that part of what globalization means resides in its relations with other social items – meta-theoretical, theoretical and practical; observable and non-observable – and, simultaneously, part of what any other social item means in the late-modern world resides partly its relations with globalization, then the widespread procedure of initial abstraction through taxonomic method engenders the misrecognition of globalization from the start. The implication of this is that recognition of what globalization means requires jettisoning taxonomy, refusing conceptualizations of globalization as a thing in itself, and developing analyses of globalization as a complex concept which refers to a set of specific relations with causal powers and causal liabilities (Sayer, 1992). This is not and cannot be a purely theoretical or abstract task, as my earlier reference to the notion of concept formation employed by Cox (1983) implies. Neither is it arbitrary, because it proceeds initially from critique. Finally, such an analysis is not pre-determined, first because it does not, and cannot, define what globalization means ahistorically and in advance of detailed historical analysis, and second, because it recognizes that although part of what globalization means is constituted in and through relations of necessity, equally, part is constituted in and through contingent relations, and the latter cannot be known in advance.

Consequently, the meaning of globalization is to be arrived at only at the *end* of a detailed concrete analysis, rather than being assumed by abstract definition at the *start* of the analysis. This does not mean that globalization has a content that can be known with certainty, or established in terms of an essential truth-value. To assume this would be to return globalization to the constraints of positivism and to the methodological landscape of *thingness* and *discreteness*, as though it had a fixed internal meaning – a set of natural properties – waiting to be discovered. What it does mean is that globalization can be assumed to have certain characteristics, and certain causal powers and causal liabilities at any particular historical moment, some of which may in principle be transhistorical. On this view, 'certain' is not a reference to resolving competing claims by recourse to testing for truth or falsity, but a reference to 'certain' meaning more or less the same as a 'definite' historically developed content, which is capable of being described.[13]

The claim that showing how the philosophical roots of the discipline in its classical realist or neo-realist manifestation misrecognizes globalization is a relatively straightforward matter and hinges necessarily upon the extent to which my analysis of 'the philosophical roots' so far is both coherent and acceptable. The focus in this section is mainly upon classical realism and neo-realism not simply because they are the most explicit representations of the philosophical roots of the discipline understood as political theory (rather than as containing a deeper structural philosophy, which I earlier argued was a generic philosophy, with transtextual capacity) but also because of my earlier argument that together, these related positions constitute the dominant orthodoxy in International Relations, and the overwhelming amount of academic production in the discipline is, to varying degrees, within their discourse. I think it is relatively straightforward now because the grounds for the demonstration are implicated in core elements of the critique, or problematization, of the philosophical roots I have developed already.

First, at the most general level, classical political realism and neo-realism misrecognize globalization not so much because they construct it as part of the assumed-to-be external reality of international relations (although they do), but more because there is no space for a reflexive consideration of their own constitutive relationship with globalization as a potential object of inquiry. To put this another way, classical realism and neo-realism must from the start (although not necessarily intentionally) strive to render globalization meaningful in terms of the core concepts, timeless truths and salient issue areas of the philosophical roots of the discipline, of which classical realism and neo-realism are the primary and explicit bearers. Consequently, to the extent that these positions are prepared to conceptualize globalization at all, this can be done only by bringing the latter into some relationship – ideally of identity or correspondence, and at least of congruence – with the domain of orthodoxy in international relations, rather than into the problematic domain of the boundary between the doxy and the doxa. And this is to assume that theory and practice are necessarily separate domains.

Second, there is a set of particular constraints inscribed within classical realism and neo-realism (although in apparently different ways) which, taken together or singly, lead to the misrecognition of globalization. As a set, these particulars are incapable of specifying what, if anything, is 'global' about globalization, without transforming the meaning of 'global' into already articulated and understood concepts. The first of the more specific constraints is the categorical separation of subjectivity from objectivity. This dichotomy is a necessary element in establishing and reproducing the categorical distinction between theory-practice itself. However, there is more than simply a meta-theoretical or theoretical dimension to this dichotomy. In order to maintain consistency with earlier parts of my argument, I need to show that there is a practical or substantive dimension to the issue. The subjectivity-objectivity separation is probably better known in International Relations as the distinction between the 'psychological environment' and the 'operational environment'.[14] Derived dualisms such as beliefs–facts, thought–action, mental–material, insider–outsider and so on have not only embedded themselves throughout the textuality of political theory and international theory, but have become firm chorus lines too in the language and debate of statespersons, soldiers, diplomats, business people, journalists and travellers.

In both the discipline of International Relations and the practice of international relations, therefore, the privileging of the objective over the subjective is essential to the reproduction of the philosophical roots of the discipline as the dominant orthodoxy within theory, and to the social reproduction of the ownership by dominant groups of what can be called 'objective' and therefore 'real' in concrete international practice: for example, claims about the relationship between wage-labour rates and competition for inward foreign direct investment (FDI). So long as classical realism and neo-realism hold the view that globalization (or for that matter the international) is located with the external environment of actors and is thus a part of the objective conditions of essentially subjective policy-making, then analysis from these positions will misrecognize globalization by only recognizing some of its observable symptoms. Furthermore, these positions can only then conceptualize actors, in this case usually states, as reacting to the perceived conditions of globalization. The possibility that state formation, in a diverse variety of forms and transformations, may be part of the concrete development of globalization cannot be contemplated.

In addition, and consistent with the theory-practice and subjectivity-objectivity dichotomies, these versions of the philosophical roots of the discipline hold strongly to a categorical separation between the domestic sphere and the international sphere. In political terms, the 'domestic' is seen as the defining site of order, community, law, legitimate government, citizenship and security, and it represents 'territory at rest'. The agent predominantly identified as maintaining and realizing coherence between these dimensions of social practice is the modern state, while the capacity of the state presupposed in this overall coherence is that of sovereignty (M. Williams, 1996: 109–22). Against this, the 'international' is usually seen as the defining site of disorder, lack of government, non-citizenship, insecurity, no overall law, and other, foreign 'territories at rest'. What norms there are that transcend territorial boundaries, together with international public laws, sets of peaceful transactions, regulated competition, free movements of persons, goods and capital, and so on are seen as quintessentially temporary and voluntary arrangements, consciously entered into by the knowing agents of states. They do not arise from enforceable commands of a supra-state authority, but from sets of interactive agreements, and are therefore subject to continuous review and potential rejection. On the basis of this assumption the domestic is in tension with the international, and with the regional. The global cannot be conceived except as other than the domestic, and as no more than an increase in the geographical and observable spread of international interactions. Globalization on this view adds nothing of qualitative or analytical value to the interactive concept of internationalization, and is then redundant.

The second particular constraint within the realist and neo-realist orthodoxy is a complex compound effect of their shared mode of abstraction. It arises out of the deeper generic philosophy of empiricist epistemology, and it is this continuous transtextual potential which will allow a later argument that neo-realism covers a wider part of the doxy than it is usually considered to, and, that other positions not part of the realist and neo-realist discourse are nevertheless still located within the doxy. Consequently they are subject to the same or similar limitations so far as conceptualizing globalization is concerned. The mode of abstraction common to realism and neo-realism – and, as I will argue later, to almost all other positions within the heterodoxy – is a double form of reductionism. One part of this, which I will call vertical reductionism, is the way in which realism, and neo-realism (including within the latter the attempt by Waltz in 1979 to develop a systemic or structural realism), have sought to resolve the relationship between parts of a system and the system as a whole. This problematic is now generally referred to, following Wendt, as the agent-structure issue (Wendt, 1987; Hollis and Smith, 1991, 1994, 1996; Carlsnaes, 1992; Jabri and Chan, 1996). Briefly, this has been resolved in realism and neo-realism by the adoption, either explicitly or implicitly, of methodological individualism, which in general holds that facts about social relations or social phenomena as a whole can only be explained in terms of facts about individuals.

It is perhaps both ironic, and pertinent to the long historical scope of classical political theory, that this position was first clearly articulated by Hobbes, who asserted that 'it is necessary that we know the things that are to be compounded before we can know the whole compound, because everything is best understood by its constitutive causes' (Hobbes, quoted in Lukes, 1973: 110). So far as conceptualizing globalization is concerned, the possibility that it may represent a structural condition, related causally with but not reducible to the aims, intentions, capabilities and interests of individual units in the world (whatever they are) is methodologically disallowed from the start. Furthermore, the concept of globalization on this view is meaningful if and only if it is capable of being translated directly into observational statements, which means that claims about globalization which include consideration of non-observable elements are also rendered unintelligible.

The second part of this double form of reductionism, which I will call horizontal reductionism, is the characterization of relevant phenomena in International Relations as political. This is overwhelmingly the case in the realist and neo-realist orthodoxy, and in International Relations more generally, notwithstanding a great amount of recent critique, which is to be found in its most sustained form in the field of IPE. I will argue shortly that the dominant forms of conceptualization in IPE do not resolve this form of reduction, but replace the strict separation of politics from economics with an interactive account of politics and economics, wherein these two analytically distinct spheres of social relations are still related in terms of difference.

Such a privileging of politics underpins the predominant tendency in realism and neo-realism to focus upon the state as both the major actor in international relations and the core unit of analysis in International Relations. Equally it was the privileging of questions about individuals' obligations to the state, power and order, citizenship, the origins of the modern state and sovereignty, which enabled the earlier establishment of a tradition of political theory which was both separated and different from a tradition of economic theory. Conceptualizing globalization as a largely or mainly political phenomenon entails an unnecessary narrowing of the complexity of the late-modern world, and leaves other important contexts of contemporary social practice such as trade and poverty, technology and science, gender and ethnicity as no more and no less than marginalized practices to be brought under political control. More importantly in my view, it means that insofar as globalization is contemplated at all, it is problematized in terms of a necessary opposition and tension between, for example, state sovereignty/autonomy and the alien forces of globalization (Ohmae, 1990, 1995), or between states and firms (Stopford and Strange, 1991) or as more recently between states seen as the source of competitive strategies in an environment of global economic processes (Jessop, 1993; Palan and Abbott, 1996).

The third particular constraint generated by the orthodoxy of the philosophical roots arises from the conception of time and space inscribed within it. The first point here has strong links back to my earlier discussion about the assumed distinction between normative theory and empirical theory, which has become a generally accepted motif of both the political philosophy and the generic philosophy that together make up the philosophical roots of the discipline. It also has strong links back to my earlier discussion about the state as a defined territory – what I called earlier 'territory at rest' – and the 'international' seen either as non-territory, or territory in dispute (e.g., the earth's near atmospheric space), or simply the globe as a geographical, three-dimensional whole. I argued earlier that the distinction between normative and empirical theory rested on the security of the logical and formal distinction between evaluative statements and descriptive statements: more crudely, between claims about what 'is' and claims about what 'ought' to be. I concluded that this distinction is strictly meaningful only as an analytical truth, but is nevertheless of overwhelming importance in respect of the connection between appropriating the conditions of 'reality' on the one hand, and systems of power and hegemony in the world on the other.

It is of course possible to translate the logical distinction between 'is' and 'ought' into its presupposed temporal and spatial characteristics. 'Is' here refers to what is the case now, that is the present, or by extension, to a set of repeated 'nows' or 'past-presents'. There is also an ontological assumption that what 'is' is observable, which is to say it occupies some describable or measurable three-dimensional space. Against the firmness of the 'is' of social practice, 'ought' is assumed to be in opposition to 'now': that is, as a reference to what things are not now, but should or might be in the future. Even in those cases where the 'ought' is an injunction to continue some present practice or behaviour – as in, 'the UK ought to remain in the United Nations' – the reference is to projecting what is now the case into the future. On this standard view, time is seen as capable of being split into pieces, or slices: usually the past, the present and the future. Three implications of this reveal constraints upon recognizing globalization.

First, time and space are assumed to be independent factors, in the sense of being unaffected by what goes on within them. Consequently, they are seen as fixed or absolute environments of activity, as natural. Second, by distinguishing the 'is' of International Relations (as what is in the present and therefore also what is 'real'), from the 'ought' of International Relations (as what is not yet the case, but some future state of affairs and therefore also not yet 'real') the 'is' – or by extension the 'was' of International Relations – is privileged over the 'ought' of International Relations, because there is no possibility on this view of holding that the 'ought' things (e.g., that there ought to be peace in the world, or that there ought to be no starvation in the world) are already contained within, already a part of, the 'is' or reality of International Relations. There *are* already spaces in the world which are more or less continuously peaceful, and there *are* already spaces in the world where starvation is more or less continuously absent. If it is the case that globalization refers not only to the global empirical spread of ways of doing things, but also to the transfer of causality from local space to non-territorial space while none the less reproducing the unequal distribution of peace in the world, and of starvation in the world, within local space, then analyses which fail to theorize the meta-theoretical elements of time and space, normally constructed so as to legitimate the world as it appears to us, will also fail to recognize globalization fully.

These two points together imply a third, namely that within the discipline orthodoxy, that which can be characterized as real, because it 'is', is thereby deemed to exist. Because of the pervasive conflation of what is real with what is empirical, that which is deemed to exist is deemed also, and necessarily, to occupy some space, which is defined exclusively in the discipline as territory. Conversely, that which can be characterized as not-real because it is deemed an ought-to-be project – which would include *all* critical theory and most feminist theory – is also seen as not yet capable of occupying space, territorial, three-dimensional or otherwise. It is spaceless but not timeless, and can be deemed therefore to be metaphysical or idealistic.

Two things are important here. First, the orthodoxy is not only able to exclude oppositional views as they arise, it is also and ironically able to police future possible views in advance of their articulation, because the categorizations of 'is/now' and 'ought/future' are constructed paradoxically, as ahistorical criteria. They apply to past, present and future texts, and this is a significant power of exclusion. Second, because of these deeply embedded assumptions of time and space within the orthodoxy of the philosophical roots of the discipline, what is 'global' about globalization can only be constructed so long as it is congruent with a territorial conception of space. This allows a certain coherence in the orthodoxy for the opposition of domestic and international or state and non-state actors, because 'international' can be constructed as foreign territory, or interaction between discrete domestic territories, while non-state actors can be coherently characterized as occupying some territory – being in some place – but without the quality of legitimate sovereign control over a defined territory. Consequently, and moving beyond the inherent circularity of this view, the 'global' is seen either as the extension of what is meant by international, but of no qualitative difference, or as some possible future condition such as a simple, geographically global super-territorial state. Again, the possibility of the 'global' being real but none the less non-territorial, or more precisely now, non-three-dimensional, is not allowed.

Within the orthodoxy at large, that is to say beyond its realist and neo-realist manifestations, the site of observable behaviour, which *is* necessarily territorial or three-dimensional, is conflated with the site of causality, which is assumed also to be, but is *not* necessarily, territorial or three-dimensional. Indeed, the possibility of causal items which are non-three-dimensional is already ironically contained within the orthodox account of time and space. In order for the orthodoxy to dismiss emancipatory theory or opposition on the grounds that it is normative, an ought-to-be thing, residing in the future and therefore spaceless, the concept of 'spaceless' is already conceded, indeed it is essential (although unspoken) to their critique. Furthermore, the deep philosophical structure of the orthodoxy – what I have called the generic philosophy of empiricism – although historically initiated in territorial space (which is why it is meaningful to refer to Anglo-Saxon analytical philosophy, or the Vienna school of logical-positivism, or the Chicago school of economics) has now become global in the sense not only that it has spread geographically to receiver locations, but in the more important sense that it is no longer tied to *any* particular territory. This proposition, it should be noted, in no way applies in the case of empirical examples drawn from other existing philosophies of epistemology, such as islamic, confucian, scientific realist or marxist variants.

Thus we have one specific candidate for knowledge construction, in this case empiricism, which has shifted from its territorial and historical location as an outcome of the long period of the Enlightenment, to become the taken-for-granted ahistorical and universalizable criterion for evaluating all attempts at knowledge construction. In this sense, empiricism has become timeless, spaceless but in spite of this (or because of this) it has enlarged and confirmed its causal content in respect of the inclusive and exclusive powers of the orthodoxy, if not in respect of its own explanatory power. In more accessible terms, it can be briefly stated that the orthodoxy of the discipline has constructed time as chronological history, space as geographical and political territory, and each as separate from the other. Moreover, it is historical rather than spatial frameworks which have been privileged in the discipline, at least until recently, as new conceptions of political geography developed in geography, urban studies and sociology have begun to spread beyond their initial disciplinary boundaries (Kofman and Youngs, 1996). However, the impact of this work is as yet slight. Time in the form of chronological history remains at the core of the orthodoxy, and it remains separated from space.

Clearly then, the construction of time and space within the orthodoxy is atomistic, linked to observable conditions, biased towards chronology and sequence, and towards territorial definition. Consequently, globalization can only be recognized by rendering it consistent with this particular time-space framework. This means either that the concept of globalization is brought within the domain of the doxy, and rendered safe as a variant of internationalization, or excluded as simply redundant. Alternative constructions of globalization seen as a wholly meta-theoretical but none the less real structure in the world, with causal powers and liabilities, and located in *n*-dimensional space, are then evaluated at best as misconceived and at worst as unintelligible.

It can now be seen that the philosophical roots of the discipline represents a consistent system. The appearance of debate is maintained. Whether Hobbes, or Machiavelli, or Locke, or Kant, or Marx, best help us to understand contemporary international relations is taken still to be a relevant area of contestation. I have argued that the philosophical roots of the discipline in its most accessible forms – that is as explicit classical international political theory, or its transformation to neo-realism – can only misrecognize globalization and will be likely to dismiss claims about globalization as premature, mistaken, misplaced, empirically unsustainable or at best, limited. However, the argument I have made requires the exposure of what I call the deep philosophical structure of the orthodoxy, which has developed historically through the establishment of the tradition of political theory, but cannot be said to be reducible to it. It is a powerful epistemology, partly because it has been reciprocally related to the gradual dominance of science in modernity, through the application of technology to society.

The orthodoxy is consequently more extensive than its appearance in the discipline would at first sight imply. In its classical form, the realist view reads international relations as mainly relations between states; it sees the state as a rational unitary actor; constructs the domestic as wholly different from and separate from the international, and it sees the latter as anarchic and a site of continuous danger, within which the security of citizens depends upon the security of the state, and the security of the state depends in the end upon military capacity, either singly or in alliance. On this view, globalization is more or less incomprehensible. From out of its deeper philosophy, classical realism steps into line not only with its transformation to neo-realism, but also with other positions in the orthodoxy such as transnationalism, behaviouralism, IPE, 'new normative' theory, and post-modernism. And it does so on the basis of a set of shared assumptions, which I have analysed as likely to lead to the misrecognition of globalization. The major elements of this I have identified as a consistent, highly connected disciplinary device within the discipline, and I have also argued that this set is causally connected to real relations of power and hegemony in the world. The most significant dichotomies within this set are the separations of theory from practice; of subjectivity from objectivity; of agency from structure; of politics from economics; of the domestic from the international; and of time from space.

I want to conclude this section with a brief two-part discussion of where this critique might now lead. The first part can be characterized as an ironic inversion. Although it must be clear by now that my view is that the philosophical roots/intellectual tradition in International Relations leads to the strong likelihood that globalization will be misrecognized, I have not argued that the recognition of globalization must therefore come from outside the discipline. My central thesis has been that in order to develop a convincing account of globalization, analysis must start from a critical account of the discipline's existing relationship with the concept of globalization, on the grounds that part of what globalization means resides in existing theorizations of it. This is the movement within critical theory methodology to metatheory, namely that making a concept concrete is not a matter of evaluating different theories *about* it, but evaluating at the start the relationship *between* existing theories and the object of inquiry.

This is the task represented in orthodox research projects as a literature review. In critical theory method, the task of review appears similar, in that it involves the identification and evaluation of relevant existing academic work on the issue. However, it is fundamentally different from a literature review as normally understood in two respects. First, a critical review involves analysis of the relationship between the existing academic work and the object of inquiry as a causal relation, not simply one of empirical validity and internal coherence. Second, and following from this, a critical review is not a pre-theoretical, pre-research task, but is an essential part of the real research from the start. In this way what is problematic about globalization can then stand as the basis for a new (but not arbitrary) conceptualization. This is why my claim in the introduction that some very prominent views of globalization fundamentally misrecognize globalization does not entail either that I have a uniquely privileged and known to be correct view of globalization in advance of such a critique, or that there is a single correct view on the matter.

On the contrary, what I have tried to do is to show that there are two dimensions of philosophy involved in the philosophical roots of the discipline: one apparent and derived from classical political theory, and one embedded and linked to the generic philosophy of empiricist epistemology. Consequently, we are able to reach a point at which we can argue not only that analysis of international relations in general, and globalization in particular, necessarily requires attention to the philosophical content of the discipline, but that any critical conceptualization of international relations necessarily depends upon a reconstruction of that philosophical content. Philosophy here is not removed, but relocated, from its orthodox position where it is assumed to be outside, and inherently disinterested in, its object of inquiry, to its real position which is that of the deep, obscured philosophical or meta-theoretical content of everyday social practices. In the genuinely critical method philosophy shifts from its causal role of constraint and discipline in the reproduction of the dominance of doxy over doxa to an emancipatory causal role as the first step to disrupting the taken-for-granted naturalness and arbitrariness of the doxy-doxa boundary.

There is a further element to this inversion, although not so ironic. Here, the analysis of how the orthodoxy in the discipline engenders a misrecognition of globalization simultaneously confronts the International Relations discipline. This is because by posing the central elements of the orthodoxy against plausible possibilities of the meaning of globalization, the extent to which the latter presents major conceptual, theoretical and practical difficulties for the existing orthodoxy is also revealed. It would be unkind to leave the argument here, as though the whole of the classical political theory tradition were unyielding in the face of claims about globalization. A recent book (H. Williams, 1996) contains a perceptive, at times striking (if also gentle) critique of the classical political theory tradition. Although the title of the book – *International Relations and the Limits of Political Theory* – implies critique, it is only in the penultimate chapter that the grounds for this emerge fully and clearly. I will not go into detail here, for two sharp assertions by Williams will show the line of argument. First, he argues (H. Williams, 1996: 143) that while political theory maintains a 'vague intimation that its insights were applicable both to internal and international politics ... there is not a great deal in political theory as it presently stands to back up this hunch'. Although he acknowledges that political theory must change with the times:

> The suggestion that political theory may need to undergo a radical change seems to contradict the most recent flowering of political theory which has taken place in the United States and Britain. After its apparent demise in the 1950s, political theory has made a remarkable leap to prominence through the work of individuals like John

> Rawls, Robert Nozic, Bruce Ackerman, Brian Barry, Charles Taylor and, more polemically Roger Scruton and the revival of Hayekian political thought ... The form of this recent writing has remained as ever upon the relationship between the individual and the state.
>
> (H. Williams, 1996)

Williams is not a critical theorist, and his criticisms are careful, leading to a demand not so much for fundamental change in political theory as for the kind of changes that would allow some explicit reconciliation between the still individual and state-centred orthodoxy of the classical tradition, and the demands of globalization. However, there is no doubt at all that here is a notable contributor to the classical political theory tradition in International Relations acknowledging that globalization, whatever it is, presents severe difficulties for maintenance of the tradition in its present form.

The second part, or implication, of my critique so far is that a great deal of recent work in International Relations which would not normally be located within classical realism or neo-realism, some of which furthermore identifies itself as explicitly opposed to the philosophical roots of the discipline, can now be shown nevertheless to be firmly located within the orthodoxy of International Relations. This is not to say they are not critical of the intellectual tradition, for they often are, but only at its level of appearance, namely classical political realism and neo-realism. Consequently, they do not advance a fundamental opposition to the orthodoxy because they fail to confront the embedded generic philosophy of empiricist epistemology. In my argument, they do not and cannot represent critical theory proper. This is not to assert they have nothing useful at all to say about globalization, for they do. However, what they do say is truncated, because analysis remains fixed at the level of the appearance, or observable consequences of globalization, and this represents still a misrecognition. This is so on my argument because by seeking to recognize and conceptualize globalization through a process of reconciliation with the existing and established domain of the discipline's heterodoxy, what is problematic about globalization is seen mainly as residing within globalization. On my view, specifying what it is that is problematic about globalization requires a simultaneous specification about what it is that is problematic, in epistemological and meta-theoretical terms, about the International Relations discipline itself.

Substantiating such a contentious claim as this is important if it is not to be left purely as assertion. However, there is no need for this to be extensive and detailed because, first, I have referred to this element of the discussion in various earlier sections of the chapter and second, what I have to say here is already strongly implicated in the argument so far. Consequently, the core elements of this substantiation can be argued from a basis of correspondence with those items already exposed as constituting the deeper, or generic philosophy of knowledge embedded in, but also extending beyond, the classical political theory component of the orthodoxy. If it can be shown that other apparently critical positions in International Relations share assumptions which are in common with the classical realist and neo-realist positions, and which are at the same time central to the reproduction of the discipline's orthodoxy as heterodoxy, albeit in a variety of degrees of explicitness, extent and rigour, then a prima facie substantiation is confirmed. In what follows, I will refer only to academic work which explicitly addresses the issue of globalization, but would make the point in passing that this argument of correspondence applies in principle to much of the recent work in International Relations that has other projects in hand.

Although Scholte (1996: 43 and 45) has recently asserted that 'today the vocabulary of globality occupies a notable place in the everyday parlance of commerce, governance, academe and entertainment', and that 'questions of globalization have become a concern across the academic spectrum in the 1990s', there is not yet a great amount of published academic work on globalization, even though such work is likely to increase. Also, what exists is spread across a range of disciplines, in particular sociology, international relations (including international political economy), political science, international business studies and political geography.[15] In none of the disciplines where analysis of globalization has emerged can this work be seen as central, or discipline-shifting, in the fundamental sense I have specified, and this is particularly so in International Relations. It is understandable that academics interested in globalization from any one of these disciplines will tend to talk to, write with and against, meet, and generally engage with similarly interested academics from other disciplines more perhaps than with academics immune to the globalization bug within their own discipline. Nevertheless, there is clearly a danger here of self-enclosure: that is, the possibility of the development of an interdisciplinary academic ghetto of globalization. If, as globalization theorists assert, globalization is of central importance in making sense of how the late-modern world is organized in the ways it is rather than in some other conceivable ways, then a 'ghettoized' academic location on the margins is likely to develop further. This is so in my view until and unless globalization is theorized in such a form as to confront the orthodoxy within each discipline, and that deep element of it which constitutes what I referred to earlier as the silent but effective transdisciplinary epistemological alliance of empiricisms. Support and acknowledgement from other academics is an important part of academic existence but, if it is based upon the exile of like-minded people, it is bound to reinforce marginalization and exclusion rather than dismantling the grounds of that exclusion. It is in this sense that I assert the need to move from an interdisciplinary account to an anti-disciplinary account of globalization.

I have argued at length that the 'philosophical roots' of the discipline, as a tradition, is the bearer of two connected philosophies: classical political philosophy, and an embedded epistemology of empiricism. This was not just an argument that classical political theory, and its modern extensions, depend upon empiricist assumptions about how we come to have knowledge of the world, how we might best evaluate knowledge claims about the world, what kinds of things can be properly said to exist in the world, and what opportunities there might be for bringing about change in the world. It was also an argument that the establishment of the intellectual tradition as a *particular* tradition was (and still is) a causal element in the development of empiricist epistemology, and its eventual achievement of academic and social hegemony. I have shown how it is that the philosophical roots of the discipline, mainly in its political philosophy form, but with assistance from its deeper transtextual philosophy, has severely constrained the potential for classical realism and neo-realism to conceptualize globalization to the extent of misrecognition. In broad terms, this misrecognition is close to being absolute, in that the very possibility of the development of globalization, as a qualitatively different and historically recent phenomenon, is either rejected or translated as a limited enlargement of already existing practices adequately dealt with through the concepts of 'regional' and 'international'.

In interrogating other positions in the discipline, the *form* of misrecognition will be shown to be different, and more complex. This is so because work which seeks to explain globalization already concedes globalization as a problematic requiring attention, specification, explanation and evaluation. This is a minimum level of agreement for particular analyses do vary in their conceptions of what globalization means, what its main elements are, its extent and importance in

International Relations, and whether globalization is a good thing or a bad thing. Consequently, this contestation within and between writings on globalization is an important first part of explaining why it is that even if such work claims explicitly to confront the classical tradition as part of its account of globalization (e.g., Shaw, 1994; Saurin, 1995; Spike Peterson, 1996), it nevertheless (and necessarily) reproduces one of the conditions of heterodoxy.

This reproduction of the heterodoxy, however, is not enough in itself to substantiate a claim of misrecognition. In order to do this, the argument I have developed has to be accepted as relevant, and in principle sustainable. It then has to be moved from its present status as 'abstract research' to that of 'concrete research' (Sayer, 1992: 146–51). This means returning the critical analysis, developed up to this point by concentrating on the abstract or meta-theoretical possibilities of conceptualizing globalization, back into the substantive world which gives it meaning and space. This is not a procedure of empirical testing, because the substantive context itself is given new meaning through abstraction, while establishing the meaning of the concept at the same time. Furthermore, on this view already existing analyses are part of the substantive context of globalization, and not external to it. To accomplish this movement, I will take the conditions of the deep philosophical structure of the orthodoxy, outlined so far in general terms, and examine whether or not they are inscribed within other positions in the discipline.

The first important element in this evaluation of International Relations literature on globalization is how, if at all, the relationship between theory and practice is articulated. In the introduction to their recent edited collection entitled *Globalization: Theory and Practice*, Kofman and Youngs (1996: 1, emphasis added) refer to their volume as representing 'the second wave, as it were, of globalization studies. These are characterized by a dissatisfaction with the current state of global play, *both theoretical and practical*.' Reference is then made to 'the range of critical issues which need to be addressed in relation to *the theory and practice of globalization*' (emphasis added).

There is here then a clear and explicit concern to deal with the theory-practice relation. In a later chapter, for example, Youngs (1996: 58–9) asserts that 'theory and practice are intrinsically and problematically related' and declares 'the importance or regarding theories of international relations as dimensions of the practice of world politics'. However, the resolution is achieved by declaring that theory is not separate from practice, but itself already a practice. This is ambiguous, and could be simplistic. This is so because it would be absurd to deny that theory production is a part of total social practice. But if this is what Youngs means, and such an interpretation is heavily implicated when she declares 'These kinds of questions indicate the extent to which *theorizing is a practical human activity, distinct from but not totally separate from other forms of activity*' (Kofman and Youngs, 1996: 63, emphasis added), then what is at stake here is whether or not theory and practice can be categorically differentiated and located alongside the categorical differentiation of subjective and objective. Youngs's formulation does not help, for it is linear: theory is a practice, and not just some theory but all theory. This does not allow us to differentiate which theorizations are part of dominant practices, or to explain why some theories in the world are incompatible with some practices. The issue of whether or not practice is also and equally a part of theory is left unspoken.

Throughout the text, there are many more examples of analyses based on the categorical separation of theory from practice than there are attempts such as Youngs's to integrate the relation between theory and practice as part of recognizing globalization. With reference to the formation of trading blocs, the reader is asked to note that 'such a strategy represents a political response to economic globalization'. Here we see the separation of theory from practice, the construction of globalization in observational terms, the separation of economics from politics, and the separation of the domestic from the political. These attempts are thus firmly located within the heterodoxy of the discipline, sharing the assumptions and practices of neo-realism and empiricism, and dealing only with the symptoms of globalization.

A different approach has been developed by Martin Shaw (1994) in *Global Society and International Relations*. Although a sociologist strictly speaking, this work arises from what Shaw (1994: iv) describes as 'a period of engagement with international relations'. Shaw's aim (1994: 4) is to fundamentally challenge and reconceptualize the field of International Relations 'from the point of view of sociology in general, and the sociology of globalization in particular'. He characterizes globalization 'as the way in which social relations become defined by specifically global contexts' but then seems to conflate 'globalization' with global society, within which some 'genuinely global' specific systems have formed (Shaw, 1994: 18–19).

The question which should concern us here is what allows Shaw to distinguish items which are 'genuinely global' from those which remain 'restricted to national or local contexts'? What is clear is the overwhelming taxonomic framework. Global is separated from international, and both of these from the local and the national. The global economic system is separated from the global political system; both of these are separated from the global cultural system, and all of these are separated from the global civil society (Shaw, 1994: 21–2). In the end, globalization is conceptualized as a geographical, measurable item, which still allows the idea of the state as a discrete entity in the form of 'inter-state relations' (1994: 5). The problem running through all of this, which is why globalization is a radical issue for Shaw – as well as for International Relations and sociology – is the heroic struggle to render globalization distinct from other concepts, definable in itself, and capable of being operationalized. The power of empiricism to specify the terrain upon which this struggle is waged is revealed fully when Shaw (1994: 17, emphasis added) asserts: 'While global society in this sense [no more or less than the entire complex of social relations between human beings on a world scale] contains all social relations not all relations are *actually defined at a global level*.'

It would be incredible in my view if *any* social relation was actually defined at the global level, for all social behaviour in the sense of observable practices is necessarily (and for all intents and purposes always will be) located at the local level, precisely because social items, agents, actors *can* only operate in three-dimensional space. The only way in which Shaw's statement can make sense is to assume 'the global' is some non-national, non-territorial, yet *still* three-dimensional place or site of social practice. The problem arises here because the term 'actually' is seen as non-problematic and indicates too a confusion and conflation of the site of observable events and behaviour with possible sites of explanation.

From this particular sociological perspective, globalization is misrecognized. The impulse to understand (perhaps we should say control) a concept through definition remains strong in 1997. Baylis and Smith (1997: 7), for example, feel compelled to define globalization in ahistorical and abstract terms at the outset of their edited volume: 'By globalization we simply mean the process of increasing interconnectedness between societies, such that events in one part of the world more and more have effects on peoples and societies far away.' This is very close to an earlier definition offered by McGrew (1992b: 13–14):

> [globalization is] the multiplicity of linkages and interconnections that transcend the nation-state (and by implication the societies) which make up the modern world system. It defines a process

> through which events, decisions and activities in one part of the world can come to have significant consequences for individuals and communities in quite distant parts of the world.

In both cases, these definitions appear more or less identical with the rash of definitions of international relations as a system, which appeared first in the late 1950s and 1960s (Kaplan, 1957; Burton, 1972).

If globalization means nothing more or less than the interconnectedness of parts of the international system, albeit increased, then it adds nothing to our understanding of globalization as a qualitatively different phenomenon in the world. In addition, such conceptualizations simply state the obvious, because 'the interconnections of parts' is what it means to describe something as a system. The world here is seen as a geographical whole, and globalization is then seen as the increased geographical spread of ways of doing things. What is 'global' about these processes cannot be distinguished from what is international, and places in the world are no different from space in the world; that is to say, they are all by implication territorial.

In a similar vein, Scholte (1997: 14) refers to globalization as those 'processes whereby social relations acquire relatively distanceless and borderless qualities, so that human lives are increasingly played out in the world as a single place'. Here again, the definition is ahistorical and wholly abstract in form. What is 'global' about globalization is not made clear. Instead, globalization is translated into its main manifestations: communications, organizations, ecology, production, military, norms and everyday thinking (Scholte 1997: 15–16). The choice of these, rather than say gender, or food, or labour, or consumption, or culture, or race is never justified, and consequently remains arbitrary. They may indeed be globalization's main manifestations, but in the first place, those chosen are not evaluated in relation to other possible candidates; second, discussion of what the 'main manifestations' of globalization are in empirical detail cannot account for what explains 'distanceless' and 'borderless', and conflates globalization as a thing to be explained with globalization as a causal concept. Again, the bases for misrecognition are clear.

Baylis and Smith pay significant attention in their introductory chapter to a recent text by Hirst and Thompson (1996). This is not surprising, given the rapid and extensive influence the book has had. Such influence is, however, in my view, difficult to explain for Hirst and Thompson's argument is severely flawed in a number of important respects. First, they pose the globalization thesis in its extreme and idealized form. They focus on extreme views because 'these extreme views [are] strong, relatively coherent and capable of being developed into a clear ideal typical conception of a globalized economic system' (Hirst and Thompson, 1996: 3–4). This justification can stand if and only if they can show that none, or few, of the not-extreme views on globalization are not strong, relatively coherent and capable of being developed into clear ideal type conceptions of a globalized economic system. It is interesting in this regard that Hirst and Thompson do not refer in their opening chapter to *any* extant texts on globalization. Even a cursory examination of the literature in this area shows that there are very few analysts of globalization that are extreme in the Hirst and Thompson sense. I can think of only three such texts – Ohmae (1990, 1995) and Phillips (1992) – and it is noteworthy that their influence is felt most sharply in the discipline of international business studies and disseminated through seminars for international business people.

The Hirst and Thompson justification can be seen therefore to be a rationalization. This does not mean necessarily that the rest of their analysis is without merit. However, in my view, it is seriously flawed throughout on the following grounds. First, it assumes that the question of globalization (or not) is a question of measurement, and therefore can be settled empirically: that is, they declare (1996: 2) the 'absence of a clear model to measure trends' to be a significant objection in itself, as is the lack of agreement as to 'a commonly accepted model of the new global political economy'. This is a sloppy argument, for it presupposes that agreement *to* model globalization and then agreement about *a* model of globalization is necessary in order to conceptualize it in the first place. Here, Hirst and Thompson's view of what is necessary to conceptualize globalization properly is offered as a general view about what is necessary, which in my view is simply a case of academic terrorism.

Other instances of poor argument inhabit the entire text. For example, the whole question of globalization is begged from the start. What I mean here is that Hirst and Thompson seek to measure the extent of globalization, as against continuing national or territorially based causes, on the basis of criteria of measurement which are national or locally derived indices. Consequently, the conclusion that globalization is not nearly as extensive as some argue is built into the analytical framework from the start. Further theoretically impoverished items abound: the reduction of globalization to *economic* globalization on the grounds of belief alone (1996: 3); the assumption that transnational corporations are not major agents of change because the majority of companies are nationally based (which is like arguing that the advanced political economies in the world are not major agents of change because the majority of political economies in the world are not advanced). This is absurd because it equates the influence of *X* with the number of *X*s. They assume that regional trading blocs are necessarily and unequivocally evidence against globalization, when they could equally be evidence for it (see Chapter 9 in this volume). This text is empiricist, reductionist in both vertical and horizontal terms, its conclusions are embedded in its premises, its conception of global is geographical and territorial, and it seeks to conceptualize globalization in terms of correspondence with a model defined in advance, rather than developing a concept of globalization out of the practices and conditions of social life in the world.

If this critique is sustainable, then the question as to the influence of this text seems central. I argued earlier, in respect of the classical tradition of political theory, that we cannot evaluate or comprehend a text only as a literal thing in itself. All texts have contexts, today as then, and a large element in this is the potential receptivity for a text. And it is this in my view that best explains the significance attributed to the Hirst and Thompson text. We cannot say that this significance comes only because the text is elegant, endowed with a clarity of language and argument, or compelling internal coherence, for it has few of these qualities. It is replete, however, with the motifs of the dominant discourse of empiricism: it separates theory from practice and politics from economics; it reduces the 'global' to the aims, intentions and properties of individual agents; it reproduces the distinction between national and international; and finally, privileges the status of economistic theorization over other forms. Consequently, Hirst and Thompson, without intention, locate their text at the centre of the deep transdisciplinary orthodoxy, from whence a deep resonance secures its audience.

One final example of the extended disciplining power of the orthodoxy will complete this section. The recent text by Palan and Abbott (1996) is perhaps the most interesting in terms of the hegemony of the orthodoxy in International Relations and its continuous reproduction through and by new texts. Of the texts examined so far, this is by far the most eclectic, and it stands as an ironic analogue with the framework developed in this chapter. One could argue that particular texts (like states) are in competition with each other for a market share of the discipline's orthodoxy: that is, a certain intelligible place within the heterodoxy, or the universe of discourse, which is the space of debate. International relations is not only concerned now with things considered from a global point of view, it has itself become a globalized social science. It can thus be seen as a practical everyday environment for the activities of individual scholars, who (like states) must react and adapt to what they see as the defining characteristics of the academic environment. Academics (like states) respond by devising a number of strategies of competition: realism was at one stage a successful competitive strategy, and became part of the infrastructure of the discipline's orthodoxy (i.e., simultaneously a response to, and a part of, that orthodoxy).

Changes in the environment signalled a demise of realism's competitive force, and a 'new' strategy – neo-realism – was devised, representing 'new' forms of adapting. It was never to be expected that all academics would respond (adapt) in the same way, but it is clear that (as with states) some possible strategies have turned out to be mistaken: that is to say, they represent failed adaptive strategies. As several scholars have shown,[16] Marxism as a competitive but emancipatory academic strategy has little to offer the discipline, and has not 'contributed to an entire new infrastructure' of the International Relations 'environment' (Palan and Abbott, 1996: 6). The point, however, is that Palan and Abbott fail to offer an account of *why* it is that some strategic responses of states (like academics) are 'effective in terms of improved competitiveness' but some are not. To do so, the environment (in this case 'globalization') has to be explained, particularly in respect of how it came to be mediated through a discourse of competition.

Although declaring an interest in exposing the relations between 'competitiveness' and 'globalization', it is competitiveness only which is described. What it is that is 'global' about globalization is not explored, except in the limited sense of its empirical manifestations. The form of eclecticism is extreme, representing a position-of-no-position. Marx and Braudel are the basis, it seems, of the analysis of institutions and structures; Porter (1990) is the source of an operational definition of globalization; while Cerny (1990, 1994b) and Strange (1988) are the major voices from which 'many of the basic assumptions upon which the competition state is based' are derived (Palan and Abbott, 1996: 15–26 and 36).

This text claims a radical eclectic position, but such a position is not available. There is the demand for the discipline to be more relevant, more critical, interdisciplinary and historically nuanced. But no coherent or distinctive concepts are presented for analysis. Instead, attention is paid to 'what governments *are doing*' and 'to the processes by which such complex social entities as states *respond to and adapt to the changing global environment*' (Palan and Abbott 1996: 12, emphasis added), and to the development of a 'more nuanced approach [than those in which the environment is deemed to be an external force that determines behavioural patterns] in which the perception of the environment is possibly the main cause for changing patterns of behaviour' (Palan and Abbott 1996: 32). Although the general tendency in the radical eclectic approach is to employ a Marxist terminology mixed with concepts and methods drawn from orthodox social science, in the Palan and Abbott text, Marx and Braudel effectively disappear after page 19. This form of scholastic theory-hopping necessarily leads to sophistry, not only because of the superficial view of concepts and concept formation involved, but also – and importantly so far as my argument is concerned – because such eclecticism is itself a strong representation of the very nature of orthodoxy represented as heterodoxy.

Such conceptual wanderings are allowed because of the unwarranted assumption that a position of 'no preconceived position', or of 'disinterested inquiry' is possible, and that existing theories can be drawn upon as seen fit by the researcher. The resulting mix, however, as shown in this text, is necessarily haphazard with respect to theory. Rather than presenting the possibility of a synthesis, it is properly understood as a position of ideological intervention. Like classical political theory, it is implicitly critical of theory that is constructed out of a political or evaluative, or 'interested' position. Indeed Palan and Abbott (1996: 13) are explicit about such positions being unsatisfactory:

> It is the second position which is particularly worrying, because it has bedevilled much of the globalization literature. As a result, the globalization thesis is often employed as a prescriptive notion, propagated by business gurus and company directors to push through such ideas as 'down-sizing or 're-engineering' – all of which usually lead to sacking people from their jobs, and doing so in the name of a changing global environment which (and that is the beauty of the concept) is unfortunately out of their control.

Quite apart from the problematic status of the core claim here about the extent of appearance of this position in 'the globalization literature' – in my view, this can only be sustained in respect of the globalization literature specific to international business studies – Palan and

Abbott are forced, because of their implicit denial of any autonomous theoretical base, to enter confrontations and disputes only on the basis of terms established by other ideological positions. The mere use of words such as 'capital', 'market', 'circuits of capital' and 'dialectic' does not ensure that they are used as analytical categories within a systematic and coherent theoretical framework which gives them their content, and which poses its own questions about social reality. From page 19 onwards, the book comes firmly 'back to the past and back to the future' of empiricist epistemology. The economic remains separated from the political, except in interactive terms; the existence or not of globalization depends upon empirical evidence; behaviour is reduced to the 'more nuanced' site of perception, reproducing the deep orthodoxy of the empiricist distinction between subject and object; and taxonomy is the defining motif for revealing the multiplicity of *forms* of adaptation through competition.

Furthermore, competition itself is never theorized, and the set of states is deconstructed, as simultaneously an ideal-typical form – 'The competition state theory is therefore essentially an "ideal-type" description of the activities of the state based upon four essential assumptions' (Palan and Abbott, 1996: 37–9) – and as discrete competitive forms. In the end, as with Hirst and Thompson, Scholte and Shaw, globalization is reduced to a set of manifestations, and the site of behaviour or agency is conflated with the site of causation. What the book does succeed in doing is describing how and in what ways different kinds of states have reacted to globalization, in the sense of what they are presently doing in terms of policy formulation. But, to understand states, globalization and competitive strategies, we need to analyse what possible strategies are *not* chosen, or even not thought of, and explain why this is so.

The Palan and Abbott text is not a critical or radical text because ultimately it fails to answer its core question: namely, what is global about globalization. Rather, this question is transferred to the domain of reactive agents, predominantly states, and thus prompts Palan and Abbott to misrecognize globalization. Consequently, the text is successful in a second sense: that is, as an adaptive academic competitive strategy. Like the other texts interrogated here, rather than presenting a basis for real opposition to the doxy-doxa boundary which sustains the philosophical roots of the discipline beyond its political philosophy surface, these contributions fall just as firmly (although not perhaps so obviously as classical realism and neo-realism) into the embrace of the orthodoxy seen as heterodoxy.

I have identified the core elements of this transtextual hegemony in theory as a set of initially constructed dichotomies, or categorical separations: theory from practice, subject from object, politics from economics, domestic from international; agency from structure, and time from space. But, I have argued at the same time that it is only by exposing the deep structure of the philosophical *roots*, or intellectual tradition of the discipline and its disabling properties, that we can move to a non-arbitrary, critical and emancipatory construction of philosophy, namely new philosophical *routes*, as a necessary part of articulating an analytical framework which may recognize globalization better. This task I will attempt in the final section.

Philosophical routes to globalization

Although I have adopted the convention in this chapter of section headings, I have done so only in order to emphasize the initial analytical distinction between philosophical *roots* of, and philosophical *routes* to, globalization. The two sections do not represent sets of different arguments, or a significant turn in the overall argument. Instead, they represent simultaneous moments of one argument. In the introduction, I said there was an important space for philosophy because it is already embedded within the concept and practices of globalization. But I have also argued that what globalization means is not fixed: that is to say, it could be otherwise than it is presently thought and practised. This last proposition presupposes that conceptualizing globalization is not simply a matter of describing how practitioners – statespersons, business people, diplomats, soldiers, citizens and other sites of agency in international relations – think and practise globalization (although it includes this), but also a matter of conceptualizing the mediated, complex relationship between academic theorizations and those observable practices. In other words, explicit academic theorization is constitutive of the object it seeks to comprehend, and this both accounts for and follows from the central analytical weight I have placed upon the theory-practice dichotomy within the orthodoxy of International Relations.

The argument of this chapter, while so far concentrating on how it is that the philosophical *roots* of the discipline necessarily engender a misrecognition of globalization, is simultaneously an argument for a reconstruction of orthodox philosophy to radical philosophy: that is, an emancipatory form of philosophical *routes* towards recognizing globalization. Consequently, this section requires no further substantial argumentation. In addition, I have argued, from the basis of critical theory methodology, that the content or meaning of social concepts, in this case globalization, cannot be generated by defining the concept in question in abstract terms (i.e., torn out of its context which is part of what it means) and ahistorical terms (i.e., without reference to time or place) as a supposedly secure starting point of analysis. From a critical point of view, such meanings can only be arrived at as the conclusion of a detailed concrete historical analysis. For both these reasons, this section will be relatively brief, for it is already the bearer of extensive argument. I have set out all the core elements which together make up the doxy-doxa relationship within the philosophical roots of the discipline, and I have done this in respect of constraints upon the assumed content and scope of the discipline, and upon some particular texts about globalization. All that remains now is to set out, first in broad terms, what general misrecognitions of globalization are inscribed in the literature. Then I will offer a new analytical framework which represents a project for recognizing globalization on the basis of philosophical *routes* which are not outside globalization, but an obscured transformable content of the everyday taken-for-granted practices of globalization.

The misrecognition of globalization, which emerges from the disciplining reach of the International Relations orthodoxy once it has been interrogated, can be summarized as follows:

1. Globalization is generally assumed to be a 'thing', a process, or an effect of other conditions, and therefore as something empirical to be explained. Consequently, it is generally located in a linear causal process, and assumed not to have causal powers or liabilities itself.
2. Globalization is generally assumed to be predominantly political, or economic or cultural, and therefore not a complex discourse which structurally determines and mediates the diverse possible relations *between* these dimensions (and others) of social practice. It is important to note here that the concept of determination in this sense does not mean either predetermined or inevitable. Instead it refers to the Marxist sense of a set of conditions which set limits to what kinds of policies, objectives, and projects can be conceived, and how they can be realized. Thus there is no implication at all here that determination entails evidence of the observable homogenization of social practice. This may of course develop in certain areas at certain times: trade liberalization, privatization and de-regulation, scientific anatomical medicine and rational choice policy-making frame-

works, for example, are prominent contemporary examples of this. What it does mean though is that there is an increasing silent homogeneity: that is to say, a homogeneity of what is *not* thought, *not* disputed, *not* chosen, and *not* practised.

3. Following from points 1 and 2, globalization is usually conceived of as an outcome of the observable interactions of discrete units, mainly states and firms, but also international organizations, especially at the present time regional economic unions and treaty arrangements. In methodological terms, globalization is usually abstracted on the basis of methodological individualism, and this is to privilege agent over structure from the start.
4. There is a dominant tendency to conflate globalization with internationalization, or interdependence, or both.
5. Globalization is normally conceived of in geographical-territorial terms: that is, if it exists at all, it must occupy some position in time, and some three-dimensional space. This is of course consistent with its characterization as something empirical or, if not, something metaphysical and therefore not real. Underpinning this misrecognition is an absolute conception of time and space: that is, the assumption that time and space are both independent of each other, and of objects. This implies further that space could in principle be empty, and that objects are located within it. But this is incoherent, because 'what is empty is nothing, and nothing cannot be' (Sayer, 1992: 147).
6. As a corollary of points 1, 3 and 5, globalization is invested usually with limited ontological status, which is to say it is generally assumed to be meaningful if and only if it can be translated directly into observational statements. Consequently the possibility that globalization might be itself (and strictly) a non-observable item but none the less real, and possessing causal power, is not allowed (MacLean, 1981a: 55–7).
7. Finally there are particular elements of misrecognition that are embedded in the post-modernist view of globalization. Usually, post-modernists see their conception of globalization as radical resistance, because it is assumed to be a political project outside, and therefore a real alternative to, the perceived disabling consequences of globalization: that is, its anti-democratic and discriminatory character. However, insofar as globalization is a condition of late-modernity (Giddens, 1990; 1991) then it is conceivable that post-modernism, in its artistic, architectural and literary forms, and as an assumed analytical posture, is both a strict causal consequence of

globalization, and a causal element in its social reproduction. On this view, post-modernism can best be seen as one more example of a fundamentalist reassertion of tradition against globalization, in particular the reassertion of self, of identity, of choice, or more generally of bourgeois possessive individualism. To the extent that post-modernism is influential (and it seems to be increasingly so) it reinforces its own misrecognition of globalization by ironically focusing on uni-dimensional aspects of globalization such as fragmentation (thus missing unification and integration), individual identity (thus missing collective identity), agents (thus missing structures), localities (thus missing the global), turbulence (thus missing calm), micro-circuits of power (thus missing hegemony), femininity (thus missing gender) and so on. Rather than developing a generalizable resistance to globalization, post-modernism (and, to a lesser extent, post-structuralism) contribute to its reproduction.

The potentially critical analytical framework I promised is already implicated in (although it is not the premise of) the argumentation of the first section, and the exposure of the main fixing points of the misrecognition of globalization in this section. Consequently, all that remains in this chapter is to set this out in its bare form. This does not, and cannot represent a detailed concrete analysis of globalization. However, it does stand as a basis for the working up of such analysis, and I will from time to time say what I think globalization, as 'an hypothesized entity', but nevertheless a real entity, might mean (Harré, 1972; Bhaskar, 1975; Keat and Urry, 1975; MacLean, 1981a).

There are five analytically distinct abstract elements in my view which together constitute the concrete condition of globalization. These are as follows.

First, *the hegemony of tradition within the International Relations discipline*. This postulates that at least part of what 'globalization' means, besides its relations with other social items, is its already existing forms of theorization. To put this in practical research terms, the initial question is not so much what might explain 'globalization', abstracted from its social theoretical context, but what are the meta-theoretical, theoretical and subjective historical conditions necessary for 'globalization' to emerge at the time, and in the specific form that it has. Here, one deals with the theory-practice and subject-object relation. Following Marx's meta-methodology of political economy (cf. MacLean 1988b: 300–7), the supposed constitution of 'globalization' in other diverse elements – say the states, firms and societies – are abstracted first in thought, and then combined together to produce a formal concrete specification of 'globalization', which will be different from that assumed at the start. This further means that the classical project of political economy needs to be recovered.

Second, *'globalization' is a historical phenomenon*. This does not mean that globalization has a chronological starting point in time, which can be dated and constructed as part of a more general periodization (Scholte, 1997: 16). This could only be established if time was absolute, and if social views were capable of being fixed in a slice of it. Neither of these requirements holds. Because they do not hold, there will always be disputes about when globalization did or did not begin. To ask such a question is like asking when precisely did life begin, or when precisely did capitalism begin, or when precisely did realism fail, or when precisely did Hobbes enter the tradition. Such questions can never be resolved. However, if 'globalization' is to be properly understood, it needs to be historicized. This means asking what kinds of conditions, necessary and contingent, were historically necessary for 'globalization' to occur. Globalization on this view does not have a chronological history, but emerges as a structure when other possible forms of political-economy organization (e.g., Socialism or Islam) no longer stand as a basis for possible alternatives for organizing the *global* political economy, although they may continue to maintain limited local histories. That is, 'globalization' is a form of political economy which establishes a structural history as well as a local history. It becomes a framework in terms of which other possible forms of political economy and integration are described and evaluated (see Chapter 2 in this volume).

Third, *globalization is constituted through a specific resolution of the agent/structure problem within concrete social practices*. This means that the agent-structure issue is not resolvable at the level of abstracted meta-theoretical discussion alone, as many have sought to do. Rather, it is continuously and historically resolved through the concrete social establishment of what are taken to be the limits of social reality, by social agents and by academic practice, as the earlier discussion following Bourdieu has set out. In concrete terms, for globalization to develop in the form it has, certain initially subjective practices and forms of knowledge have to be transformed into global normative structures – and global here does not mean the same as universal, but rather non-territorial causal powers – which present themselves to agents as the 'natural' or objective conditions of social life. This means not so much a requirement to address the 'relationship between the "particular" and the "general"' as one of the 'theoretical questions [about globalization that] have been largely ignored', as Palan and Abbott (1996: 12) assert, but rather to analyse what subjective interests have become transformed into objective conditions, which means that particulars are contained within universals, and necessarily so, although obscured.

Such transformations relevant to making 'globalization' meaningful include the social practices of the assumed superior efficiency of trade liberalization; of non-socialized health; of war over peace; of private property over collective property; of science over tradition; and so on. It is this kind of simultaneous theoretical and practical transformation which invests 'globalization' with hegemonic quality, and allows the reconciliation of so-called American hegemony with hegemony in general. For the USA is hegemonic not so much in terms of its identifiable – that is, measurable local or unit-level capabilities, objectives and personal history (although these count) – but more in terms of the close correspondence between originally 'subjective' American interests, and those which occupy the content of what presents itself as the objective, natural, or taken-for-granted conditions of the global political economy as a whole, for the USA and other dominant agents, as well as for subordinated agents.

This means that the agent/structure issue is really a story of two connected structures. Structure I is a reference to the observable institutions, rules, norms and conventions in and through which social practices – agency in general – are realized in any particular historical period. Structure II is a reference to the simultaneous meta-theoretical elements which are embedded in the practices of Structure I, but taken for granted, and which are never themselves capable of direct or indirect observation, only of specification in terms of observable consequences. These include items such as gender, private property, time (space) and rationality. As with concepts like gravity or magnetism or time (space) in the natural world, these are purely meta-theoretical, but without them explanation of the relations of observable items is not possible, or at least, is severely limited.

Fourth, *globalization is not located in a particular time or place*. This means that in order to recognize 'globalization' account must be taken of its structural history (as in Structure II above) and its non-territoriality: that is, globalization cannot be characterized as a 'thing' which necessarily occupies three-dimensional space. Instead, it is *n*-dimensional, and although engendering certain historical forms of agency, it is therefore not reducible to its empirical or substantive manifestations alone. This means it is coherent to refer to 'globalization' as universal, not in the sense of being identifiable everywhere in the world as a single place, but as the dominant framework within which the possibilities for agency are both articulated and evaluated.

Finally, *globalization has constructed new non-territorial and non-sovereign forms of governance, while simultaneously confirming the sovereign state, transformed from its original historical form as the defining, territorially located site of central and legitimate government, to a new form of local and regional 'subsidiary' government.* This implies that the development of international organization, especially since 1945, has been misrecognized and marginalized in the discipline as an inadequate 'non-state' actor. In order to recognize 'globalization', a generic conception of public *and* private organization is more relevant, such that the orthodox categorical separation of international organizations from states is disrupted and the state itself brought back into the category of world organization. The problematic then shifts from the issue of what the role and significance of named international organizations is in the late-modern world, to the question of how and why did the world become organized in the way that it has, rather than in some other conceivable way: for example, organized for realizing social need rather than profitability, or organized for realizing unequal redistribution rather than equal distribution.

It also implies that 'globalization' is a structure which has evacuated the traditional content of Western (and therefore global) political theory and political practice. At first sight, an economistic expert-knowledge based form of rational-technical politics has developed, which partly explains the re-emergence, or 'recent flowering of political theory that has taken place in the United States and Britain' that H. Williams (1996: 146) refers to. What is important here is that this work (Rawls, Nozick, Ackerman and Barry, for example) represents the heartland of 'new' rational public choice theory and neo-institutionalist conceptions. This is not an argument that politics is being *replaced* by economics within globalization, but rather that it is being *reinvented*. There is not the space here to develop this point fully, but it implies a contra-distinction with the long and carefully established tradition of Western classical political theory, while still returning analysis to the individual and to the problem of choice.

My assertion here is that a central dimension of 'globalization' is the reconstruction of business and management practices, including ethics, as a dominant normative structure (Structure II) which is coming to be seen as appropriate not only for application to the domain of private ownership of economic goods and services, but equally to the domain of public political, social, legal, and cultural goods and services. To put it another way, globalization has appropriated and recolonized the very centre of one part of the historical origin of the separation of politics from economics, namely the normative, and therefore potentially critical discourse and practices of government and the nature of ethics within it. Today, liberal political and ethical concepts are socially maintained, but with a new, reinvented historical content, by means of which they re-present themselves socially as technical-rational: that is to say, as scientific concepts. This means that scientific-technical reason no longer stands only as the assumed maximally reliable basis for determining the optimum *means* for achieving separated political or ethical *ends*, otherwise and normatively settled upon, but comes to appropriate, through apparently informed and rational consent, the very basis for establishing what *can* be objectively articulated as constituting the ends of societies.

This is a stunning feat of and within globalization, and it represents at the same time an increasing marginalization of normative prospects in the world, at least in their classical form as potentially emancipatory projects based on the possibility of enhancing equality of access to goods and decision-making, or more simply basic human needs. Politics has become transformed from participation in policy-making to the consumption of policies; from the potential disruption of power as inequality and systemic privilege, to the individualism of self-empowerment.

* * *

To conclude, I have argued that globalization is generally misrecognized, and that a necessary element in this is to be found in the disciplining authority of the International Relations discipline as an orthodoxy. I have shown how this capacity resides partly within a double meaning of the 'philosophical roots' of the discipline: first, a particularistic philosophy, that of politics; and second, a universal (or generic) philosophy, that of empiricist epistemology. I have also shown that these 'philosophical roots' cannot achieve such hegemony on their own, but depend upon the repeated agency of academics for their reproduction and transformation.

However, I have also demonstrated that recognizing globalization depends upon the development of an alternative, critical analysis, but where this is not developed as though it is a complete and coherent alternative at the outset. Instead, I have shown how this must be developed out of the already existing conditions of globalization, theoretical and practical, so that the philosophical *roots* of the discipline might be relocated as new philosophical *routes* to globalization. The analytical framework presented in the final section of the chapter has been developed out of critique, but it has not yet been rendered fully concrete. However, I have given some indications of what I think are the core abstract, constitutive elements of globalization, in the late-modern world. On the basis of this, I am able to temporarily conclude that globalization, whatever else it might be, is the most obscured but also most systematic form of disciplining strategy yet developed in the world. If this is the case, then the implication for International Relations scholars is that recognition of globalization, meaning partly the articulation of possible real alternatives, requires that the starting point for analysis is not the concept of globalization itself, but a reflexive appreciation by scholars of the possible forms of their own existing relationships with globalization.

Notes

1. The author would like to thank participants at the 'Globalization and its Critics' workshop for helpful comments on an earlier draft.
2. Throughout this chapter, I shall use 'International Relations' to refer to the discipline, and 'international relations' to refer to the substantive activity, events and practices which are supposed as the basis and rationale of the former. This is adopted to enable greater precision of argument. It does not imply at all a categorical separation/distinction between the two; if there is one core proposition upon which this chapter is based, it is that the discipline, and substantive international relations (as I would argue also to be the case for all Social Science disciplines, although not in precisely the same way), subsist in a complex relation of reciprocal causality. However, this relation, as I shall demonstrate, is generally an indirect or mediated relation. A consequence of this core proposition, from my stand-point, is that the main task for international theory is not so much to evaluate competing attempts to explain international relations activity, as to explain its own relationship, at any particular point in time, with that activity.
3. I first developed this argument of derivation within the International Relations tradition in MacLean (1981b). I shall refer to this argument again in the first section.
4. See, for example, Wight (1946), Wolfers (1956), Forsyth, Keens-Soper and Savigear (1970), Bull (1966, 1977), Parkinson (1977), Donelan (1978, 1990), Vincent (1981), Williams, Wright and Evans (1993), H. Williams (1996), Rengger (1988, 1995), Navari (1991), Jackson (1990, 1996), Burrell (1990), Thompson (1992), and Beitz (1979).
5. See, for example, Morgenthau (1948), Kaplan (1957), Waltz (1959, 1979), Keohane and Nye (1972, 1977), Nicholson (1970, 1996), Gilpin (1987),

Strange (1988), James (1989), Shaw (1994), Krasner (1983), Vasquez (1983, 1993, 1995), Buzan, Jones and Little (1993), De Porte (1986), and Mann (1986, 1993).

6. I describe the term 'traditional critical theory' here as odd, mainly because this is not a direct reference back to the early work of the Frankfurt School theorists such as Weil, Grossman, Pollock, Marinuse or Horkheimer, or to the later work of Habermas. Rather, it is a recognition that even though the explicit critical theory intervention in International Relations, which did see itself as linked explicitly to the Frankfurt School project, only occurred in the very early 1980s, it has since then been rapidly overtaken by, and for most observers, conflated with, the post-positivist and post-modernist interventions which appeared a short time after. Consequently, it seems to me, most observers see critical theory in the discipline as synonymous with post-positivism or post-modernism or both. I do not, but recognize that the latter has almost completely appropriated what is seen as critical radical conceptualization in the field. This itself is a very interesting development, which requires explanation. I shall not attempt to do much about this in this chapter, but will simply assert that in my view, post-modernism in International Relations represents a powerful deradicalization of the critical theory project and that this itself requires explanation.
7. This is not to say that radical methodologies were not available for the analysis of international relations before 1980. Classical and contemporary Marxist theories are a case in point, as Krippendorf (1982: ch. 2) has argued. However, even though the International Relations discipline has never been slow to adopt approaches, concepts or models developed initially within other disciplines, it is equally clear that it has done so in an extremely selective manner. Approaches or conceptualizations that might have confronted and displaced the steady development and deepening of the traditional orthodoxy have not received much of a welcome. I have developed this argument more fully in MacLean (1988b).
8. See, for example, Wolfers (1962), Forsyth, Keens-Soper and Savigear (1970), Parkinson (1977), Gallie (1978), Donelan (1978, 1990), Vincent (1981), Walzer (1992), Brown (1992), H. Williams (1992, 1996) and Jackson (1996).
9. There is an unwitting irony here contained in Jackson's use of the noun 'pantheon'. The origin of this term is the construction of the Pantheon, a circular temple built in Rome in 27BC by Agrippa, and dedicated to all the gods. It was rebuilt by Hadrian between 120 and 124AD, and since 609AD has been used as a Christian Church, dedicated consequently to one God. This shows that Pantheons have a clear capacity for fundamental transformation without changing their name.
10. See, for example, Forsyth, Keens-Soper and Saviglar (1970), Parkinson (1977), Donelan (1978, 1990), Vincent (1981), Burrell (1990), and more recently Brown (1992), H. Williams (1992, 1996) and Jackson (1996).
11. Examples of this 'weak version' include Morgenthau (1948), Aron (1962), Wight (1979, 1991), Waltz (1979), Bull (1977), Keohane and Nye (1972, 1977), Gilpin (1981), Strange (1988), Rosenau (1990), Doyle (1986, 1993), Buzan, Jones and Little (1993), Shaw (1994), Hirst and Thompson (1996) and Palan and Abbott (1996).

12. See, for example, Ashley (1981), Cox (1981), MacLean (1981b), Krippendorf (1982) and Linklater (1986).
13. Here, it is important to note that I am not using the verb 'to describe' as it is usually understood in social science, namely as a *pre-theoretical* first step towards the construction of knowledge, in terms of which the analyst-as-observer sets out the observable features, characteristics and properties of the thing to be explained, and then develops relevant hypotheses to be tested against an assumed external reality. Instead, I am using 'to describe' in the context of Marx's meta-methodology of the totality, in terms of which description refers to building up the complex set of relations and history which together constitute the appearance of social items and social practices. Hence, within this meta-methodology, description is not a technical pre-theoretical device, but an essential element *within* the processes of conceptualization and theorization; that is to say, it is a part of theory construction itself.
14. See, for example, Sprout and Sprout (1957), Snyder *et al.* (1962: 51–5), Burton (1972: 55–78), Reynolds (1980: 171–2), and Kegley and Wittkopf (1993: 10–20).
15. See, for example, Walker (1988b), Dicken (1992), Ohmae (1990), Giddens (1990), Featherstone (1990), Sklair (1991), Sassen (1991), Robertson (1992), Shaw (1992, 1994), Taylor (1993, 1996), Dunning (1993a), Scholte (1993), Cerny (1995), Kofman and Youngs (1996) and Baylis and Smith (1997).
16. See, for example, Krippendorf (1982), Thorndike (1978), Linklater (1986), MacLean (1988b) and H. Smith (1996).

2
Globalization in Historical Perspective[1]

Randall D. Germain

> History cannot be compared to a tunnel through which an express races until it brings its freight of passengers out into sunlit plains.
>
> E. P. Thompson (1978: 296)

Globalization is considered by many to be the key social, economic and political development of the late twentieth century. Its significance is often presented as a challenge to both modernity and capitalism, the twin foundations of the contemporary era. Where modernity is bound up with the triumph of the modern state, globalization works to dissolve the bonds of identity which lie at the heart of the state's claim to authority. And where capitalism is predicated upon a particular relationship of market to society, globalization threatens to undermine and recast these relations. Globalization, such claims run, both relocates the efficacy of the state and recasts the constitution of the market. In this sense modernity, capitalism, globalization and its consequences are part of a train of developments which have taken us from a modern into a post-modern age. Like an express train racing through a tunnel, they have clear origins and transparent trajectories whose meanings are easily acknowledged and well understood.

This chapter questions the ease and clarity of these meanings by placing globalization into a 'historical' perspective. This perspective, however, contains a double meaning. At one level it means that the analytical framework to be used embraces what is here called the *historical mode of thought*. This type of reasoning takes its starting point to be the historicity and transformability of all human practice, including the way in which it is embedded in layers of patterned collective activity. Its concern with human practice in all of its dimensions makes it perforce multidisciplinary in scope. At another level it means stretching the analysis of globalization both longitudinally, back in time, and latitudinally, across a range of social hierarchies which constitute the ensemble of the contemporary period. By reaching for this dual perspective, the historicity of globalization is confirmed even as its received meanings are challenged in terms of the variegated structures of social life.

To ask these questions I will consider globalization from the vantage point of the discipline of IPE. The first step in this analysis is to outline the theoretical foundations of the historical mode of thought. These foundations highlight three principles which are used to guide subsequent analysis. The second step is to explore the historicity of globalization. This involves examining the emergence of what can be described as 'globalizing' social practices in the early modern period, most importantly around the military dimension of the state and the financial dimension of international commerce. Commerce and conquest are two of the most important touchstones of social life in which globalized social practices have been pervasive throughout the modern period.[2] Having established the historicity of globalization, the focus of analysis then shifts to the contemporary period, where the extensiveness of globalized social practices across a number of social domains is examined. Here Fernand Braudel's controversial use of the triptych of capitalism, the market economy and material life is deployed to distinguish between those domains of social life where globalization is a driving organizational dynamic from those where it is less dominant.[3] Finally, the chapter closes by reflecting upon the advantages offered by the historical mode of thought for understanding the phenomena of globalization.

International political economy and the historical mode of thought

As a branch of knowledge, IPE is most commonly associated with methods employed by either economists or political scientists to study the interaction of markets and states as alternative ways of organizing authority (Lindblom, 1977). Indeed, economics and politics can both lay claim to IPE as their special intellectual progeny: many political scientists claim to study the politics of international economic relations (Spero and Hart, 1997), while economists often advance the claim that the public choice approach to IPE can yield particularly rich dividends

(Frey, 1984). Despite the different entry points to IPE for these scholars, however, they share many traits: they embrace a positivist and behavioural approach to the question of acquiring knowledge; they agree on the overall constitution of the international economy as the sum total of exchange between national economies; and they focus primarily on public policy issues as perceived by state actors. Whether the starting point is state or market, IPE is here largely conceived of as a 'problem-solving' enterprise, a means of understanding the precise balance between state and market so as to delineate more clearly the implications for public agents.

There are strands of scholarship, however, which view IPE in a less overtly public policy and discipline-specific light. Some within IPE accept the centrality of state and market as analytical categories, but employ them without unduly privileging one over the other (Strange, 1988; Schwartz, 1994). For the purposes of this chapter, however, those scholars who reach beyond the categories of state and market to account for how the global political economy is organized will be highlighted. The work of three groups of scholars is particularly important in this regard.

First, those scholars whose work is based explicitly on a historically-sensitive set of methodological premises provide the ontological foundations for the historical mode of thought.[4] These foundations are built around the transformative possibilities of human activity in its individual and collective manifestations, and suggest that the appropriate method of inquiry for the historical mode of thought comprises a constant dialogue between conceptual apparatus and historical evidence, in which concepts display extreme elasticity and allow for great irregularity (Thompson, 1978: 46).

Second, those scholars whose work sets out and extends a Gramscian analysis of the global political economy offer a set of tools which can usefully integrate the material and ideational dimensions of social life into a sustained inquiry of the institutional cohesion of world order.[5] In Craig Murphy's words, the Gramscian turn in International Relations (IR) and IPE allows us to recognize 'sites of regulation of the world economy at levels other than those of the nation-state and the state system' (1994: 13). This is most important with respect to understanding the constitution of institutions within the global political economy.

And third, those scholars whose work contests dominant representations of space and identity provide tools capable of recovering silenced narratives about the past.[6] The social world is a historically constructed environment rather than a given one, and our representations of it provide a powerful point of entry into considering how and where its relationships might be challenged.

Taken together, these elements of the historical mode of thought suggest three principles to guide our inquiry into globalization. First and foremost it suggests that globalization should be considered as a particular type of social practice bounded by identifiable social hierarchies. Most definitions of globalization echo to a greater or lesser extent Waters's recent formulation, namely that it is 'a social process in which the constraints of geography on social and cultural arrangements recede and in which people become increasingly aware that they are receding' (1995: 3). While thinking about globalization as a process certainly helps to categorize some of its systemic characteristics, it also imbues our thinking about globalization with a homeostatic quality. Because processes and systems are often seen as self-reproducing mechanisms, defining globalization as a process obscures both the entrenched obstacles which globalization has been confronted with historically and the possible instability of globalized social practices today. It is akin to thinking about history as a train racing through a tunnel towards an opening, with only one possible direction and no impediments.

Considering globalization in terms of bounded social practices, on the other hand, allows us to think about globalization as set within multiple contexts, which are themselves collective patterns of activity that structure individual practices and shape outcomes without mechanistically determining them. Robert Cox (1981) invokes the metaphor of a historical structure to capture the non-deterministic and two-way relationship between individual and collectively patterned practices at both the material and ideational level. This metaphor is followed here in order to strengthen resistance to thinking about globalization as an inevitable or inexorable process beyond human control, without at the same time losing sight of the larger patterns of thought and activity which constitute the historical structure of globalization.

Second, this approach suggests that the institutional dimension of globalization warrants further attention. This attention can be focused on different domains or levels of institutional activity. It can, for example, be directed at the level of the state. How (meaning through what kinds of practices) does the state uphold, extend or undermine the practices of globalization, and what has been its role in their spread? At the same time, assuming that the state is the only institutional bulwark to globalization should be resisted. To adopt a

Gramscian focus, the way in which institutionalized practices within the economy and civil society uphold, extend or undermine globalization should also be explored.

It would be inadequate, however, to distinguish only between polity, economy and civil society in terms of institutional behaviour. In order to strengthen the way in which individual and collective motivations are incorporated into this schema, these distinctions can also be layered with those used by the French historian Fernand Braudel, who organized his historical inquiries around the domains of material life, the market economy and capitalism (1973: xi–xv). He explored each of these domains as the natural constituency for particular kinds of institutional activities and the motivations which encourage such behaviour. Such a method allows for a complex and nuanced consideration of where and how the social practices constitutive of globalization are most likely to be reproduced. It is also the case that Braudel places these domains in relation with one another within the overall context of a *world economy*, a bounded social totality exhibiting a strong sense of organic coherence (1984: 22). Considering the institutional dimension of globalization from this point of view provides a suitable entry point to mapping what we might call the terrain of globalization.

Finally, the historical mode of thought suggests that those representations which see globalization as accounting for every stitch of the social fabric must be challenged. These representations, often imbued with the logic of technological determinism, distort both the scope and scale of globalization in today's world. Without minimizing in any way the profound impact of globalized social practices on the organization of the world economy, the equation of modernity with globalization must be severely qualified in the sense that social life is multifaceted and defined by many different types of activity, not all of which can be equated with capitalism *per se*. Here it is helpful to consider Braudel's rather controversial use of the term 'capitalism' to refer to the domain in which the quest for massive accumulation largely through speculation prevails. If globalization is equated with capitalism, it should be clear that capitalism itself is restricted to a select number of institutions and the arenas in which they participate. Adopting this perspective allows representations of globalization as a totalizing process to be contested, and points to where and how it can (and should) be resisted.

The historical mode of thought thus offers a useful avenue of inquiry into the question of globalization. It builds upon a conception of globalization as a particular type of bounded social practice to ask where, how and through which types of institution it is sustained. It also inquires into the reverse: namely where, how and through which types of institution is this kind of practice resisted. And finally, it is deeply imbued with a conception of human beings and institutions as highly transformative, allowing for change to be introduced into the structural parameters that are the logical outgrowth of persistent patterns of individual and collective behaviour. The three distinctive pillars of this approach – its transformative view of human beings, its insistence on considering both the ideational and material basis of social practice, and its focus on institutions as the most useful vehicle through which these practices can be apprehended – thus suggest that acquiring a historical perspective on globalization is a valuable and indeed even necessary intellectual task.

The historicity of globalization

Globalization and time

There are many conceptual and theoretical issues at stake in the debate over the origins of globalization, one of the most important being whether globalization is a relational or a literal/absolute representation of historical experience. Where globalization is conceived of as a single uninterrupted process (the 'train in the tunnel' model) – albeit replete with swings, dips and cycles – it is usually dated from about the fifteenth century. In Robertson's influential formulation, this was the germinal phase of globalization (lasting in Europe until the mid-eighteenth century), in which the seeds of globalization were sown in terms of the emergence of national communities, the concept of the individual and the idea of humanity (1992: 58–60). Subsequent phases included the incipient phase (lasting until the 1870s), in which the unitary state, citizenship, formal international relations, nationalism and internationalism became crystallized; the take-off phase (lasting into the 1920s), in which a number of globalization issues were for the first time systematically thematized, global communication arose, global competitions such as the Olympics and the Nobel Prize were initiated, and the First World War occurred; the struggle-for-hegemony phase (lasting into the 1960s); and finally the phase of uncertainty (reaching a crisis in the 1990s). In each of these phases the process of globalization became further consolidated, bringing larger portions of the world into contact with one another and raising awareness and consciousness of the planetary environment in its social, physical and ecological dimensions. It is precisely this unilinear account of globalization that a historical perspective questions, especially where the process of globalization is imbued with a teleological and almost ahistorical inevitability.

An alternative reading of the time of globalization begins by recasting this unilinear account of its progress. Globalization did not enter the historical tunnel in the fifteenth century destined to exit in full running order in the twentieth century; rather, it has had a significant temporal presence in successive world economies from at least the thirteenth century. Janet Abu-Lughod, for example, reminds us that contact between regions of the Old World flourished between 1250 and 1350, forming the basis of her claim that the interconnections between these regions constituted a genuine world system (1989: 3). Accepting such a view of globalization, however, means relaxing a central assumption of globalization that equates it with the literal world: that is, that global equals world-wide.

A more nuanced and *historicized* understanding begins from the Braudelian proposition that a world economy is a bounded social totality which may or may not be world-wide in scope. Here, globalization refers to the reach of particular social practices *throughout* an extant world economy. Global is in this sense a relational rather than a literal term, one which expresses a relative and fluid social relationship rather than an absolute and static one. And while the relational and absolute representations might overlap under the condition of a world-wide world economy, we should privilege the relational representation of the term over an absolute one. A brief appraisal of the historic presence of globalization within the key social practices of commerce and conquest will demonstrate the significance of a relational representation even in eras not usually associated with extensive globalization.

Commerce

Commerce, or the exchange of goods, services and credit, has a long and well-preserved global dimension. While much trade of course has been strictly local or regional in scope, there have always been long-distance traders who have provided scarce or desired products to those with the resources or prestige to command them. It is the creation and exchange of credit, however, which has most consistently provided examples of intense and wide-ranging global commercial practices throughout successive world economies. Two examples will be offered here.

The first example of globalized social practices can be seen in the constant creation and recreation of global credit networks since at least the twelfth and thirteenth centuries. These credit networks tended to be coterminous with the dominant world economy, centred in one particular city, often based on the activities of a handful of bankers or banking houses, and required complex financial instruments and accounting codes to flourish. In the twelfth century, sophisticated financial instruments allowed overlapping regional circuits of exchange to develop into what Abu-Lughod (1989) has called a single world system. In the thirteenth century, sets of bankers provided the credit infrastructure for European international trade by congregating during the great medieval fairs to conduct their business, thereby helping to turn these events into cosmopolitan experiences (Braudel, 1982: 81–94). In the fourteenth and fifteenth centuries, vast amounts of Papal funds were recycled through the Europe-wide credit networks established by the Italian banking houses of the Bardi, Peruzzi and Medici. They financed, among other things, the growing expenditures of princes and the movement of English wool to Rome (de Roover, 1963). In the sixteenth century much of Spain's imperial effort was financed by South German banking houses operating out of Antwerp and dependent upon the intake of silver from the New World (Ehrenberg, 1958). Within the context of the creation and recreation of 'global' credit networks, in other words, there is much to suggest that globalization had an intensity and scope that was as profound in relation to past world economies as it is to the present one (Germain, 1997).

The second example of extensive globalization can be found in the relationship between the major financial centres of the European world economy in the seventeenth and eighteenth centuries. If globalization is consistent with the relaxation of geographical constraints on economic arrangements, then the price sensitivity of shares and debt traded on the London Stock Exchange and Amsterdam Bourse had virtually no geographical constraints during this time. To all intents and purposes, they moved as one, given the communication technology of the time. Moreover, significant cross-border holdings existed for the debt of major companies such as the Bank of England, the Dutch East India Company and the South Sea Company: by one calculation, nearly 20 per cent of outstanding English public debt was owned by the Dutch in 1750 (Neal, 1990: 147). Such cross-border holdings were facilitated and encouraged by the ease of dividend and capital bonus payments between London and Amsterdam, a practice which clearly contributed to the 'globalized' world of finance during this time.[7] Through much of the seventeenth century, in fact, the core of this 'global' capital market also reached out to include Paris, at least until the onset of financial panics associated with the collapse of the Mississippi and South Sea Bubbles in 1720 (Schubert, 1988). And finally, financial centres in Hamburg, Brabant, Antwerp, Copenhagen, Vienna and elsewhere were all closely tied to events and trends in Amsterdam (and to a lesser extent London): the credit crises of the late eighteenth century radiated outwards from Amsterdam towards other European centres of finance (Braudel, 1984: 267–73). Within the world of finance, then, neither the existence nor the extent of globalized social practices during the seventeenth and eighteenth centuries can be disputed. As a guiding practice of what Karl Polanyi later called *hauté finance* (1944: 9), globalization was a reality long before the term was invented.

Conquest

There are two axes along which the global dimension of conquest can be charted. What is of concern here is not so much the act of conquest, which has of course been associated with conquering far-away lands for thousands of years; rather, attention is drawn to what makes conquest possible in the first place, namely how it is organized and the practices through which it is prosecuted. The first axis along which the global dimension of conquest can be charted, then, is the widespread use of mercenaries and foreign military commanders within increasingly nationalized armed forces throughout much of the modern period. Vestiges of this historically globalized practice can still be found in the institutionalized command structures of multinational forces such as NATO and UN peacekeeping missions. The second axis along which the global dimension of conquest is visible, today as in the past, is the swift and widespread diffusion of military strategy and organization. When viewed from this perspective, conquest has been organized around a set of globalized social practices since at least the advent of modernity.

The use of mercenary armies in western Europe arose during the early modern period in line with the increased demands of war on changing state structures. The small personal armies of kings and princes, or the citizen-armies of independent cities, became insufficient to bear the increased burden of war-making over the course of the seventeenth century. But until states could either entice or enforce their citizens to become soldiers, their only recourse was to purchase soldiers on what Tilly has described as 'the international market' (1992: 81).[8] Particularly important in this regard were the Swiss, but they were joined by many other princes and states who literally rented out armies *en masse* (Tilly, 1992: 79–84; Howard, 1976: 27–9).[9] Ironically, it was the non-national character of states during this period which allowed such a form of globalized social practice to flourish. As state structures became more efficient, increasingly nationalized, and larger, the use of mercenaries correspondingly declined, although a strong degree of internationalism prevailed among the professional officer class.[10] International mobility among this class was not completely eliminated until well into the nineteenth century, when nationalism finally assumed its imperial character.

Although the globalization attendant upon the use of mercenary armies and commanders subsided over the course of the nineteenth century, the globalized social practices associated with the diffusion of military organization and strategy continued. History provides clear examples of how quickly superior military organization and strategy spread. Both King Gustavus Aldophus of Sweden and Maurice of Nassau (Prince of Orange), for example, introduced significant reforms into military affairs in Sweden and Holland during the seventeenth century (McNeill, 1982: 118–39). Crucially, these reforms were immediately picked up and refined by military leaders throughout Europe. And although some were more (and others less) adept at the art of war, all were aware of important recent developments. This state of affairs resulted in the eventual convergence of military strategies among adversaries. By the outbreak of the First World War, what Tuchman calls the 'doctrine of the offensive' (1962: 31) had crystallized as the dominant strategy upon which military planning proceeded in all of the principal European states.

If globalization is considered as a relational rather than an absolute representation, it is evident that globalized social practices have existed within successive world economies since at least the fifteenth century. Financial practices have always had a significant 'global' dimension, not least because one of the key objectives of high finance includes transmitting money and credit across political borders. Moreover, in many ways these practices have been as sophisticated and global in the past as they are currently. Few banks today have the international operations boasted by the House of Fugger during the sixteenth century, while the mental horizon of Polanyi's *hauté finance* was no less global in orientation than J. P. Morgan's today. But commerce is not the only touchstone of social life that has been marked historically through and through by what is now called globalization. The organization and practices of conquest have been equally globalized for a long period of time. Not only does an 'international market' for mercenaries have a long and noble connection to modernity, but military strategy and knowledge have spread with remarkable speed and intensity for centuries. Both commerce and conquest are spheres of social life that have been deeply imbued with the logic and ethos of extensive globalization from before the fifteenth century.

Globalization and social hierarchies

If the time of globalization is open to challenge, so too is the representation of those social hierarchies around and through which globalization is organized. To explore the extent of globalization within the contemporary organization of social life, Fernand Braudel's conceptual distinction between the domains of material life, the market economy and capitalism will be deployed. The case for using Braudel's triptych rests upon his view of the multilayered complexity of social life, and the way his model is able to distinguish between the dynamics and motivations that inform historical subjects active within and across different social *milieux*. This conceptual framework will be briefly outlined and then used to consider some of the structural constraints faced by globalization today.

Although Braudel developed what he referred to as his 'grammar' with respect to the period between the fifteenth and eighteenth centuries, he was not adverse to considering how well such a model might navigate periods for which it was not explicitly constructed, such as the present. And in point of fact, whenever he reflected on the contemporary era, he was firmly convinced that his model was still capable of generating important insights into the organization of social life. As he put it at the end of the third and last volume of *Civilization and Capitalism*:

> So we should not be too quick to assume that capitalism embraces the whole of western society, that it accounts for every stitch in the social fabric ... It is still possible ... to use the three-tier model whose relevance to the past has already been discussed. It can still be applied to the present. (Braudel, 1984: 630)

From the perspective of considering globalization, one of the key attributes of Braudel's 'grammar' is its capacity to embed the motivational differences that distinguish one social domain from another into a holistic conception of 'global' social order . Thus he argues that we should consider the world economy as the primary unit of analysis because it has a central coherence which serves to connect its several different social domains. With respect to the sixteenth-century world economy, for example, Braudel (1984: 22) argues that 'it bestrode the political and cultural frontiers which each in its own way quartered and differentiated the Mediterranean world'.

Yet, even while a world economy has an overarching coherence, its different domains are for Braudel constructed around competing sets of social practices. If we follow Braudel in conceptualizing a world economy in a pyramidal form, the bottom and largest layer represents the slowly changing modalities of everyday life. He calls this the domain of material life, and argues that it is composed mostly of the routines and rituals that both govern our daily relationships and inform the way we characterize our environment. Many of these rituals are free of the profit motive, and are directed towards satisfying those aspects of people's lives which are not easily subjected to cost-benefit analyses rooted in the price mechanism. In the past these rituals have been shaped powerfully by people's immediate physical environment, and in some of his work Braudel has placed great stress on these constraints in accounting for the construction of social order. This stress has led one critic to argue that Braudel's work is a form of 'geohistorical structuralism' (Kinser, 1981).

In the modern period, however, these physical constraints on everyday life have receded (for most of those in the industrialized world, at any rate), allowing other constraints to become more prominent. One of these constraints is what Braudel calls the *mentalité*, or the mental horizons of historical subjects. In terms of everyday life, mental horizons are generally linked to the past and dependent upon received wisdom; hence people's reliance on the security of rituals and routines to guide behaviour from day to day. *Mentalités* change very slowly and often only under great duress. They are mental maps useful precisely because they fix the parameters of social order and the place of the individual within it. To change them abruptly is to throw our place within the world into question.

Another constraint which works to hold back the pace of change is the role of personal relationships in the construction and reproduction of local communities. The communal structure of everyday life is shaped as much by the breadth, depth and limits of our relationships among family and friends as by the mental horizons we share and the technology at our fingertips. Braudel's point about the durability of the domain of material life is precisely its embeddedness within the slowly woven fabric of these relationships. They are circumscribed by family histories, social roots and personal mobility, and for many change only marginally over a lifetime. And even though some are bound less than others by the general inertia of daily living, Braudel is correct to draw attention to the considerable constraints imposed by routine and ritual upon the organization of social life. To consider globalization as the keystone of social organization is to neglect the power of these other conflicting dynamics.

The second layer of Braudel's social hierarchy is the domain of the market economy. Braudel's use of the term should be distinguished here from its more widespread meaning as a realm in which the uncontrolled pursuit of private profit occurs without consideration of social consequences. This understanding of the market economy can be found, for example, in the work of Karl Polanyi, who argued that the nineteenth century witnessed a bold and ultimately unsuccessful attempt to transform 'society into a market economy' (Polanyi, 1944: 101). Whereas for Polanyi, Marx and many others the market economy is a homogeneous and indivisible set of social relations, Braudel takes great pains to distinguish the market economy from the domains of material life and what he calls 'capitalism'. At one level, the market economy is the realm of commercial exchange in which the profit motive plays a central role. At the same time, however, the kind of commercial exchange Braudel has in mind is associated primarily with the straightforward application of supply and demand dynamics, in which products are grown, manufactured or purchased for stable markets and where investment returns can be easily calculated.[11] They are markets which are subject to change on a regular and cyclical basis, in line with the slowly fluctuating needs and demands of producers and consumers.

As a social realm, Braudel considers the market economy to be a more privileged set of social relations than the domain of material life because of its increased scope for movement and change. The social relations at the heart of the market economy are less bound by family and domicile (although not devoid of them), and less subject to the encrusted grip of tradition. They are more open to encouraging personal mobility and forging new social relationships. At the same time, most participants within the market economy share a mental horizon dominated by stable expectations about the future. It is a *mentalité* which accepts the cyclical nature of change and considers the profit motive in line with personal and/or family security. In other words, even though the profit motive is an integral element of activities within the market economy, it is one which is largely bound by the needs and requirements of maintaining a livelihood or the competitive pressures inspired by stable demand and supply expectations. Those who follow the dictates of such a profit motive help to create a transparent economic environment in which knowledge about the particular costs and benefits of engaging in trade is widely diffused.

The domain of activity which stands over the market economy is the realm for which Braudel prefers to reserve the term capitalism. It is starkly differentiated from the market economy in three ways. First, where the market economy is characterized by transparent commercial exchange, the domain of capitalism is dominated by non-transparent exchange. By this Braudel means that few transactions at this level become regularized or routinized. Markets both materialize suddenly and disappear quickly, and their characteristics cannot be assumed beyond the short time span. Assessment of the costs and benefits of participation involves judgements about the kinds of developments over which few people have adequate knowledge or control. In short, it is an arena of action subject to extreme contingency and risk.

Such contingency and risk introduce the second way in which capitalism is distinguished from the market economy. Here Braudel highlights speculation as the lifeblood of capitalism, and argues that it is largely absent from the way in which the profit motive works within the market economy. For Braudel, it is misleading to compare as capitalists both the self-employed corner baker and the venture capitalist, as each is driven by entirely different motivational dynamics. Although they may be part of the same world economy, their own economic and social worlds are marked by stark discontinuities. Finally, these discontinuities are accentuated by the logic of capital accumulation. Within the domain of capitalism, the profit motive takes the form of the quest for massive accumulation, which seeks to reproduce capital in terms of itself. Whereas the profit motive in the domain of the market economy encourages savings and consumption linked to the reproduction of livelihoods, for capitalists it is the reproduction and expansion of capital itself which defines their domain. It is not so much a system of production as a terrain of activity, and – for Braudel at least – a rather narrow one at that.

As a terrain of activity, therefore, capitalism is distinguished by its logic of accumulation, its speculative dimension and its lack of transparency. It is the arena in which predators roam, using information and capital to exploit opportunities in which the possibility of large-scale profit is directly related to the degree of risk involved. Crucially, this correlation between risk and reward, which is an integral element of the definition of capitalism, also serves to limit it. Capitalists, Braudel contends, will ultimately choose only to be active where the rewards are consonant with the possibility of massive accumulation. While such choice is one of the chief privileges of capitalists (and the realm of capitalism more generally), it also means that there are many types of activity which fall outside the interests of capitalists. For Braudel, it is the consequences of these kinds of structured choices which differentiate the domains of material life, the market economy and capitalism, notwithstanding the overarching coherence imparted to their relations by the social parameters of the world economy.

Globalization, capitalism and the market economy

Considering globalization from a Braudelian-inspired historical perspective draws attention to two important points. First, as a social practice globalization is largely restricted to the domain of capitalism. This is the arena of activity in which the drive for massive accumulation predominates, and in which the kinds of information differentials necessary for speculation exist . Where globalization is considered as an economic phenomenon, it is most closely associated with large institutions engaged in the search for massive accumulation via speculative ventures. They are the institutions which have the resources, motivations and capabilities to roam the world searching for the kind of opportunities which promise lucrative rewards. These opportunities are usually found in markets characterized by few players, rapidly changing norms of behaviour, and unknown horizons. Prominent contemporary examples would include those markets associated with knowledge-intensive products such as telecommunications, biotechnology, pharmaceuticals and computer programming, as well as the more traditional preserves of speculation such as property development, insurance, stock market trading and investment banking. Certain large-scale illicit activities, such as narcotics and racketeering, would also fall into this category. Defined broadly, this is the principal terrain of capitalism today.

If the first point of importance draws attention to how the terrain of globalization is constituted, the second point emphasizes the healthy competitive dynamics of the market economy and the importance of protecting it from the predatory incursions of capitalism. Protecting the market economy is important because it is the arena in which most of the products and services which people use on a daily basis are produced, exchanged and purchased. It is the domain of social life most clearly connected to how people live their lives.[12] What is particularly significant in this respect is the relative transparency which the production and exchange of goods and services enjoys within the market economy. Because of the widespread diffusion of information, the ease of entry into its commercial practices, and the limitations placed on the profit motive by its openly competitive framework, the market economy is the realm in which most basic needs are expressed and met, and around which the fabric of daily life is most tightly woven. From this perspective, it is perhaps not too much to say that in the contemporary period the market economy is the basic sub-stratum of society.

However, protecting the market economy from capitalism can no longer mean simply exalting the national over the global. One of the broader implications of employing Braudel's triptych concerns the way in which the significance of geographical and political boundaries can be recast. In the sixteenth century, for example, the constraints of geography served as one of the principal determinants of the contours of the Mediterranean world economy. By the eighteenth century, the Amsterdam-centred world economy had overcome the constraints of the Mediterranean, although the limits of technology at that time meant that the vagaries of oceanic transport remained important. Today, the geographic constraints on the world economy have been largely eliminated: a single global world economy is now in existence. This means, of course, that the contours of the market economy have also changed over time. In the sixteenth century, the market economy was largely a local domain, stretching at most to a few days' travel across self-contained trading basins. During the course of the eighteenth and nineteenth centuries, however, the consolidation in Europe of national economies associated with the formation of the modern state allowed the market economy to become national in scope. Political boundaries thus played a crucial role in determining the extent of the market economy.

Capitalism, as it strengthened during this era, flourished in and around the interstices of geography and politics: that is, beyond the market economy. This is one reason for capitalism's international character, which Braudel believes has been one of its biggest strengths from its earliest days (Braudel, 1982: 554). He also insists that capitalism did not begin to invade the market economy until capitalists began to see in the means of production the possibility also of reproducing capital, which did not take place until the full force of the Industrial Revolution had been felt (Braudel, 1982: 372–3). It was only after this, moreover, that the state became a full participant in the domain of capitalism. Until then it was content mostly to license capitalists where the interests of capitalism and the state coincided. The state did not whole-heartedly favour the terrain of capitalism until capitalism had reconstituted itself in order to imbricate capitalists within the very hierarchy of the state. It was at this point that capitalism and the state became natural allies.

In the contemporary period, however, there is no longer a necessary relationship between national boundaries and the market economy. On one hand, the market economy has outgrown the national economy. Routine trade of a wide variety of everyday consumer products now takes place across national borders. The two clearest examples of this are the single market in Europe and the North American free trade area. In both cases all manner of small-scale firms trade on a regular and routine basis across markets defined on a continental scale: the market economy today is broader than the national economy. On the other hand, the market economy is also less than the national economy due to its extensive penetration by capitalism. National economies are amalgams of all three of Braudel's principal social domains, even if the balance between them is constantly shifting. This balance was obscured, however, during the middle decades of this century, when the national economy became broadly identified with the market economy.

This temporary configuration of the national economy was part of the reason for the regulatory success of post-1945 Keynesianism. A producing and trading environment contained within national political borders and marked by stable and transparent dynamics lent itself to relatively successful macro-economic regulation. This was aided immensely by the stunted nature of capitalist speculation during this time; its international thrust had been deflected as a consequence of the inter-war period. Capitalists did not regain their speculative and international dynamism until the late 1960s, by which time the logic of massive accumulation (within the largest industrialized economies at least) in the guise of Fordism had penetrated deep into national economies. The terrain of capitalism, in other words, had become reconstituted after 1945 to span parts of the national economy and the world market.

If it is appropriate to consider globalization as the social practice which most clearly identifies the terrain of capitalism today, what constraints does it face? The Braudelian perspective adopted here suggests that the structural organization of the world economy presents two kinds of constraints to the further spread of globalization. These constraints are located within the competing dynamics of the domains of material life and the market economy. Acknowledging the value of these domains as bulwarks against globalization suggests strategies for resistance to globalization which neither accept the logic of globalization nor exalt the national over the global. These strategies instead recognize that resistance to globalization will be most successful where it builds upon the constraints presently faced by globalized social practices, in order to secure more fully the space within which everyday life can be freed from the disruptive incursions of capitalism (and globalization).

One such strategy, targeted at the domain of material life, would therefore be to empower the family as an institution, to endow it with a capacity to overcome the sudden economic dislocations which are often the consequences of speculative behaviour. Such empowerment has traditionally taken the form of income support to insulate the purchasing power of families from sudden swings in currency parities or interest rates, which often translate directly into job losses. Alternatively, and more innovatively, it could mean ensuring the provision of the kinds of health, leisure and community-related services which serve as anchors for stable communities. Crucially, this would require accountability for and control over these services to pass to local communities, in order to empower them to arrange their lives and the services which affect them according to local priorities. In either case the goal would be to provide a safe and secure environment in which family and community relations can develop without fear of sudden disruptions to the social fabric.

Any strategy of resistance to globalization, nevertheless, must enlist the power of the state to insulate the market economy from the speculative logic of capitalism. This strategy, which must build on the strengths of the market economy as it is currently constituted, requires at least two prongs. The first prong must be a macro-economic one which should seek to enlarge and entrench the market economy beyond the confines of the national economy. Seen in this light, trends towards regionalism within Europe and North America assume a healthy perspective, for one of their cardinal achievements has been to establish a transparent and competitive trading environment in which firms of all sizes can participate on a level playing field. And while it is clearly the case that large corporate firms are a main beneficiary of this development, so too are many smaller firms which are not engaged in the quest for massive accumulation, and who do not seek to realize speculative windfall savings through the implementation of dramatic economies of scale. What the new enlarged regional markets provide is a bigger and more transparent environment in which to do business, thus securing a space for a market dynamic to flourish which is not necessarily speculative in character and directed towards massive accumulation. In macro-economic terms, therefore, trends towards regionalism strengthen the market economy by politically securing its extra-national foundations.

At the same time, these foundations will wither unless a microeconomic prong is not included as part of the strategy of resistance. Here some combination of taxation and fiscal policy designed to privilege and/or encourage small businesses is required. Small family-owned businesses comprise the bulk of participants within the market economy, and subject to size and/or profit limits, they ought to be encouraged to participate to their fullest extent within this domain. Such encouragement could take two forms. At one level, taxation policy could be formulated to privilege the ownership structure of small businesses, making them advantageous from a tax point of view provided they were undertaking certain kinds of activities. There is little need, for example, to encourage or privilege a small business structure in the hair salon and corner store market, as this largely exists already. But preserving a role for small businesses in the retail service markets associated with providing everyday essentials in the community might be very advantageous from the perspective of ensuring the preservation of strong and stable communities.

At another level, carefully targeted fiscal policies aimed at strengthening the link between finance, production and consumption within the market economy could help to insulate it from the depredations of capitalism. Focusing on the provision of financial resources to small businesses, for example, could strengthen this sector of the market economy by ensuring access to reasonably priced start-up and/or expansion capital (once again, subject to a size or profit threshold). Publicly owned development or community banks are one example of such fiscal policy at work, as are insurance and export promotion schemes aimed at small businesses. Taken together, the two prongs of such a strategy might help to secure a suitable space within which the institutional pillars of the market economy could evolve progressively. Such a development would ensure that as far as possible the structural constraints of the market economy would continue to circumscribe the reach of globalization.

The main weakness of such a strategy, of course, is its reliance on the state as the key empowering agency within the market economy. In many respects the state has become a capitalist enterprise, designed to encourage and defend the terrain of capitalism. During the middle years of the twentieth century, for example, the state largely directed its efforts towards consolidating capitalism on the home ground of the national economy, which in the industrialized world meant promoting a welfare apparatus and encouraging forms of labour relations supportive of large-scale industry. But the attempt to weld capitalism to the framework of the national economy has come unstuck, and the state is now engaged in a renewed attempt to reconstitute and entrench capitalism on a global level. Government support for globalization has indeed been one of the clearest indications so far that as an institution the state must be considered a genuine and enthusiastic participant in capitalism (Helleiner, 1994). Channelling resistance to globalization through the state will be a problematic venture until this paradox is confronted.

Nevertheless, it is within the realm of political accountability that resistance to the malign affects of globalization must begin, as electorates across the world push for more control over their local communities. Enlisting state support for these initiatives can and ought to be pursued through the ballot box, especially where such efforts can be allied to a rethinking of community within the context of global pressures. In today's world, recasting the relationship between capitalism and the market economy requires nothing less than rethinking the role of the state within the context of globalized social practices.

Globalization and the historical mode of thought

To some, the history of the past half-century has followed a narrow path which has brought its precious cargo through the dark tunnel of the Depression and the war years out on to the sunlit plains of a fully globalized world. This particular express train is most commonly known as globalization, and despite the occasional challenge it is largely accepted as an accurate portrayal of the leading dynamics of social organization today.[13] This chapter has sought to unsettle that portrayal, and to inject into our representation of globalization an awareness of both its historicity and its uneven presence across the social structure of today's world. It now remains to reflect more broadly on the advantages of adopting the historical mode of thought as one possible theoretical foundation for our inquiry. Three advantages are emphasized.

The first advantage to be gained lies in bringing a concern with what Braudel called social time into the analysis of globalization. This concern has been styled here in terms of the historicity of globalization, in order to highlight the presence of extensively globalized social practices throughout the entire modern period. Alternatively, the social time of globalization could be understood in terms of the long, medium and short term, and its significance assessed against different temporal frameworks (Helleiner, 1997: 93–6). In either case a linear conception of globalization's development is denied, and a more fluid set of possibilities marking the pathways open to these globalized social practices put in its place. Such a concern with the time of globalization allows for analyses which not only see its consequences as differentiated, but which also see the 'home ground' of globalization – its natural constituency, so to speak – as a time-bound realm. To use the historical mode of thought, in other words, is to refuse to accept the prevailing orthodoxy that globalization represents above all a 'space/time compression' (Harvey, 1989: 284–308). Even in a post-modern and globalized world, time refuses to be compressed: its impact upon thought and action is multilayered, uneven and complex.

The second advantage to be gained by employing the historical mode of thought as conveyed here is a heightened awareness of the level of institutional differentiation within the modern global political economy. Most proponents (and critics) of globalization consider every institutional form to be subject to its central dynamic, without regard to the market they participate in or the cultural context of their activities. This predilection is especially evident in analyses of finance, which reduce all financial institutions and markets to those of 'global finance'. And while it is certainly true that global investment banks, big bank holding companies with powerful investment banking arms, some private banks and pension funds, large mutual or unit trust funds, and some insurance companies do control the vast majority of internationally mobile funds, it is also the case that many aspects of finance are left to small, local or national financial institutions, with little or no competition from 'global finance'. Even full-service financial conglomerates such as Citicorp or HSBC contain within themselves multiple and often conflicting dynamics associated with those parts of the institution that participate in differently organized markets. A signal contribution of the historical mode of thought, then, is an awareness of this institutional differentiation and its consequences for how we understand the broader patterns of social organization.

The third advantage considered here is the flipside of taking time and institutional differentiation within the social world seriously, namely to acknowledge the transformative possibilities engendered by collective agency. Because of its focus on particular social practices as the defining hallmark of globalization, the historical mode of thought refuses to endow globalization with a transhistorical or predetermined character. What we understand as globalization today is nothing more than a form of globalized social practice inherent to a particular terrain of social activity, a terrain which, although it has expanded over the past century, remains nevertheless bound by certain constraints. Moreover, it is the mapping of this terrain and the recognition of these constraints which empowers collective agency through institutional channels in the first place. In terms then of informing resistance to globalization (where this is warranted), the immediate task is to identify the boundaries of social organization over which globalization does not hold sway, and to support those dynamics and institutions which protect and promote the stable relationships of the market economy. One part of this task might lie in enlisting the support of civilizational viewpoints inimical to the modern Western consumer ethos that drives globalization, while another part may lie in mobilizing counter-hegemonic social forces to challenge the thrust of globalization. In either case, employing the historical mode of thought strengthens efforts to encourage transformations in collective social practices so as to counter and contain the more predatory aspects of globalization.[14]

Understood as a specific type of bounded social practice embedded within a particular institutional form, globalization is clearly one of the most significant constituent factors contributing to the contemporary structure of the global political economy. Coming to terms with how it shapes expectations and informs ways of thinking is critical to a full comprehension of this important phenomena. Insofar as the historical mode of thought encourages an appreciation of how globalizing dynamics fit into the wider organization of social life, this way of thinking can be an integral element of the general attempt to understand globalization. Fernand Braudel was concerned to understand the broad structure of social order, and argued that it was impossible to do so unless one was prepared first to consider society in terms of a 'set of sets': that is, an interlocking set of economic, cultural, political and social practices subject to multiple and conflicting dynamics. To isolate a single dynamic as the driving force behind the construction of social order is for Braudel to present a misleading portrayal of how order is achieved over time. That advice, first offered during the course of an attempt to understand the mainsprings of social order between the fifteenth and eighteenth centuries, remains sound today, and we would do well to follow it in our analyses of the complex subject of globalization.

Notes

1. For their comments and suggestions, the author would like to thank participants at the 'Globalization and its Critics' workshop and the 1997 annual workshop of the International Political Economy Group of the British International Studies Association.
2. It should be noted that the trade in ideas and knowledge are other touchstones of social life that have an inherently global dimension, as is of course the practice of theorizing itself (see Chapter 1 in this volume).
3. For explications of Braudel's triptych within the context of IPE, see Gill (1991b), Germain (1996) and Helleiner (1997).
4. Work in the political economy tradition which falls into this category would include Barraclough (1967), Braudel (1984), Hobsbawm (1968), Polanyi (1944), A. K. Smith (1991) and Thompson (1978). This work in turn draws on historiographical and philosophical reflections broadly associated with the current of historicism, such as in Carr (1961), Collingwood (1946) and Vico (1968). Femia (1981) provides a succinct overview of key aspects of historicism.
5. Examples of such work include Cox (1983), Gill (1993) and Murphy (1994).
6. Work in this tradition includes geographers such as Agnew and Corbridge (1995) and Taylor (1996), as well as that recently done by constructivists such as Wendt (1994).
7. The term 'globalized' is used here because a close examination of the international financial interests of the Dutch capitalist class during the seventeenth and eighteenth centuries reveals a wide-ranging and extensive set of holdings throughout the known trading world (Barbour, 1963: 104–29).
8. As Howard notes:

   > whatever the rationale of wars during this period, ... they were carried out by a largely international class of contractors on a purely commercial basis ... [These armies] were raised, maintained, and led into battle by a class of entrepreneurs whose only bond of loyalty to their employer was the assurance of cash payment, punctually and in full. (1976: 24–5)

9. War *materiel* was also available on the international market. During the seventeenth century in particular, Amsterdam's reputation (and ability) as a supplier of war *materiel* to all sides, including countries with which the Dutch were at war, was unrivalled (Barbour, 1963: 35–42).
10. This internationalism, for example, is evident in the career of the French artillery commander Jean Baptiste Vacquette de Gribeauval, principal architect of France's artillery modernization efforts in the mid-eighteenth century. He was sent in 1752 to Prussia for military training, and then after 1756 served with the Austrian armed forces during their conflict with Prussia. He only returned to France in 1763 (McNeill, 1982: 174).
11. Braudel (1982: 457) notes as an example of trade within the market economy that of oil and wine between the merchants of the Mediterranean

and northern France. He uses the observation of an eighteenth-century writer to make his point: 'The real treasures of France among the fruits of the earth, are wines and oils. The whole of the North needs them and the North cannot produce them. So a trade becomes established, carves itself a channel, ceases to be speculation, and becomes routine.'

12. Two hundred years ago, the domain of material life would have been the most important arena of activity in this regard. One of the signal developments of the past two centuries has been the increasingly circumscribed nature of this domain, which has been penetrated and overlaid by the relations of the market economy and capitalism.
13. Two analyses which do challenge the empirical claims of the leading proponents of globalization are Kapstein (1994) and Hirst and Thompson (1996).
14. Two recent volumes which attempt to undertake this task are Mittelman (1996) and Gill and Mittelman (1997). The journal *New Political Economy* has also devoted a volume to the question of the politics of globalization (Gill, 1997), while Cox (1996) has explored the role of civilizations in world politics partly in terms of resistance to globalization.

3
Globalization and Cultural Political Economy

Nick Stevenson

The contemporary debate in respect of the changes taking place in world cultures would have us make a choice between universalism and difference, sameness and plurality and homogeneity and diversity. Often identical examples can be called upon to make a case for either argument. The development of 'world music' is a good example. On the one hand, we might argue that the main beneficiaries of the global traffic in music are the large conglomerates who market and sell commodities to customers. Walk into any large record store and you will be able to choose selections of music from English folk to the latest dance tracks by Madonna.

Some might argue, however, that this offers only the 'illusion' of diversity, in that the music has been similarly packaged, presented and manufactured in order to be immediately reproducible on the consumer's audio technology. The capitalist economy converts all musical forms into products to be bought and sold in the market place. The most important aspect about contemporary culture is not its aesthetic value, but the profits it is able to generate for a transnational business class. Such arguments might also be linked to the notion that traditional musical forms, such as Irish music, have become 'colonized' by the standardized and repetitive nature of much Western popular music: that is, the Irish music that is made available is either incorporated into more established musical genres or converted into an easily consumable form through the establishment of 'greatest hits' packages. Hence in place of 'world music' we might read global commodification and reification.

On the other hand, this narrative could be read somewhat differently: the arrival of 'world music' means that music is now more difficult to classify than ever before. A great deal of contemporary music exists as a hybrid form promoting culturally cosmopolitan tastes amongst its consumers through the intermixing of different genres, styles and types. The arrival of post-modern culture has meant that previously held distinctions between high and low culture have largely been displaced. In listening to a single record we might be able to discern the influences of Latin jazz, African drums, the Irish harp, a string quartet and even a Yorkshire brass band. Music cultures in this reading are not so much flattening out as providing new opportunities for artistic bricolage.

The problem with such debates is that they force us to simplify complex and uneven cultural processes. As the above 'local' example spells out, we can just as easily make a case for the fact that the world's cultural systems are growing in diversity as we can that they are homogenizing. Many of the transformations sweeping through global cultures incorporate elements of both homogeneity and difference: that is, it is not enough to *read* cultural processes through the optic suggested by either of these categories.

My account will remain distinct from the tendency of merely describing global cultures through a form of uncritical pluralism. Instead, I suggest that renewed emphasis is placed upon what I shall call a framework of cultural political economy. By this I do not simply mean that relations of cultural production and reproduction have to be 'represented' in discourse, but that cultural processes are simultaneously being reconstructed and deconstructed by a number of forces and tendencies that can be associated with both modernity and post-modernity. I shall focus my remarks on five themes:

1. *The thesis of McDonaldization*, where the emergence of an instrumental and technical rational culture is evident within the meanings and practices fostered by global capital and bureaucratic systems.
2. *The thesis of cultural imperialism*, where the relationship between world economic power and global culture stresses the predominant position of the USA today.
3. *The thesis of post-modernization*, where the development of a world-wide spatially disoriented culture has emerged within late capitalism.
4. *The thesis of democratization*, where the institutions and practices of liberal democracy have triumphed over its rivals.
5. *The thesis of nationalism*, where the arrival of modernity has been accompanied by the conversion of the globe into a mosaic of national cultures.

All of these perspectives are attempting to articulate a broad conception of how global cultures are changing beyond the reach of the template that has traditionally equated the nation with society. They each offer a partial picture of global culture. Yet in seeking to do this all of the perspectives have a number of blind spots. Taken together, it might be possible to begin the complex task of tracing through the different levels of mediation that any attempt to capture broadly defined cultural processes must inevitably encounter. This strategy is particularly important in that it attempts to distance itself from the excesses of certain post-modern arguments that perceive the more stable elements of modernity to have disappeared, as well as the modernist search for the one paradigm that will reveal the true nature of existing cultural relations. My argument therefore emphasizes both cultural complexity and ambiguity along with a more traditional institutional analysis of society.

Arguably, I could have chosen other aspects of cultural development to illustrate my argument. For reasons that will become apparent, however, the features I identify below seem to be the most sociologically significant. That there is ample evidence for all of these processes will not deter me from offering some critical remarks in respect of the evident limitations of such viewpoints. Notably, most of the features described by these frameworks have their roots in modernity, rather than a fully fledged post-modernity. However, as my discussion will demonstrate, many of these features are the subject of contestation and challenge within the modern era, and are often more culturally complex than many of the authors allow.

The idea that we are simultaneously witnessing the continuation of modernity as well as the development of more post-modern features will guide my discussion. Here I shall seek to provide the beginnings of an explanatory framework within which we might begin to map uneven social and cultural developments. Finally, I shall use one theorist to illustrate each perspective or thesis in question. This should not of course be taken to indicate that many of these views are not often combined with others, or that the particular theorist I have chosen to highlight does not also endorse a number of the other perspectives that will also be discussed.

McDonaldization

One of the most persistent fears that can be associated with the growth of modern bureaucracies and rational calculative reason is that the world is being emptied of human difference, meaning and spontaneity. From the classical sociology of Max Weber to the early Frankfurt school and beyond, the growth of expert systems has been represented as having a rationalizing and ordering effect upon modern life. The pervasiveness of formal rationality, it is claimed, has constructed a dehumanizing iron cage which holds modern subjects prisoner. This view has been recently most persuasively stressed by George Ritzer's (1992) study of the American fast food giant, McDonald's. Ritzer is clear that the book is not only meant to be indicative of a particular way of processing and delivering food, but a wider culture that is slowly penetrating the globe.

The fast food industry can be identified with four basic components of formal rationality: efficiency, quantification, predictability and the displacement of human labour. These principles of bureaucratic organization have not only colonized food production and consumption, but are evident in the university, hospital, supermarket and the cultural industries in general. The McDonald's culture offers efficiency in that it seeks the quickest method possible to satisfy the consumer's demands for entertainment, nourishment, information and transport. In an increasingly fast-paced world consumer needs have to be satisfied quickly, and with the minimum amount of personal disturbance. In terms of media cultures, the development of the Internet offers a fast and streamlined way of receiving up to the minute news, without (it seems) the inconvenience of having to search through cumbersome newspapers for the reports that are of interest. The McDonald's culture also offers a service that can be quantified and numerically counted. Culture in this climate is increasingly subject to the procedures of calculation; rather than focusing upon the 'experience' a piece of music opens out, we are persuaded to assess our purchase in terms of its value for money, the length of the recording and even the number of easily recognized songs it contains.

The prevailing McDonald's culture takes predictability as its hallmark. Each time I settle into my armchair to watch the latest American situation comedy, I expect the experience to be exactly the same as the previous hundred or so times. This homogeneous streamlined culture encourages the desire for psychically comforting sameness, and promotes the avoidance of other more troubling questions and experiences. The daily flow of television news programmes, in this reading, only superficially appear to be 'different'; viewed more critically, they rely upon well-tested formats, and easily consumable sound bites. Finally, the rapidly spreading McDonald's culture replaces human beings with technological forms of mediation and control. Human labour that can never be made perfectly predictable is replaced by technology in the workplace, in areas of social control and other avenues of social life.

The McDonaldized culture has sought to provide highly efficient systems of service delivery, although this is often achieved by making the customer do more of the work. For example, the old grocery store, where the shopkeeper gathered the items of purchase, has been replaced by the supermarket where the unpaid labour of the shopper predominates. The growth of a self-service culture de-skills service workers while imposing drudgery upon the consumer. The ultimate consequence of this process is the elimination of human contact altogether. Indeed this is precisely what is promised by home shopping television channels. Viewers are able to travel around the virtual store without ever leaving their own home or, more importantly, without encountering the 'presence' of another human being. Technology therefore is being used to create a culture of distance and indifference by isolating the 'consumer' from the concerns of her neighbour.

New media technologies can also be utilized as surveillance mechanisms whether we are out shopping, attending a sporting event or even sitting in our own home. Such mechanisms are more efficient than their human equivalent in that they do not become bored, fall asleep or avoid work. Taken together, the McDonaldized world is ushering in a cultural environment based around consumer efficiency, calculability, predictability and the replacement of human capacities with technological devices. Such practices offer a smooth seamless culture with few shocks or surprises; they encourage a kind of stupefied mass conformity.

These processes undoubtedly point towards important features that can be connected to the rationalization of modernity. However, many have recently come to doubt the extent to which the world will ever comply with this model. As I indicated, the fear of a completely bureaucratized and rationalized life-world has been an important component which has shaped many people's understanding of the world. However, while the cultural industries exhibit many of these features, it is not currently evident that these projections are any closer to fruition than they were at the turn of the century. The argument that the modern world is increasingly becoming culturally unified as well as rationally controlled is misleading. If we now inhabit, to use Beck's (1992) phrase, a risk society, given the potentially catastrophic consequences of global warming and nuclear meltdown, then this is something other than a predictable universe. Indeed many of the features which seem at first to be elements of an increasingly predictable and controlled social world inevitably contain less rationalized elements.

For instance, the development of global news events could be read as fostering a culture of sameness, whereby the diverse nature of political currents is flattened out into the predictable rumblings of media sensation. However, such practices also inform different logics and cultural sensibilities. According to Lewis Friedman (1992), the reporting of Tienanmen Square by CNN had a greater cultural significance than a concern with the rationalized manufacture of consumable news would have us believe. The world media's 24-hour coverage of Beijing not only subjected the Chinese authorities to global scrutiny, but also, by making the protesters visible, held back the manoeuvrings of the Chinese military. Modernity, in this reading, is better represented through a dialectic of rational control and disorder. The growth in television ownership world-wide, for example, could be said to provide modern citizens with a fast, efficient and cost-effective means of communication. However, it is increasingly the case that the reporting of news stories and the construction of global media events opens up local practices to a form of global critical scrutiny provoking increasingly unpredictable consequences. The McDonaldization of modern culture somewhat paradoxically both strengthens and undermines the penetration of bureaucratic reason into the far reaches of modern society. As we will find with the other cultural theses explored below, what is lacking is a more enhanced dialectical appreciation of modern culture.

Cultural imperialism

The only culture that can properly be considered to be a global culture is American culture. Whether we are thinking about films, television programmes, popular sayings, comic books or music, it is American culture that has the broadest reach globally. One way of accounting for this has been through what Schiller and others have called the cultural imperialist thesis. In Schiller's (1996) most recent defence of this argument, he focuses upon the capitalist-driven nature and commodification of American popular culture before transferring this model to the rest of the world. The globe, it seems, is being remade in America's own image. American capitalist culture, according to Schiller, is one of the purest currently in existence, its internal development in post-war society being fostered by the expansion of credit, rampant consumerism, advertising and the systematic displacement of traditional forms of constraint.

Capitalism American style has largely arisen in a national context that lacks any recognizable tradition of social democracy, and where working-class labour organizations have only the weakest public presence. Such an environment has fostered the integration of information and culture into the dominant structures of the finance economy. Popular culture in America is driven by capitalist accumulation strategies. Economic forces are the main structures behind technological developments such as the super information highway and the Internet, and they also help determine the superficiality of much of mainstream mass culture. The dominance of the economic system over other social spheres helps foster a culture of conformity rather than critique, sensation rather than substance, and technique rather than reflection. Cultural concerns, other than for a small intellectual elite, are run, managed and determined by the parameters of economics. For this reason, American culture carries ideological messages of consumerism and promotes acquisitive behaviour in the host and the world population in general. Mass forms of entertainment, therefore, act as a form of compensation for a disintegrating communal life, while encouraging the displacement of critical questions connected to a divided society. Schiller argues that the expansion in entertainment services not only provides new markets for advertisers, but masks important social issues such as the growing underclass, widening social divisions and a spiralling prison population. Mass culture thereby helps to insulate the well-off from the poor, and is utilized increasingly by private as opposed to public interests.

Schiller maintains that while America has declined in terms of its overall position within the world economy, it has maintained its hegemony over global culture. Since the 1980s, culture everywhere has become increasingly Americanized and penetrated by economic reason. The increasing integration of media products into the global market and the rapid deregulation of public cultures have promoted world-wide processes of Americanization. This has been achieved through the direct promotion of American products, and the local copying of American television styles and formats. Just as American capitalism was able to marginalize oppositional structures at home, so with the running down of public cultures abroad it has been able to penetrate into new markets.

Commercially-driven media, the main carriers of American products, are currently overrunning a passive world. Significantly, it is the global economy rather than the nation-state which is the new mechanism of governance. In the face of networks of global capital, the nation is struggling to maintain its cultural autonomy and preserve the distinctiveness of internally constructed social identities. Indeed the development of global communications has been driven less by individual states than by the world's rich and powerful seeking to cordon themselves off from the poor. In this reading, again mirroring developments within American society, the globe's wealthy consumers will become the targets of accumulation strategies, thereby repressing questions concerning deepening global inequalities which will inevitably be avoided by overtly capitalist controlled media structures. A world dominated less by the governance of the nation, and more by the commercial imperatives of global capitalism, will foster a social environment where a few prosper and many are marginalized.

The cultural imperialist thesis has many parallels with notions of rationalization presented earlier. Both perspectives represent the diverse cultures and practices of the globe as being overtaken by a homogenizing hegemony which is being driven by a systemic logic. Indeed, if notions of rationalization can be traced back to Weber, the imperialistic expansion of the capitalist economy has its roots within Marx. Again, however, the main problem with the analysis, which undoubtedly cannot be dismissed out of hand, is that it fails to articulate the complexity of cultural processes that can be associated with globalization. Another point worth noting is that while criticizing the engulfment of culture by economics, Schiller's own critique reproduces a similar trope on a theoretical level: culture is here thought to mirror economic practices.

Although they are clearly related, in Schiller's account globalization becomes confused with universalization. Cultural processes of universalization thus suggest that the world is becoming progressively unified through the spread of commodification. Indeed much of the evidence points towards the argument that the global capitalist economy is not so much expanding into previously unexploited world regions, but is intensifying in a number of world economic centres. For instance, Latin America's and Africa's current share of world trade is in decline due to the *deepening* rather than *widening* of capitalist networks (Castells, 1996; Hoogvelt, 1997). Globalization, however, is not purely an economic phenomena, but must also be associated with the strengthening of cultural interconnections between world regions. Giddens (1991: 64) has offered a good rule of thumb definition: 'Globalization can thus be defined as the intensification of world-wide social relations which link distant localities in such a way that local happenings are shaped by events occurring many miles away and vice versa.'

Schiller's hermeneutic therefore both misrepresents global economic trends and marginalizes other more cultural patterns. For example, Robertson (1992) has pointed towards a growing political and cultural realization that critical questions related to AIDS, nuclear disasters and ecological degradation are truly global questions. The rich and powerful are of course in a much better position to be able to shield themselves from the negative impacts of such developments, but there remains a sense in which they are *everyone's* responsibility. These dimensions arguably offer a more nuanced understanding of the new identities being fostered by processes (such as the technological development of the media) that cannot be captured by patterns of consumerism alone. Indeed, we might go further and suggest that the intensification of the capitalist economy has produced both cultural homogeneity as well as cultural difference. In this instance, Harvey (1989) argues that the increasing liquidity of capital means that a stronger emphasis will be placed upon the distinctiveness of social spaces that might attract capital. Such processes, which are undoubtedly evident within tourism, would seek to attract potential consumers and flows of capital due, at least in part, to the distinctive features one space was able to offer over others.

Why, then, is Schiller seemingly so blind to these developments? Part of the answer to this question must be a consequence of his tendency to assume that economic and cultural developments are both moving in the same direction. This is also exaggerated, a point I shall return to in the next section, due to Schiller's tendency to universalize the experience of his host national culture. It remains the case that Schiller's economistic Marxism fails to unravel the complexity of rapidly globalizing cultures. Baudrillard (1975) argues that it is characteristic of Marxist notions of political economy to suppose that economic dimensions directly determine cultural signs and meanings. Marxist frames tend to reduce particular activities of, say, watching the television, to the interests of capitalist commodification. While Baudrillard can be accused of pushing this argument beyond the limits of what is proposed here, the point remains one of significance (Stevenson, 1995). The practice of gathering around the television could equally be connected to certain family rituals, national days of celebration, or even a way of becoming informed about significant world events. These questions will be returned to in the final section when I seek to develop a model of cultural political economy that seeks to recognize the increasing significance of the economy in cultural production without reproducing the theoretical problems that have rightly become associated with economic determinism.

Post-modernization

Post-modernism, according to Frederick Jameson (1991), is the cultural expression – or logic – of a particular phase of capitalism. Jameson takes the global collapse of culture into economic forms of production as the starting point for his analysis. The effacing of high modernism and mass commercial culture has been achieved by the colonization of the cultural sphere by the operation of the market. The integration of aesthetic production into commodity production has delivered a new culturally dominant post-modernism. The aim of classical modernism was to shock and deride the bourgeoisie through cultural production. In the post-modern era, however, modernist formations have become canonized in university departments and have thereby lost their subversive temper. Meanwhile, contemporary art forms that seek to subvert the system, such as punk rock, are quickly made safe through their commodification and reification. Most artistic production has now become tied to the market place and takes achievement to equal commercial success. For Jameson, the deathless fluidity of much of modern culture is the direct consequence of multinational capitalism.

What, then, are the distinctive features of post-modernism? One way of illustrating this is to compare it with other modes of artistic production. Jameson, in this regard, offers a comparison between Van Gogh's well known painting of peasant shoes and Andy Warhol's print called Diamond Dust shoes. Van Gogh's work invites a traditional interpretive approach that refers to its context of production and possible moment of transcendence. The vivid colours of the painting offer a utopian gesture, while the content speaks of material deprivation. Such an interpretation could not be offered of Warhol's effort; for one, the shoes in the print are a random collection of objects that float free of any larger context. Jameson muses that the shoes could have been left behind after a dance hall fire or be the ghostly remains of a concentration camp. That we have no way of knowing is embodied by Warhol's artistic disposition, which Jameson (1991: 10) describes as 'gratuitous frivolity'.

These concerns mirror those of contemporary theory that have become suspicious of depth models of interpretation. The notions of signifier and signified, not to mention sign and referent, have been replaced by concerns with discourses and codes. Warhol's shoes, in distinction to Van Gogh's, have no stable or obvious relation to the domain of the real. Hence an interpretive approach could return the peasant's shoes to a notion of totality that is strikingly absent within Warhol's project. The freeing of regimes of signification from their original material contexts is a crucial part of the global post-modern culture.

The superficial culture of the market has also erased the notion of individual style. Developments in modern theory around the death of the subject have run parallel to the disappearance of the 'inimitable' styles of modernism. The commodification of the social world has led to the proliferation and fragmentation of social codes. Since discursive heterogeneity has become the norm, modern culture is best represented as 'blank parody' or pastiche. By pastiche, Jameson means that social codes can no longer be the subject of parody in the traditional sense. Parody implies, by definition, a critical reception of the social codes and norms being utilized by the cultural producer. This is no longer possible as the fragmentation of cultural styles has not only dispensed with the idea of individual creative genius, but also with the notion of linguistic normalcy. Pastiche is 'without the satirical impulse, without laughter, without that still latent feeling that there exists something normal compared to which what is being imitated is rather comic' (Jameson, 1988: 16).

Much of popular post-modern culture can currently be read as a pastiche of the 1970s. Codes are currently being utilized by a number of popular cultural forms to signify a nostalgic rerun of the decade of the 1970s. The cultural artefacts which are generated by a means of representation that detaches them from their original social location (the splitting of signifier and signified) can thus be seen to herald a breakdown in temporality. Popular culture here becomes a schizophrenic array of codes that are no longer able to represent a past as the other of the present. The 1970s become a form of 'pastness' that is conveyed through certain 'imaginary and stereotypical idealities' (Jameson, 1991: 19). The real 1970s have been symbolically erased through the intertextual play of codes that seek semiotically to simulate the decade.

Paradoxically, historicity is erased as this decade becomes rearticulated through music, films, fashion and clothing and other cultural artefacts. The 'pastness' of popular culture is seemingly contradicted by the 'nowness' of the cultural codes. The1970s revival currently sweeping the nation has collapsed definite stylistic distinctions that could be made on the basis of period. For instance, musically we are currently experiencing the rebirth of 1970s soul, punk and Abba (including bands that imitate them) all at the same time. The endless recycling and mimicking of old styles has become a central feature of corporate music culture. According to Jameson, the fracturing of signifiers and signifieds evident within this process means we are now living in a perpetual present.

Elsewhere, Jameson (1988) argues that the electronic media generally, through their rapid turn over of news and events, quickly relegates recent experiences to a distant past. The suggestion is that the ideological effect of the media comes through its form rather than its content. The conversion of reality into autonomous regimes of signification and the electronic speed of information circulation deprives the subject of a sense of historical process. However, as a dialectician, Jameson argues that the media and modern culture also contain a more critical potential. He readily accepts that the new forms of public visibility heralded by communication technologies have restrained certain repressive regimes, while large-scale media events, such as President Kennedy's murder, retain a utopian impulse. The new communication technologies both contribute to a pervasive historical amnesia and occasionally to more collective forms of 'communium'. For Jameson utopia is prefigured through the symbolic representation of collectivity. Whether it is through televised spectator sports, attending a rock concert or running in a fun marathon, these events articulate a collective sensibility that is denied expression within the reifying culture of commodity capitalism.

Such a sliding fragmented culture of film production, while articulating moments of transcendence, is unable to represent the global mode of production. Just as a work of art is no longer able to conceptualize the whole, so the phenomenological experience of the subject is unable to position itself within the global co-ordinates of capitalism. The relation between the social structures of late capitalism and our social experiences have become increasingly polarized. The growing complexity of systemic levels of analysis has meant that the subject becomes 'limited to a tiny corner of the social world' (Jameson, 1991: 411).

Spatially disorganized capitalism demands a new radical form of politics Jameson calls cognitive mapping. Such a venture would realize that while the 'real' cannot be directly represented it could be mapped. New cultural forms are required that are able to represent the spatial dimensions of multinational capitalism helping to build a new class consciousness. This is especially necessary in a spatially confused culture that has witnessed the suppression of critical distance. The information barrage of modern communications has collapsed private spaces of critical reflection into a reified commodity culture. It is then only through Marxist science and potentially radical art, Jameson argues, that this situation can be grasped. The interrelations between locality, the nation and the globe can only be thought at this level, while the subject remains fractured and isolated.

The globalization of consumer capital has thus fostered new relations of social control and internationalized class domination, while also providing new imaginary spaces that point towards its transcendence. Unlike the other two theories reviewed so far, Jameson is able to bring to his description of contemporary culture a dialectical sensibility. While Ritzer and Schiller describe an increasingly one-dimensional society, Jameson is at least alive to the possibility of the contradictions evident within the present. But, despite the sophistication of Jameson's cultural theory, he remains a traditional Marxist in many respects. Indeed, his argument that the dominance of the capitalist system depends upon the psychic fragmentation of the proletariat can be traced back to the early Lukacs. He insists that it is both cultural and material forms of separation that ensure the dominance of multinational capital. Just as important as cultural fragmentation, in this frame of reference, is the radical separateness of the practices of consumption and production (Jameson, 1991: 315). The reification of these social domains ideologically erases the less fortunate from the image of dominant social groups. In a culture that has lost its ability to express historicity and totality, this materially prevents the development of geo-political relations of solidarity.

Of course Jameson's formulations encounter their own peculiar difficulties. Here I will mention only a few. Reading Jameson's prose I am struck by its American origins. His emphasis upon the economic dominance of the cultural sphere seemingly makes less sense in other social contexts, which as I have indicated could also be said of Schiller. Jameson's theory, in other words, says more about American culture than it does about global culture. Said (1993) has argued that it is a characteristic illusion of the pretensions of American intellectuals to assume their own nation to be the centre of the globe. Jameson, despite being a Marxist, offers much of the confidence that is usually associated with an imperial vision. While Jameson partially protects himself from this objection by arguing that post-modernism has not yet fully arrived, his theory lacks an appreciation of certain cultural and institutional mediations that restrain the economic.

Such a concern, viewed more globally, would want to look to the maintenance of traditional artistic practices, the continuation of relatively decommodified zones and public cultures that remain state-protected. In seeking to represent the 'globalness' of post-modernism, Jameson actually succeeds in reminding us that American culture is the world's dominant culture, and that Marxism retains a traditional blindness to the continued power of the political sphere and national cultures.

Democratization

In the 1960s social theorists debated the so-called end of ideology, meaning that there no longer remained a realistic alternative to liberal forms of democracy. The 'end of ideology' debate, however, had to be revised as Marxism gained popularity amongst intellectuals during the 1960s, and especially after the political protests of 1968. Since the Eastern European revolutions of 1989, many of the themes of the earlier discussion have been replayed through the 'end of history' debate. This discussion, inspired largely by the writings of Fukuyama (1992), argues that since the collapse of actually existins socialism, liberal forms of democracy are the most rational forms of political organization on offer. The end of history is not the arrival of a perfect system, but the elimination of any realistic alternatives to a liberal civil society and a democratic state. Fukuyama's book points towards the global spread of liberal democratic culture with the collapse of Eastern European socialism and the increasingly widespread acceptance of democratic norms and procedures.

In this context, Fukuyama explains the relationship between capitalism and democracy in terms of an individualistic theory of human motivation. That we are biological/material creatures means that we will prefer the most efficient means of economic organization. The regulatory desires of socialists to plan centrally and rationally control modern economies have been an unqualified failure in this respect. The complexity of modern globalized economies has meant that the global market is more efficient than nationally controlled socialism. This is because the information flows of modern capitalism are so vast they cannot be co-ordinated by one central organ. For example, to make an aeroplane requires thousands of parts from all over the world; therefore, rather than the state seeking to set the price for and make each part it is arguably more efficient to leave this to the operation of an unco-ordinated market.

Fukuyama argues that those economies since the Second World War that have adopted liberalized markets (e.g., South Korea, Taiwan, Hong Kong, Singapore, Malaysia and Thailand) have been the most successful. Yet Fukuyama rejects the idea that there is a necessary functional relationship between capitalism and democracy. For example, one such argument is that capitalism produces democracy in that it allows for the emergence of a middle class that demands political participation and equal rights. However, such a view presupposes that democratic publics will necessarily make rational economic policies. Here Fukuyama recognizes that democracy puts restraints on market capitalism in that it allows 'economic losers' to influence state policy.

The other key element of human nature mentioned by Fukuyama is the desire for recognition and respect satisfied by political democracy: that is, we can say that history has come to an end when we are able to satisfy *completely* the basic human longings for recognition from others. This need for recognition cannot be met by economic prosperity alone. Fukuyama argues that human beings have an essential need to be able to make authentic moral choices and to have those recognized by others. Racism, for example, is resisted not only because of the economic forms of deprivation that are often associated with it, but more importantly because it denies the equal recognition of a fellow human being. Liberalism is to this extent universal (it grants recognition to all) and homogeneous (it creates a classless society by abolishing formal distinctions between masters and slaves).

Yet Fukuyama also realizes that this argument has a problem in that some people wish to be recognized as superior to others. This drive is more evident in aristocratic societies, since in liberal democracies it has been mediated by the economization of life (the ability of citizens to make rational career plans and market choices) and democratization (the equal recognition of others). At the end of the twentieth century, the real threat to liberal democracy comes not so much from the re-emergence of socialism as from the possible rebirth of a dissatisfied striving for dominance. In other words, the triumph of liberal democracy may be short lived as it leaves unsatisfied the human need for absolute values.

Paradoxically, then, the triumph of liberal democracy could lead to a certain boredom and the revival of more exclusionary social movements. If this pursuit is not to threaten liberal democracy's commitment to a peaceful world order, such an impulse must be contained within the private sphere. Sporting events and entrepreneurial activity, for instance, allow us to secure superiority without openly clashing with the values of liberal democracy. An emerging global liberal democratic culture can only thrive, in this reading, as long as the economic sphere remains committed to the free market, and the polity to universal forms of equal recognition. A possible future world of liberal democratic nation-states would thus need to balance the needs we all have for recognition and glory.

Although written from a different political perspective, Fukuyama's thesis on liberal democracy has much in common with Ritzer, Schiller and Jameson. They all point towards the global triumph of American life-styles, institutions and cultural patterns. Fukuyama's arguments, however, are slightly different in that they speak of an economic and a corresponding *political* culture. The other critics mentioned so far seem to assume that all culture is economically driven, and that the *political* need to achieve basic civil, political and cultural rights has not been a major cause for concern within excluded social groups. Fukuyama's writing could also be taken as a warning against many of the overt nationalist movements that are seeking to ethnically cleanse public space and thereby introduce illiberal shared cultural spaces. The rise of fundamentalism and overt nationalism all threaten the historical achievements that can be legitimately associated with liberal democracy. The culture of liberalism remains important in this respect, as it upholds the virtues of tolerance, freedom of thought, belief and expression. The political and cultural desire for equal forms of recognition can on this reading be associated with a diversity of social movements from disabled people's rights to feminism.

Nevertheless, four critical observations can be made here, each one pointing towards considerable difficulties with some of Fukuyama's overblown projections. First, although Fukuyama points to the achievements of liberal democracy, he displays a myopic neglect of its more negative heritage. Western liberal democracy has presided over a world where the gap between rich and poor is accelerating, and new questions concerning ecological sustainability have yet to be addressed. Indeed Fukuyama's distance from such questions is evident in his advocation of 'actually existing' liberal democracy as a model for 'Third World' nations. Given some of the present forecasts on material scarcity and ecological degradation, the global spread of 'actually existing' liberal democracy cannot but have long-term catastrophic consequences. In ecological and social terms, the prosperity of North America and Western Europe requires the misery of the rest of the world. Liberal capitalism has structural problems which it has yet to solve.

The second observation is that Fukuyama ties the future of democracy to the nation-state. Such an assertion seems to be blind to the fact that large multinational companies, globalizing communication structures, ecological perspectives and AIDS all pose questions that cannot be resolved by national forms of governance. Contrary to Fukuyama, these developments would suggest that the possibilities implicit in the struggle for a generalized democratic culture are far from complete.

Third, it is likely that if Fukuyama were to rewrite his book today, only a few years after its conception, its conclusions could well be less upbeat. Despite the problematic relations between democratic principles and free market economics which have been pointed to by a number of radical critics, it is unclear that the current 'new world disorder' is witnessing a strengthening of liberal democratic principles. As conflicts in Kosovo Bosnia, Northern Ireland, Rwanda, East Timor, Sudan and Palestine have amply demonstrated, the world continues to be infested with war, death and human misery. That democratic principles have only the slenderest of footholds in these and other contexts is too easily passed over by an optimistic vision that takes its lead from the collapse of the Berlin Wall.

Finally, the individualistic culture of liberal democracy has been criticized by communitarians, feminists and post-colonial critics alike. The overwhelming concern here has been that the notion of atomized individuals all pursuing their individual notions of the good disallows wider, more community-oriented sets of identifications, builds upon an overtly masculine logic, and takes the cultural particularity of Western society as the norm. In other words, liberal democracy has grown up with, and helps to promote, an overtly individualistic culture that stresses individual rights rather than the obligations that are owed to overlapping communities. If the culture of liberal democracy has been hegemonic over the twentieth century, there are now signs – in both the growth of social movements that stress obligations over rights and in the critique of masculinity and Eurocentrism in general – that we are not so much witnessing liberalism's triumph as its radical questioning.

Nationalism

The perspectives reviewed so far can all be associated with optics that have a strong connection with American culture. This neatly leads us on to the view that the 'culture' which has the deepest resonance globally remains national culture. That the globe can be divided up into different nations and states (not always the same thing) has more far-reaching cultural consequences than the perspectives viewed so far seem to be aware of. Indeed, A. D. Smith (1990, 1994, 1995) argues that despite all the current talk in respect of global cultures, national cultures are far more permanent and durable constructions than many current theorists seem to realize. It is one thing, Smith maintains, to point to the ways we are regularly exposed to a diverse cultural traffic through the development of technologically diverse communications systems and other mechanisms, but quite another to suggest that they compare with the continued emotional resonance of the nation. Conversely, national sentiment has deep historic roots that can be traced back to the ancient world, where humanity was divided up into fluid ethnic communities. These ethnic identities later came to be refashioned into national identities, thereby presaging the emergence of self-conscious nationalist movements which in the nineteenth century sought to claim the title of 'nation'.

Nations and nationalist movements have all sought to impose a homogeneous identity by articulating a sense of continuity between the generations, thereby preserving a collective store of memory and inculcating a sense of collective destiny. When compared with the ability of nations discursively to compose a terrain of collective myth and memory, the possibility of a new global culture looks superficial by comparison. The proliferation of new information networks may inform us as to events both spatially and temporally distant from our everyday lives, but what it cannot do is preserve a continuous sense of who we currently are, what we have been in the past, and what we might become in the future.

The national ideal is able to maintain its hold over modern subjects precisely because it is able to configure a sense of cohesiveness in the face of cultural fragmentation; offer subordinate peoples a sense of pride and emotional gratification despite their lowly international status; and mark out a set of inherent distinctions we hold as compared to others. Where some commentators have argued that national cultures are losing their grip over the modern subject, they have based their arguments on the assumption that cultural identities mirror patterns marked out by the transformation of economic structures. Nevertheless, Smith maintains that while capitalism may be a globalizing phenomenon, identities are still for the most part made out of more local national resources.

Smith's comments are a useful resource in the present context in that they perceive that overtly national forms of identification remain a crucial aspect of modernity that are not about to be replaced by less spatially distinct social forces. Indeed, Smith makes the case that in the face of post-modern fragmentation and the dominance of American culture, it is likely that nationalists will take even further steps to reaffirm their cultural distinctiveness. The national community remains in this respect the main focus for our collective sense of belonging, cultural identity and sense of obligation.

While in broad agreement with these points, I suspect that the current situation is more ambivalent than Smith allows. For instance, while Smith discounts the chances of a growing cultural cosmopolitanism, other writers are more optimistic in this respect. For Bauman (1992b) nationalism's continued appeal can be discovered in the fact that it provides a way of displacing ambivalence by promising an identity rooted in soil and blood. The continuation of ethnic categories is not so much located in the past, as both the nationalists and Smith claim, but by increasingly fragile borders and boundaries. In an age where identity is becoming increasingly the product of widespread cultural reflexivity, the strict division between friend and enemy offered by national cultures seemingly staves off more complex questions. Giddens (1995) similarly argues that the relative impermanence of national boundaries offers new forms of cultural intermixing, converting the self into an uncertain and risky project. On the one hand, globalization can be linked with increasing uncertainty and fragmentation, while on the other, global interdependence ushers in the possibility of the cosmopolitan acceptance of difference. Cosmopolitanism, then, offers the possibility of a dialogic negotiation of different traditions and world views which are opened out by new levels of global interconnection.

Arguably Smith, Bauman and Giddens are all overstating their respective cases. First, Smith's emphasis on the rooted nature of national cultures blinds him to new levels of cultural complexity and intermixing that are being ushered in by certain globalizing trends. The traffic of bodies and symbols across national borders has surely destabilized the ability of national cultures to impose homogeneity upon previously captive populations. New cultural spaces are certainly emerging where previously held traditional identities can be reflexively interrogated and different lifestyles experimented with. The unasked question, however, is who are the new cultural cosmopolitans? One answer is provided by Hannerz (1992), who argues that it is intellectuals who most obviously occupy this space, exercising an interpretive cultural openness to the outside world.

In distinction to a genuinely critical cosmopolitanism we might also highlight two different kinds of provincialism. The first is determined by the market and promotes a form of mindless mimicry of the newest fashions coming from the world's metropolitan centers. The second is led by the state where new ideas are treated with a mistrustfulness in preference for a safe and repetitive mediocrity. However, even here, and given some of the earlier discussions, it remains striking that many of the positions outlined on global cultures continue to take the host national culture as the main intellectual template. Despite new levels of cultural intermixing, therefore, national cultures remain semi-permanent constructs in a way that is not adequately appreciated by an overt concern with ambivalence or cosmopolitanism.

Towards a cultural political economy

The five paradigms or theses outlined above can be connected to what Bauman (1991) has described as the modern project. This is the imperative to understand the world through the use of categories that lay aside chaos and satisfy the desire to definitely define modern existence. Order is the need to achieve precision and clarity when set against more random social features. Conceptually this has been made possible through a form of self-deception that has sought to conceal the parochial nature of those elements that were once taken to be universal. That which could not be explained or categorized had to be hidden and masked from view. To understand the trajectory of modern cultures depends as much on our need to put our collective heads in the sand as it does upon how to grasp the workings of symbolic cultures.

However, if we are not left with a choice between universalism and difference, the same also applies to the distinction between modernity and post-modernity. While undoubtedly the complexities of global culture are far more uncertain and ambivalent than any of the five frames would have us believe, neither can they be discounted from an attempt to understand the way cultures continue to be shaped by multiple social processes. The problem with only concentrating upon the contingent and the fleeting experience (as Bauman understands better than most), is that it encourages the belief that modern society is free of all determining social structures. The failure to give the world a structure is as illusory as it is to claim that modern cultures can only be explained through a series of random and disconnected cultural flows. A critical understanding of 'cultural' political economy would therefore start from the view that contemporary globalization processes promote a restructuration of contemporary cultural relations.

For example, the emergence of global media in the twentieth century has witnessed the rapid development of a medium that was originally locally based and oriented around print culture. For most of this time the media has been specifically national, centralized and defined by hierarchical forms of control. However, processes of technological development, globalization and deregulation have meant that there has been a rapid increase in the total available amount of information, a spatial compression of the 'knowable' world, and a fragmentation of new consumptive communities. These developments have helped foster ideas of a global civil society, the decline of the national community and regulatory powers of the state, information overload, and the destruction of a mass culture based upon conformity. However, as we have already seen, processes of instrumental reason, capitalist economics, world regional power and national cultures remain major structuring forces. An understanding of cultural political economy, therefore, would seek to unravel the new cultural co-ordinates that are reshaping media landscapes in a way that heralds the development of new identities along with the maintenance of cultural traditions and more permanent institutional features. The globalization of the media may be driven by modernity, but this does not mean that many of the consequences will of necessity be derived from these features.

This then raises the question of a political economy of culture that is built upon complexity rather than simple, repetitive, homogeneous patterns. A political economy of culture would seek to understand newly emergent cultural patterns and more established relations that could never be completely determined by the dual mechanisms of money and power. The argument here makes a distinction between those processes that seek to model the plasticity of culture, and attempts to argue that cultures can be solely explained through their instrumentalized, commodified, post-modernized, democratized or nationalized features. A political economy of culture, in this reading, would seek to understand the workings of cultural processes through these elements without arguing, even in the final analysis, that the hermeneutic circle did not remain open to more ambivalent and less 'colonized' features and interpretations. Culture, then, is neither completely structured by the hard dimensions of modernity, nor wholly undetermined by the softer more subtle axes ushered in by postmodernity. To understand the impact that different cultural paradigms have within different social contexts means that, while remaining open to challenge and review, we must also remain sceptical of those who insist that in order to understand modern culture we must opt either for a homogenized or a hybridized social field.

How then might we begin to assemble a notion of cultural political economy utilizing these dimensions? We could start with a view of social totality that would look to the ways in which the globalization of culture was instrumentalizing cultural processes, providing new opportunities for the accumulation of capital, leading to new forms of cultural fragmentation and spatial disorientation, democratizing relations of authority and disrupting or reaffirming national forms of identification. Such a take on cultural political economy would have to take as its starting point that the sources of cultural power and authority remain centred within the economy and the state.

However, as Susan Strange (1995) makes plain, the political consequences of economic globalization are that there has been a general shift in power between states and markets in favour of the latter, and that the asymmetrical relations between states are widening rather than closing. This picture would support a view of the world whereby 'culture' is increasingly driven by economics and the need to secure new markets. The flow of cultural symbols across the borders of nation-states means that it is increasingly difficult for those states to regulate and order internal cultural relations. This of course does not mean that nations and associated cultures do not still have capacities to control information, but that the main system of governance has become the market rather than the state. At the same time, modernity has presided over the increasing power of the USA to be able to refashion cultural markets in order to promote symbolic goods which originate outside of national societies. Whether we are discussing film, television, magazines or, indeed, Internet cultures, it is the USA which dominates these cultural markets. These new dimensions of governance might then be counterpoised against a more normative understanding of cultural democracy that was based upon more reciprocal and less asymmetrical relations of cultural exchange.

Despite current debates on the subject of post-modernity, it would seem that contemporary global cultures are mostly witnessing a radicalization of elements that can be associated with modernity. The changing interrelations between the cultures of instrumental reason, commodification, post-modernization, liberalism and nationalism are all features that have their roots within modernity. Even arguments, within this analysis, around psychic fragmentation and temporal disorientation, ultimately seem to be connected to the operation of the economy and technology.

A different way of approaching these questions, however, could argue that the globalization of culture also heralds new opportunities to escape the ultimately disciplining impetus that became associated with modernity. This view would argue for a genuinely cultural democracy based upon the values of liberty and equality, as well as respect for 'otherness', difference and critical reflexivity. Such a view could point to an emergent culture whereby new cultural spaces of intermixing have undermined more traditional hierarchies and rationales. Whereas modernity has delivered a culture of capitalist-driven instrumental reason and nationally determined liberal democracy, there currently exist new possibilities for the renegotiation of Eurocentrism and other rigidly established ideologies. New global cultures seem to offer both the prospect of a new civil society while simultaneously reaffirming older structures of dominance. It is these new mosaics of possibility that need to become informed by an ethically motivated culture. Such a culture would hold out the prospect of the peaceful co-existence of all the world's peoples while respecting our mutual need for liberty, equality and solidarity. That processes of globalization simultaneously enable and disable this project is at the centre of my argument. The recognition that such a project is unlikely to ever reach an end point is reason enough to dismiss the claims that either 'modernity' or 'history' has yet to run its course.

Part II

Exploring Globalization: Beyond State and Market

4

Restructuring the Political Arena: Globalization and the Paradoxes of the Competition State[1]

Philip G. Cerny

The contemporary transformation of the nation-state into a 'competition state' is one of the most important consequences and indeed causes of globalization. This relationship between the competition state as a collective agent on the one hand, and wider structural changes in the world economy on the other, raises key questions of structure and agency in the globalization process. The transformation of the advanced industrial state from a 'national industrial and welfare state' into a 'competition state', like other structural changes, is the result of individual and group actors attempting to adjust to changing structural conditions, and thereby in turn shaping not only the processes but also the outcomes of structural change. In attempting to adapt to a range of complex changes in cultural, institutional and market structures, both political and market actors are increasingly seeking, directly or indirectly, wittingly or unwittingly, to reinvent political structures and institutions in a wider global context.

This transformation is a complex process, not a linear one, and it is therefore characterized by unintended and unanticipated consequences. It involves three central paradoxes. The first is that the emergence of the competition state does not lead to a simple decline of the state but instead necessitates the expansion of *de facto* state intervention and regulation in the name of competitiveness and marketization. Furthermore, in a second paradox, state actors and institutions are themselves promoting new forms of complex globalization in the attempt to adapt state action to cope more effectively with apparent global 'realities'. Although embedded state forms, contrasting modes of state interventionism, and differing state/society arrangements persist, such models are feasible in the medium term only where they are perceived to be relatively efficient modes of adaptation. At the same time, however, pressures for transnational and international homogenization continue to erode these different models where they are perceived to be economically inefficient in world markets.

This growing tension between economic globalization on the one hand and embedded state/society practices increasingly constitutes the principal terrain of political conflict within, among and across political systems. Thus a third and final paradox appears: the development of this new political terrain problematizes the capacity of state institutions to embody communal solidarity or *Gemeinschaft*, threatening the deeper legitimacy, institutionalized power and social embeddedness of states and further undermining the capacity of the state to resist globalization. The combination and dynamic interaction of these three paradoxes means that the consolidation and expansion of the competition state is itself driving a process of *political* globalization, further ratcheting up the pace of economic, social and cultural globalization in turn.

Globalization and politics

None of the other social sciences is as rooted in the 'modern' world of nation-state institutions and societies as political science and international relations. Political science starts from the presupposition that political actors, by finding and using institutional means to resolve conflicts and pursue some notion of a public interest, are able consciously to shape the very structures of the political world in which they operate.[2] Globalization as a *political* phenomenon basically means that this shaping of the playing field is determined less and less from 'domestic' processes operating *within* relatively autonomous and hierarchically organized structures called states, and more and more from transnational processes operating *across* states.[3] It increasingly derives from a complex congeries of multilevel games played on multilayered institutional playing fields, above and across, as well as within, state boundaries. These games are played out by different sets of actors: state actors as well as market actors and socio-cultural actors. Political globalization derives first and foremost from a reshaping of political practices and institutional structures in order to adjust and adapt to the growing deficiencies of nation-states as perceived and *experienced* by such actors. Central to this experience is a deeply felt contemporary failure of both actors and practices to achieve the kind of communal goals which have been the *raison d'être* of the Western state since collapse of feudalism and especially since the national democratic and social revolutions of the eighteenth, nineteenth and twentieth centuries (Polanyi, 1944).

In the modern era, democracy and authoritarianism, socialism and capitalism, liberalism and conservatism, have all seen their goals embodied in and pursued through the national project, and therefore rooted in the perceived common good of distinct 'peoples' or citizenries respectively sharing their own relatively insulated territorial spaces. The modern world has seen only two truly internationalist political projects, liberalism and Marxism. But dominant as they have been as social, political and philosophical movements, both were also assimilated into the confines and practices of the nation-state early in their historical trajectories, the first through the French and American Revolutions, the second through the Russian and Chinese Revolutions. Only then did they attain institutionalized power, for it was at the nation-state level that the most fundamental structures and institutions of society and politics had become embedded. The apparent history of the modern world thus was absorbed into a historiography of nation-states.

The concept of globalization in general challenges that prevailing framework in two ways. The first is through a rethinking of history (see Chapter 2 of this volume). The emergence, consolidation and rise to structural pre-eminence of the nation-state itself is increasingly understood as having been a quasi-accident reflecting the global situation of the late feudal period. The nation-state form can be seen in the *longue durée* as a quite recent development – mainly confined to the more established nation-states of the West – and one which may turn out to be as historically fragile as the empires and feudal systems which long preceded it.

The second challenge arises through a new social-scientific discourse of globalization itself. This discourse challenges the significance of the nation-state as a paradigm of scholarly research, suggesting that nation-state-based 'normal science' in history and the social sciences (sometimes referred to as 'methodological nationalism') has been so undermined by new challenges and findings that its usefulness in constituting a *prima facie* scholarly agenda is rapidly being lost. The uneven transnationalization of market structures in a range of economic sectors, the emergence of a complex global culture and the development of intricate three-level games cutting across national and international politics, all point towards not only the need for a new research agenda in social science but also a reshaping of political philosophy and its reformulation in a global context (Cerny, 1996a; cf. Chapters 1 and 5 in this volume).

In turn, the conceptions of common interest and community which have legitimated the institutional authority of the nation-state over the past several centuries – however predatory in practice its origins and developmental trajectory – have given the politics of the state an essential quasi-moral character well beyond pragmatism and 'interest' (in the narrow meaning of that term). They involve attributing to the state a holistic character, a sense of organic solidarity which is more than any simple social contract or set of pragmatic affiliations. If there is an increasing paradigmatic crisis of the state today, it concerns the erosion of this posited underlying bond, and the demotion of the state to a mere pragmatic association for common ends: what Tönnies (1887) called *Gesellschaft* and Michael Oakeshott called an *enterprise association* (Oakeshott, 1976; Auspitz, 1976).

In this reading, so long as the shell of modern capitalism remained the *national* capitalist model of the nation-state – where the welfare of the people in a capitalist society was secured at least minimally by the state and protected from the full commodification of the market by politics – then the image of a national *Gemeinschaft* as the route to the common good could persist, even strengthen and expand, over the entire globe. The 'capitalist state' as we have known it has been firmly rooted in the ideology and culture of modern nationalism. The latent crisis of the nation-state today, and the paradigmatic challenge of the globalization process, involve the erosion of that *Gemeinschaft* and the fragmenting of the political community from both above and below.

The form which this political transformation takes is the emergence of the 'competition state' (Cerny, 1990). The competition state is distinct from earlier state forms, much as its predecessor, the welfare state, too was distinct. The state as an institutional structure *per se* is not withering away; indeed, it is developing new and more complex structural forms and features in a more open, cross-cutting world. Complexity means the presence of many intricate component parts. It can mean a sophisticated and elegantly co-ordinated structure, but it can also mean that the different parts mesh poorly, leading to friction and even entropy. A globalizing world is intricately structured at many levels, developing within an already complex social, economic and political context, with many and varied dimensions of convergence and divergence. State actors confront different markets, firms and economic sectors organized in distinct ways, whether because of the imperatives of market and hierarchy (Williamson, 1975, 1985; Cerny, 1995, 1997) or as the result of different social-structural histories (Granovetter, 1985, 1992; Hall and Taylor, 1996). Even more problematic are the subnational, transnational and supra-national ethnic cleavages, tribalism and other revived or *invented* identities and traditions – from local groups to the European Union (EU) – which abound in the wake of the uneven erosion of national identities, national economies and national state policy capacity characteristic of the 'global era'.

Beyond this complex contestation, furthermore, it is important to understand that globalization does not lie merely in whether or not it can be empirically verified according to particular measurable criteria such as the convergence (or not) of corporate forms or social structures. Perhaps its most crucial feature is that it constitutes a *discourse* – and increasingly, a hegemonic discourse which cuts across and gives meaning to the kind of categories suggested above (see Chapter 1 in this volume). In this sense, the spread of the discourse itself alters the *a priori* ideas and perceptions which people have of the empirical phenomena which they encounter; in so doing, it engenders strategies and tactics which in turn may restructure the game itself. With the erosion of old axioms, 'paradigmatic selection' follows. And in this process, the concept of globalization is coming increasingly to shape the terms of the debate.

Globalization is therefore not an inexorable, exogenous process, a march to a higher – or indeed lower – form of civilization. It is a path-dependent process, rooted in real historical decisions, non-decisions and conjunctural turning points. In Granovetter's terms, social, economic and political institutions emerge in an environment where there is not one simple pathway or end point; there are in economic terminology 'multiple equilibrium points' available. However, once social relationships are established and power structures set in place in particular conjunctural settings, institutions tend to become 'locked in' and to resist fundamental restructuring. Paradoxically, in a globalizing world states play a crucial role as stabilizers and enforcers of the rules and practices of *global* society; indeed, state actors are probably the most important single category of agent in the globalization process.

From the industrial-welfare state to the competition state

State actors have acted and reacted in feedback loop fashion to the more complex structure of constraints and opportunities characteristic of the new environment. This situation is not 'hard-wired'; these constraints and opportunities do not create a rigid cage within which state and market actors are forced to work. Given changing exogenous conditions, however, this transformation increasingly entails a fundamental shift of organizational goals and institutional processes within state structures themselves. International and transnational constraints limit the things that even the best-run government can do, and this shift is leading to a potential crisis of liberal democracy as we have known it. Furthermore, a new and potentially undemocratic role is emerging for the state as the enforcer of decisions and/or outcomes which emerge from world markets, transnational 'private interest governments', and international quango-like regimes.[4]

The essence of the post-war national industrial welfare state (IWS) lay in the capacity which state actors and institutions had gained, especially since the Great Depression, to insulate certain key elements of economic life from market forces while at the same time promoting other aspects of the market. These mechanisms did not merely imply protecting the poor and helpless from poverty and pursuing welfare goals such as full employment or public health, but also regulating business in the public interest, 'fine tuning' business cycles to promote economic growth, nurturing 'strategic industries' and 'national champions', integrating labour movements into corporatist processes to promote wage stability and labour discipline, reducing barriers to international trade, imposing controls on 'speculative' international movements of capital, and so on. But this compromise of domestic regulation and international opening – what Ruggie (1982) called 'embedded liberalism' – was eroded by increasing domestic structural costs (the 'fiscal crisis of the state': see O'Connor, 1973), the structural consequences of growing external trade and, perhaps most importantly, of international financial transactions (Strange, 1986; Cerny, 1993; Andrews, 1994). The crisis of welfare states lay in their decreasing capacity to insulate national economies from the global economy, and in the combination of stagnation and inflation which resulted when they tried.

The world since then has seen the emergence of a quite different beast, the competition state. Rather than attempt to take certain economic activities *out* of the market, to 'decommodify' them as the welfare state in particular was organized to do,[5] the competition state has pursued *increased* marketization in order to make economic activities located within the national territory, or which otherwise contribute to national wealth, more competitive in international and transnational terms. The main features of this process have included attempts to reduce government spending in order to minimize the 'crowding out' of private investment by state consumption and the deregulation of economic activities, especially financial markets. The result has been the rise of a new discourse and practice of 'embedded financial orthodoxy' (Cerny, 1994a, 1994b, 1996b; cf. Chapter 7 in this volume), which are in turn shaping the parameters of political action everywhere, as evidenced by the impact of recent financial crises in South-East Asia.

Transnational factors and their translation into the domestic arena have forced four specific types of policy change to the top of the political agenda:

- a shift from macroeconomic to microeconomic interventionism, as reflected in both deregulation and industrial policy;
- a shift in the focus of that interventionism from the development and maintenance of a range of 'strategic' or 'basic' economic activities in order to retain 'bottom-line' economic autonomy – which presumes that each nation-state must possess and maintain some minimum level of self-sufficiency in key sectors – to one of flexible response to competitive conditions in a range of diversified and rapidly evolving international market places (i.e. the pursuit of 'competitive advantage' as distinct from 'comparative advantage': Zysman and Tyson, 1983);
- an emphasis on the control of inflation and general neo-liberal monetarism – supposedly translating into non-inflationary growth – as the touchstone of state economic management and interventionism;
- a shift in the focal point of party and governmental politics away from the general maximization of welfare within a nation (full employment, redistributive transfer payments and social service provision) to the promotion of enterprise, innovation and profitability in both private and public sectors.

The general rule in mainstream (classical and neo-classical) economic theory is, of course, that the state should intervene as little as possible beyond maintaining the legal framework necessary for a working market system (private property rights, sanctity of contracts, etc.), a currency system, defence, and so forth. State intervention can also be justified in this context, however, where it attacks or restricts obstacles to efficient market behaviour or counteracts 'market failure' for example, through demand management at the macro-economic level and/or regulation at the meso-economic and micro-economic levels. A further widely-accepted exception to the rule is the argument that some activities – for example, natural monopolies, public goods, or 'strategic industries' – are simply not amenable to being organized and run according to market principles in the long term, or are in particular danger from 'exogenous shocks'. But these activities are essentially pathological. The market mechanism is seen to be 'natural'. The state is an artificial imposition to remedy specific defects, and its interventions are prone to serious opportunity costs. The modern IWS combined a series of such interventions. However, this combination was linked with, articulated through, and mobilized by more specifically political factors such as the organizational and electoral influence of the working class, welfare-type goals of social solidarity and so on, and the organizational logic of the bureaucratic apparatus established to carry out these tasks. Nevertheless, welfare spending, for example, can be 'justified' in mainstream economic terms by its demand management role, stabilizing the economic system and thus permitting the maximization of growth-oriented market choices. Market-enforcing regulation, such as anti-monopoly legislation or stock market regulation, is justified not only by norms of public interest, but also as preventing unfair competition and anti-competitive (and thus anti-market) behaviour by monopoly firms, cartels, or organizations such as trade unions. And more direct, non-market control or regulation is legitimized by reference to the need to organize production by natural monopolies, to provide public goods and services, or to maintain basic or strategic industries.

This is a powerful package of potential interventions indeed, especially when galvanized by social and political objectives such as full employment, social justice or increased economic growth. All these forms of interventionism have one thing in common, however: they take for granted a fundamental division of function, even an incompatibility of kind, between the *market*, seen as the only really dynamic wealth-creating mechanism in capitalist society (despite its susceptibility to 'market failures'), on the one hand; and the *state*, seen as a hierarchical and essentially static mechanism, unable to impart a dynamic impetus to production and exchange (except in wartime), on the other (Gilpin, 1987). The state is thus seen as characterized by a mode of operation which undermines market discipline and substitutes 'arbitrary prices' for 'efficiency prices' (Lindblom, 1977): at best a necessary evil, at worst inherently parasitic on wealth created through the market.

The IWS was therefore based on a paradox. It might save the market from its own dysfunctional tendencies, but it carried within itself the potential to undermine the market in turn. From a market perspective, then, the IWS had to be both restrained in its application and regularly *deconstructed* – deregulated – in order to avoid the 'ratchet effect' which leads to stagflation, the fiscal crisis of the state and the declining effectiveness of each new increment of demand reflation and functional expansion. If this were not to be done, the result would be the emergence of a lumbering, muddling, 'overloaded' state. In this context, of course, the international recession of the 1970s and early 1980s had dramatic consequences for the economic policies of advanced industrial states generally. Its perceived lessons, as assimilated by political actors and major social groups, have undermined the legitimacy of a wide range of policy measures identified with the welfare state. Political decision-makers have undergone a fundamental learning process which has altered the norms according to which they operate on both a daily and a long-term basis. This process affected the Right first, but is now also dominant on the Left, as evidenced by the policies of the UK Labour Government under Tony Blair.

This 'overloaded' state was seen to bump up against four main types of constraint. In the first place, chronic deficit financing by governments in a slump period was seen to soak up resources which might otherwise be available for private capital allocation and to cause interest rates to increase, in ways which crowd out private investment; to raise the cost of capital; and to channel resources both into consumption (increasing inflationary pressures and import penetration) and into non-productive financial outlets. Second, nationalized industry and tripartite wage bargaining (neo-corporatism) were blamed for putting further wage-push pressure on inflation, while at the same time preventing rises in productivity and/or the shedding of newly redundant labour (given the increasing obsolescence of much fixed capital and the pressing need for reconversion), thus lowering profitability through rigidities in the labour market. Third, attempts to maintain overall levels of economic activity – to maintain demand and infrastructure, and to prevent unemployment – were seen to lock state interventionism into a 'lame duck' syndrome in which the state took responsibility for ever wider, and increasingly unprofitable, sectors of the economy. And fourth, all of these rigidities, in an open international economy, had negative consequences for the balance of payments and the exchange rate. Protectionism as a response to such pressures was seen merely to invite retaliation and act as a drag on international trade, while currency devaluation (supposedly automatic in a regime of floating exchange rates, but in fact manipulated in various ways) tended to have a knock-on effect, exacerbating the other three.

All four of these constraints were seen to interact in recessionary conditions in such a way as to restrict the capacity of private capital to perform its supply-side or productive function. Thus the challenge for state actors today, as viewed through the contemporary discourse of *economic* globalization, is to confront the perceived limitations of the state by combining a significant measure of austerity with the retention of a minimal welfare net to sustain sufficient consensus, while at the same time promoting structural reform at the meso-economic and micro-economic levels in order to improve international competitiveness. In the industrial world generally, major changes in government policy have resulted, changes which have serious consequences for the IWS model: especially a shift in the focus of economic policy away from macro-economic demand management towards more targeted meso-economic and micro-economic policies, and the restructuring of the state itself through 'new public management' (Dunleavy, 1994).

Divergences: competing forms of and approaches to the competition state

Despite the vulnerability of the IWS model, however, national policy-makers have a range of potential responses, old and new, with which to work. The challenge of the competition state is one of getting the state to do both *more* and *less* at the same time. Getting more for less has been the core concept, for example, of the 'reinventing government' movement which is a major manifestation and dimension of the competition state approach (Osborne and Gaebler, 1992). The competition state involves both a transformation of the policy roles of the state and a multiplication of specific responses to change. Some of these responses look like new versions of old responses adapted to the perceived requirements of globalization, while others are more genuinely innovative.

In terms of policy transformation, several levels of government activity are affected. Among more traditional measures being reformulated is, of course, trade policy, including a wider range of non-tariff barriers and targeted strategic or 'managed' trade policies. The core issue with regard to trade is to avoid reinforcing through protection the existing rigidity of the industrial sector or sectors in question, while at the same time fostering or even imposing adaptation to global competitive conditions in return for temporary protection. Transnational constraints are growing rapidly in trade policy, however, as can be seen in the establishment of the North America Free Trade Area, the Asia-Pacific Economic Cooperation group, and especially the World Trade Organization (WTO). But two other traditional categories, monetary and fiscal policy, are perhaps even more crucial today. Here the key change is that relative priorities between the two have been reversed: tighter monetary policy through interest rate manipulation is pursued alongside looser fiscal policy through tax cuts. And exchange rate policy, difficult to manage in the era of floating exchange rates and massive international capital flows, is none the less still essential, as the British devaluation of 1992 and the American devaluation of 1985–7 have shown; however, it is increasingly intertwined with monetary and fiscal policy (Frieden, 1991).

Potentially more innovative, combining old and new measures, is the area of industrial policy. By targeting particular sectors, supporting the development of both more flexible manufacturing systems and transnationally viable economies of scale, and assuming certain costs of adjustment, governments can alter some of the conditions which determine competitive advantage: encouraging mergers and restructuring; promoting research and development; encouraging private investment and venture capital, while providing or guaranteeing credit-based investment where capital markets fail, often through joint public/private ventures; developing new forms of infrastructure in both old and new areas (e.g., the so-called 'information superhighway'); pursuing a more active labour market policy while removing barriers to mobility; and so on. The examples of Japanese, Swedish and Austrian industrial policy have been widely interpreted in this context.

A third policy category, potentially the most explosive, involves deregulation and liberalization. The deregulation approach is based partly on the assumption that national regulations, especially the traditional sort of regulations designed to protect national market actors from market failure, are insufficiently flexible to take into account the rapid shifts in transnational competitive conditions characteristic of the interpenetrated world economy of the late twentieth century. Deregulation must not be seen just as the lifting of old regulations, but also as the formulation of new regulatory structures which are designed to cope with, and even to anticipate, shifts in competitive advantage (Cerny, 1991; Vogel, 1996). However, these new regulatory structures are often designed to *enforce* global market-rational economic and political behaviour on rigid and inflexible private sector actors as well as on state actors and agencies. The institutions and practices of the state itself are increasingly marketized or 'commodified', and the state becomes the spearhead of structural transformation to market norms both at home and abroad.

Although each of these processes can be observed across a wide range of states, there are significant variations in how different competition states cope with the pressures of adaptation and transformation. Here I will focus primarily on the more advanced industrial states; the equation gets even more complex in the developing and underdeveloped worlds. There is a dialectic of divergence and convergence at work, rather than a single road to competitiveness. The original model of the competition state was the strategic-interventionist state which writers such as Zysman (1977, 1983) and Johnson (1982) associated with France and Japan. This perspective, which identifies the competition state with strong-state technocratic *dirigisme*, lives on in the analysis of newly industrializing countries (NICs) in Asia and other parts of the Third World: the so-called 'developmental state'.[6]

However, the difficulty with this approach has been that the scope of control which the technocratic patron-state and its client firms can exercise over market outcomes diminishes as the integration of these economies into global markets and the complexities of third-level games proceed, as the recent experiences of Japan and South Korea have shown.[7] The developmental state can play a crucial role in nurturing new industries and reorienting economic structures and actors to the world marketplace, but beyond a certain threshold even the most tightly bound firms and sectors will act in a more autonomous fashion. And as more firms and sectors become linked into new patterns of production, financing and market access, often moving operations offshore, their willingness to follow the script declines. However, there are distinctions even here. Within this category, for example, Japanese administrative guidance and the ties of the *keiretsu* system have remained relatively strong despite a certain amount of liberalization, deregulation and privatization, whereas in France the forces of neo-liberalism have penetrated a range of significant bastions from the main political parties to the inner sanctums of the bureaucracy itself (Schmidt, 1996; see also Chapter 9 in this volume).

In contrast, the orthodox model of the competition state today is not the strategic state but the neo-liberal state (i.e., 'liberal' in the European sense of orthodox free-market economic liberalism, or what is called 'nineteenth-century liberalism' in the USA). Thatcherism and

Reaganism in the 1980s provided both a political rationale and a power base for a renascence of free-market ideology generally, not just in the UK and the USA but throughout the world. The flexibility and openness of Anglo-Saxon capital markets, the experience of Anglo-American elites with international and transnational business and their willingness to go multinational, the corporate structure of American and British firms and their greater concern with profitability and shareholder returns rather than traditional relationships and market share, the enthusiasm with which American managers have embraced lean management and downsizing, and the relative flexibility of the US and UK labour forces, combined with an arms-length state tradition in both countries, are widely thought to have fought off the strategic state challenge and to have eventually emerged more competitive today.

Indeed, the heady rise of Wall Street in the mid-1990s, frequently attacked by bears and doomsayers, represents, according to respected *New York Times* columnist Thomas Friedman (*International Herald Tribune*, 10 February 1997), a 'globalization premium':

> That is a sense among global investors that somehow the whole mix of America – its society, its culture, its technology, its business environment and its geography – meshes more naturally with globalization than either Europe or Japan. It is a sense that while many in Europe are still trying to adjust to the demands of globalization, and are barely up to the starting line, the United States is already around the first turn.

Nevertheless, liberalization, deregulation and privatization have not reduced the overall role of state intervention; rather they have simply shifted the means of intervention from decommodifying bureaucracies to marketizing ones. 'Reinventing government', for example, means the replacement of bureaucracies which directly produce public services by ones which closely monitor and supervise contracted-out and privatized services according to complex financial criteria and performance indicators (Osborne and Gaebler, 1992). Furthermore, the substance of regulation itself has shifted from structural regulation (i.e., *ex ante* attempts to design market structures and to control market outcomes) to regulation which penalizes anti-competitive or fraudulent behaviour through *ex post* litigation, such as 'prudential regulation' in the financial markets.[8] Finally, industrial policy is alive and well too, but rather than being manifested in large strategic projects or corporatist bargains between business, labour and the state, it is increasingly secreted in the interstices of a decentralized, patchwork bureaucracy which is the American tradition and the new British obsession.

Throughout the debate between the Japanese model and the Anglo-American model, however, the European neo-corporatist model, rooted in the post-war settlement and given another dimension by the consolidation of the EU, has been presented by many European commentators as a middle way. The exceptions prove the rule: both Gaullist and post-Gaullist France on the one hand, with its strategic state and its 'corporatism without labour' (Schain, 1980), and Britain with its arm's-length financial market system on the other, were always on the margins of European construction and indeed remain so, despite the attempts of the French to hitch their monetary horse to the Bundesbank's wagon through the *franc fort* and the new single European currency.

By bringing labour into institutionalized settings for wage bargaining as well as other aspects of the social market, by doggedly pursuing conservative monetary policies, by promoting extensive training policies, and by possessing a universal banking system which nurtured and stabilized industry without strategic state interventionism, the European neo-corporatist approach (as practised in varying ways in Germany, Austria and Sweden in particular) has seemed to its proponents to embody the best aspects of both the Japanese and the Anglo-American models. However, despite the completion of the single market and the signing of the Maastricht Treaty, the signs of what in the early 1980s was called 'Eurosclerosis' have reappeared; the European Monetary Union project is widely regarded as deflationary in a context where costs are unevenly spread; and the liberalizing, deregulatory option is increasingly on the political cards, especially in the context of rapidly rising German unemployment and the apparent beginnings of a hollowing-out of parts of German industry.

The competition state, then, comes in myriad forms, only a few of which can be briefly addressed here. The key issue is not whether these forms converge, but how they cope with a range of cross-cutting pressures to adapt to a more complex world and how they embody and shape the more diverse practices which come with globalization, in turn reinforcing and shaping globalization itself. At one level, of course, 'national developments' – that is, differences in models of state/economy relations or state/societal arrangements – as Zysman (1996) writes, 'have, then, driven changes in the global economy' as the search for competitiveness continues. Different patterns of corporate governance endure, between firms themselves and between firms and the state. However, different national *economic* models must now cope in a new environment. They will endure only so long as they are efficient in achieving desired levels of profitability and/or market share, which means so long as their competitive advantages are significant (see Chapters 5 and 9 in this volume).

Should those advantages erode, then the national settlements which have nurtured national models will come under pressure, and the competition state will no longer be able to protect failing national industrial systems from the pressures of global markets. Instead, key state actors, including finance ministers and central bank governors (Maxfield, 1997), will increasingly pressure firms to conform to international and transnational market criteria. Zysman (1996), for example, argues that the key factor in the search for competitiveness is technological development, that different 'architectures of supply' or synergies between firms and patterns of technological innovation are the key to competitiveness, and also that nation-states are still the key arena for building these architectures and promoting these synergies. However, cross-national technological synergies, especially those promoted through multinational corporations (MNCs), strategic alliances (including product-by-product alliances) and the 'new competition', are overlapping with and challenging the domination of general national models (Portnoy, 1997; see also Chapter 6 in this volume).

Pauly and Reich (1997; cf. Hart, 1992) argue that national models of corporate governance and state-societal arrangements also endure. This is only natural, as different forms of corporate governance give rise to different forms of competitive advantage in international markets. However, those 'models' are less and less purely national, and more and more transnational, in their differences. For example, the 'East Asian' extended family firm is rooted less in its national base than in the transnational base of the so-called 'Overseas Chinese', not only in East and South East Asia but also in their linkages elsewhere in the world (Kotkin, 1992; Seagrave, 1995). And US-based multinational firms, although they may have a distinctly 'American' style of operating, are increasingly 'global' both in their management ideologies and in their disjunction from traditional forms of American political power or hegemony in the world economy. The criteria for evaluating the role of so-called 'national models', then, are less bound up with domestic social and political structures, and more shaped by their international success in terms of profitability and/or market share. Should those become problematic, particular firms will shift their structures and strategies to match global competitive conditions.

At another level, of course, states and state actors seek to convince, or pressure, other states – and transnational actors such as MNCs or international institutions – to adopt measures which shift the balance of competitive advantage. Such pressures generally combine elements of neo-mercantilist self-interest, limited reciprocity, and multilateral hard bargaining, whether to limit trade in sensitive sectors such as textiles, automobiles or semiconductors, to develop new regional initiatives such as the European single market, to expand multilateral trade regimes in agriculture or services, or to reach agreements in areas such as exchange rate policy (e.g., the relatively loose Plaza and Louvre Accords, or the much tighter notion of European Monetary Union). The search for competitive advantage in a relatively open world adds further layers and cross-cutting cleavages to the world economy which may undermine pure intergovernmental multilateralism, but which increase the complexity and density of networks of interdependence and interpenetration. Finally, transnational pressures develop – whether from MNCs or from nationally or locally based firms and other interests (such as trade unions) caught in the crossfire of the search for international competitiveness – for the establishment or expansion of transnational regimes, transnational neo-corporatist structures of policy bargaining, transgovernmental linkages between bureaucrats, policy-makers and policy communities, and so on.

In all these settings – the shifting utility and effectiveness of different policy instruments, the ways that differently structured state–society arrangements adapt to and reshape complex globalization, how states interact with each other and reconfigure patterns of interdependence, and the sharp increase of cross-cutting linkages and third-level games which alter the very stakes of the political and governmental game – the state is no longer able to act as a decommodifying hierarchy. It must act increasingly as a collective commodifying agent – that is, putting activities *into* the market – and even as a market actor itself. It is financier, middleman, advocate, and even entrepreneur, in a complex economic web. Not only do the frontiers between state and market become blurred, but their cross-cutting structures also become closely intertwined and their behavioural modes become less and less easy to distinguish. National differences therefore do not so much concern the possibility of resisting globalizing trends *per se*, but are best seen instead as representing *different modes of managing a complex transition* in which emerging political and economic structures are thought to be closely intertwined but not yet clear, and the possibilities for alternative equilibria are fluid.

Under pressure from recessionary conditions in a relatively open world economy, first in the 1970s and then in the early 1990s, the problems faced by all capitalist industrial states have given rise to certain similarities of response: in particular, the shift from the IWS model, nurtured by the long boom from the 1950s to the oil crisis of 1973–4, to a more differentiated repertoire of state responses to the imperatives of growth and competitiveness. However, despite these elements of convergence, significant divergences remain, for different states have different sets of advantages and disadvantages in the search for international competitiveness. They differ in endogenous structural capacity for strategic action both domestically and internationally. They differ in the extent to which their existing economic structures, with or without government help, can easily adapt to international conditions. And they differ in their vulnerability to international and transnational trends and pressures.

Convergences: the scope and limits of the competition state

The rapid rise of the competition state, in an increasingly crowded and heterogeneous world economy, has given rise to a further paradox. As states and state actors have attempted to promote competitiveness in this way, they have – seemingly voluntarily – given up a range of crucial policy instruments. The debate rages over whether, for example, capital controls can be reintroduced or whether states are still able to choose to pursue more inflationary policies without disastrous consequences (Goodman and Pauly, 1993; Kapstein, 1994; Helleiner, 1996; Cerny, 1996b). The 'genie is out of the bottle' – Andrews (1994) has called it *hysteresis* – and states are seeing their policy capacity and political autonomy eroding in ways which may not be recuperable. Political and social development is not merely a question of frictionless rational choices and cost-benefit analyses, but is inherently path-dependent and 'sticky', a process where conjunctural shifts can have structural consequences.

Although the nation-state is not dead, its role has changed. In the first place, citizens will have to live more and more without the kind of public services and redistributive arrangements characteristic of national IWSs. 'New public management' seeks not only to reorganize the state along the lines of private industry, but also to replace public provision with private provision (pensions, prisons, etc.) and to replace direct payments for unemployment compensation, income support for the poor and so on with time-limited, increasingly means-tested or work-related measures (or none at all): what US President Clinton has called 'the end of welfare as we know it'. Furthermore, the principal goal of state actors is increasingly one of minimizing inflation, in order to maintain the confidence of the international business and financial community. Core gatekeepers such as central bankers have always played this role but today are doing so to an ever-increasing extent.

In this context, rather than acting as 'strategic' or 'developmental' states, they should be seen as 'splintered states' (Machin and Wright, 1985). State actors and different agencies are increasingly intertwined with 'transgovernmental networks': systematic linkages between state actors and agencies overseeing particular jurisdictions and sectors, but cutting across different countries and including a heterogeneous collection of private actors and groups in interlocking policy communities. Furthermore, some of these linkages specifically involve the exchange of ideas rather than authoritative decision-making or power-broking: what have been called 'epistemic communities' (Haas, 1992; Stone, 1996). The functions of the state, although central in structural terms, are increasingly residual in terms of the range of policy instruments and outcomes which they entail.

In international terms, by pursuing the goal of competitiveness states are becoming increasingly involved in what Stopford and Strange (1991) have called 'triangular diplomacy', consisting of the complex interaction of state–state, state–firm, and firm–firm negotiations. But this concept must be widened further. Interdependence analysis has focused too exclusively on two-level games and the state as a Janus-faced institutional structure. Although this is an oversimplification, I argue that complex globalization has to be seen as a structure involving (at least) *three*-level games, with a growing role for third-level – transnational – games involving behind-the-border players interacting across state boundaries. Such games include not only 'firm–firm diplomacy' but also transgovernmental networks and policy communities, internationalized market structures, transnational advocacy groups and many other linked and interpenetrated markets, hierarchies and networks.

Such changes also have a crucial socio-psychological function. As the state is likely to retain a range of key political and economic functions despite (or because of) globalization, the decay of *gemeinschaftlich* loyalty will be uneven, and in relatively stronger states this decay will proceed more slowly than in economically weaker states. For example, if Reich is correct in his analysis in *The Work of Nations* (1991), then economic globalization is likely to lead to two new kinds of socio-economic stratification: (i) between a class of 'symbolic analysts' (managers, technicians, researchers, intellectuals, etc.) consisting of about 20–40 per cent of the population in advanced societies, on the one hand, and a low-paid service sector covering most of the rest (advanced societies having lost much of their labour-intensive production to the Third World), on the other; and (ii) between countries with differential capacities for providing 'immobile factors of capital'. Some countries, because of their infrastructure, education systems, workforce skills, and quality-of-life amenities, are able to attract mobile, 'footloose' capital of a highly sophisticated kind (employing lots of symbolic analysts engaging in 'high value-added activities'); others may increasingly have to depend upon low-wage, low-cost manufacturing or agricultural production.

If the developed 'trilateral' states of the USA, Europe and Japan (along with perhaps some others) are able to provide these advanced facilities better, then *gemeinschaftlich* loyalty in those states may erode more slowly or perhaps even stabilize. On the other hand, mobile international capital may well destabilize less favoured states, whose already fragile governmental systems will be torn by groups attempting to recast those *gemeinschaftlich* bonds through claims for the ascendancy of religious, ethnic, or other grass-roots loyalties. In this context, today's revival of nationalism is not of the state-bound, nineteenth-century variety; it is more elemental, and leads to the break-up of states rather than to their maintenance. Singer and Wildavsky (1993) characterized this bifurcation of the world as leading to the differentiation of 'zones of peace' and 'zones of turmoil', but it is unclear whether the zones of peace will expand or contract. However, the outcome may depend far more on how the residual state adapts to the carrying out of its new, circumscribed range of political and economic functions than on science fiction-like attempts to relocate *gemeinschaftlich* loyalties on new but more problematic levels.

If we want to look for an alternative way of conceiving of the residual state, probably the most suggestive example is provided by American state governments. These governments can claim only a partial loyalty from their inhabitants, and their power over internal economic and social structures and forces has been limited. However, they have been required to operate over the course of the past two centuries in an increasingly open continental market, without there being such a thing as state 'citizenship' (only residence, alongside the free movement of persons within the USA as a whole). Nevertheless, like some counties, provinces and regions in other countries, they foster a sense of identity and belonging that can be quite strong. And in economic policy matters they reflect the essence of the 'competition state'.

Of course, the effective scope for policy-making and policy implementation by US states means that they can have little coercive impact on mobile factors of capital. They cannot prevent capital flight, impose trade barriers, limit the movement of labour across state lines (despite the attempts of California to prevent 'Okies' from entering the state during the Great Depression), or prevent firms from relocating elsewhere or closing down. Furthermore, their taxing and regulating power is seriously constrained by the weight and legal prerogatives of the Federal Government.[9] Nevertheless, at the same time, their ability to control development planning, their power to collect and use the tax revenues they do impose, their capacity to offer tax incentives and subsidies to industries they seek to attract, and their fundamental role in the provision of infrastructure, education and training systems, law and order and so on give these sub-national states a capacity to influence the provision of *immobile* factors of capital in significant and sophisticated ways. In their capacity to provide public and other collective goods they have far more day-to-day and long-term policy impact – and indeed general legitimate authority – than many governments in other countries, especially in the Third World.

The main focus of the competition state is the promotion of economic activities, whether at home or abroad, which will make firms and sectors located within the territory of the state competitive in international markets. Furthermore, the competition state is drawn into promoting the commodification or marketization of its own activities and structures (including the internal fragmentation of the state itself) as well as promoting marketization more widely in both economic and ideological terms. But there is a difference between promoting market activities as a general public good and the state's transformation into a market-based organization *per se*. It is in the transformation of the predominant mix of goods affected by and through state policy from public-dominated to private-dominated which in turn transforms the state from a primarily hierarchical, decommodifying agent into a primarily market-based, commodifying agent (Cerny, 1998).

At the same time that the state faces these changes, the search is on to find new ways for it to function and new roles for it to play. The most important changes can be compared with the new structures of production and distribution characterizing the Third Industrial Revolution (Cerny, 1995). The attempt to make the state more 'flexible' has moved a long way over the past decade or so, not only in the USA and Britain – where deregulation, privatization, and liberalization have evolved furthest – but also in a wide range of other countries in the First and Third Worlds (and more recently in the Second World too). Some of these changes have become controversial not only because they have challenged tried and tested ways of making and implementing public policy or confronted important cultural values, but also because their prescriptions can only be tested at the risk of failure.

Convergence in the form of privatization and deregulation is particularly important because they involve the increased interweaving of the domestic economy and the global economy. The 'ratchet effect' – the term used by Mrs Thatcher's guru Sir Keith Joseph for what was once called 'creeping socialism' (i.e., each attempt to use the state to achieve a new discrete policy goal ratchets up the size and unwieldiness of the state as a whole) has been turned on its head. In a globalizing world, the competition state is more likely to be involved in a process of creeping liberalization. State actors, in ever closer contact with 'globalizing' market actors, pursue policies which they believe will make their countries more competitive; the dynamic process at the heart of the competition state is policy arbitrage (Cerny, 1993; Laurence, 1996) and its primary mechanism is 'policy transfer' (Evans and Davies, 1998).

Reconfiguring the state from above and below

The central paradox of globalization is that rather than creating one big economy or one big polity (what has been called the 'airport bookshop' image of globalization), it also divides, fragments and polarizes. Convergence and divergence are two sides of the same coin, and the relationship between them is open to wide influence from state and other actors at many levels. Furthermore, globalization is not a single discourse, but a contested concept giving rise to several distinct but intricately intertwined discourses, with national and regional differences enduring even as they are caught in the global web. Nevertheless, the concept and the practices of globalization will undoubtedly increase in significance as the trends outlined above continue to crystallize. Indeed, the power of globalization itself as process(es), practice(s) and discourse(s) – and thus as a paradigm – lies in this very complexity.

Whatever direction the future takes, therefore, it will be a path-dependent one where hard political choices will be made and the very complexities of globalization will increasingly shape both the problematic and the understanding of potential solutions. Political strategies and projects will increasingly have to become multilayered and globally oriented at the same time to be effective. In ideological terms this is true both for the Right ('globalization' in the sense of pursuing economic efficiency in a liberalized world market place) and for the Left (a regeneration of genuinely internationalist socialism?). The post-modern irony of politics is that rather than simply being undermined by inexorable structural forces, the competition state is becoming increasingly both the engine room and the steering mechanism of an agent-driven *political* globalization process. This process requires the reinventing of politics and the construction of new forms of legitimacy, which will in turn shape the wider economic, social and cultural context and, ultimately, the qualitative kind of global world which results.

Notes

1. This chapter is derived from a paper presented at the Joint Conference of the International Studies Association and the Japanese Association for International Relations, Makuhari, Japan, 20–2 September 1996. An earlier version appeared in *Government and Opposition*, Vol. 32, no. 2 (Spring 1997). I am grateful to Kal Holsti, Randall Germain and numerous others for comments on these and earlier attempts to develop the ideas contained here.
2. The shape of the *international* playing field is likewise determined by states interacting in a 'states system'
3. Caught in the middle are those traditional 'international' processes which operate *between* states, such as bilateral relations and the activities of intergovernmental institutions. I would argue, however, that these increasingly reinforce transnational processes as governments use them to play 'catch-up'.
4. A 'quango', or quasi-autonomous non-governmental organization, is an authoritative body licensed by the state to carry out public regulatory functions but made up of appointed representatives of private sector interests. It is probably best considered to be a variant of state corporatism.
5. The industrial or corporate state was rather more complicated, often protecting industry from both external and internal market forces while at the same time seeking to expand market share and profitability (as well as occasionally pursuing domestic social goals).
6. This is the term originally used by Johnson (1982) to describe the Japanese model.
7. Not to mention the recent financial crises and their aftershocks in South-East Asia: see, for example, Alan Frieden, 'Globalization Theory Vaults Into Practice' (*International Herald Tribune*, 26 September 1997).
8. What I have elsewhere called 'Type II Re-regulation' (Cerny, 1991).
9. This sort of institutional umbrella is unlikely to be fully replicated in a globalizing world, although it *is* likely that the further development of multilateralism and the authority and autonomy of international regimes will increasingly impose common rules and standards in particular sectors and issue areas.

5

Recasting Political Authority: Globalization and the State[1]

Ronen Palan

Our era is not characterized by a new post-Fordist state (Jessop, 1993) or by the withering away of the state (Ohmae, 1990), and not even by the internationalization of the state (Cox, 1981; Picciotto, 1990). Indeed, our era is characterized by each and all, in a plethora of political experiments ranging from the reinvention of the state to the creation of regional organizations, and including developmental models, social democratic states and minute tax-haven states (Palan and Abbott, 1996). Indeed, the very space of authority, the state system, is bifurcating into two separate realms. 'Onshore' is supplemented by 'offshore', the latter marking a different level of intensity by which states propose to apply regulations and taxation (Palan, 1996).

These developments raise an intriguing set of interrelated questions: what, if any, is the relation between these experiments in political authority and globalization? Furthermore, if there is a relationship, what are the lines of causality? Are they necessary effects of globalization? Does this imply that these experiments are pre-ordained, or perhaps that they are testimony to a learning process by which new forms of governance take shape? Put differently, if we were to reverse the historical process and try again, would we end up with more or less similar conditions? Is globalization, in other words, the outcome of one set of dynamics, or perhaps is it the result of the coming together of a number of disparate dynamics? Since I would like to entertain the idea that not everything is pre-ordained, this chapter focuses on the concrete processes that contribute to these political experiments.

In the course of this chapter I will argue that while the theoretical work inspired by methodological individualism and Marxism contains important insights into the conditions that give rise to these political experiments, neither approach provides us with the necessary theoretical tools to describe the processes by which these political experiments come about. I adopt instead an approach which draws on Marxism and institutionalism in equal measure, which I have described elsewhere as neo-structuralism (Gills and Palan, 1994). For the neo-structuralist perspective the state is not a volitional unity but a transformative format in the global economy. I treat the state and globalization therefore not as contending and conflicting structures, but as mutually restructuring agents so that globalization shapes the nature of modern political authority just as much as the state shapes the nature of globalization.

Globalization and territorial rationalization

The relationship between state and globalization is intricate and multifaceted. To many scholars the critical issue appears to be the future role of the state and its continuing ability to foster economic growth and well-being. Important as this debate might be, its frame of reference is misleading. It is grounded, to begin with, in a false dichotomy between state and globalization, but also, and more fundamentally, in a misunderstanding of the nature of the state. The state, as Poulantzas (1973) argued, is not a volitional subject, but a type of political authority. Equally, globalization is not an extraneous set of dynamics which now confronts the state, but a coherent and integral aspect of the construction of political authority. Furthermore, the changing nature of political authority is creating in a complex way a juridical and political infrastructure supporting and promoting further moves towards globalization (Palan and Abbott, 1996).

While such a view is becoming more widespread, greater awareness of the intricacies of the relationship between state and globalization has so far produced little in terms of concrete and solid proposals as to the way in which political authority is changing and becoming redefined. Scholars appear to be far more interested in reaffirming entrenched positions: to most mainstream scholars in International Relations (IR), globalization is mere hype as the fundamentals of the international system have changed very little (Jackson and James, 1994; Krasner, 1994); to neo-liberals globalization offers additional evidence of the inability of the state to resolve economic issues; to Marxists, globalization is a reaffirmation of the dominance of capital and the servility of the state.

To get beyond such entrenched positions, this chapter offers one possible interpretation of how statehood is being recast. Methodologically, I strive to present an analysis in which change is not haphazard but a necessary outcome of a set of events; and yet nothing is pre-ordained, driven by forces beyond human control. To do so I will argue that 'the state', which is an abstraction, cannot react to a descriptive concept such as globalization. Such analysis places the emphasis not so much on what we take to be objective conditions, but on the social structures and political processes (including those of the state), on the one hand, and on the description of the nature of change, on the other. My understanding is that by coming to grips with 'reality', in adapting to a perceived situation, reform in effect changes 'reality' so that the process of accommodation provides us with insight into the symbiotic relationship between state and globalization.

The broad macro interpretation presented in this chapter is based on the understanding that the era of globalization is characterized by a new phase of *territorial rationalization*. By territorial rationalization I do not mean necessarily objective or structural processes, but a subjective understanding of what Foucault calls 'government' (which is better translated in English to governance).[2] According to Foucault governance is a set of practices regarding 'how to govern oneself, how to be governed, how to govern others, by whom the people will accept being governed, how to become the best possible governor' (Collins, 1996). Governance in this sense relies on 'knowledge' in the broad sense. Theories of governance have undergone important changes exemplified in diverging principles of territorial rationalization:

- the post-feudal and absolutist state settled its territorial boundaries through dynastic marriages and/or war;
- the nation-state of the nineteenth century sought to correct and settle its territorial boundaries on the principle of 'national self-determination';
- the modern 'competition state' is increasingly presented as the most economically competitive form of political incorporation.

There is, of course, no clear line separating one phase from the other. The third phase, the 'competition state', for instance, draws inspiration from theories and practices which go back at least as far as Colbert. Indeed, it appears to me that it takes at least a century for one principle of territorial rationalization to achieve clear dominance over another so that a number of principles tend to merge at any given historical moment. Diverging general principles of territorial rationalization imply that state formation can be narrated in terms of a conflict between one principle of rationalization and another. Thus the post-feudal principle of territorial rationalization had to negotiate its feudal inheritance. The nation-state inherited many of its problems from absolutism, and now, this chapter argues, the modern 'competition state' is negotiating a social structure and a set of political institutions inherited from the period of the nation-state. The processes of reformation and adaptation can be understood therefore at a macro level as processes of *negotiation* or transition from the second to the third phase of territorial rationalization. These consist simultaneously of processes of *destruction* and *construction*: the destructive set of processes are often mistaken for the demise of the state; the constructive aspects are by and large ignored.

Globalization and the state

The state raises a series of conceptual difficulties not least because the concept serves as a proxy for many sociological, political and philosophical debates. Notwithstanding this, I propose to begin an examination of current literature on the state and globalization with some general comments on the nature of the state. Broadly speaking, the relationships between the state and globalization are handled in three different ways, corresponding roughly to three different sets of methodologies. Methodological individualism has tended to perceive the state and globalization as incompatible if not conflicting trends; Marxist methodologies view the state as instrumental of class interests and therefore enhancing and promoting globalization; institutionalist approaches place the stress on learning processes, institutional adjustment and their constraints.

These three schools of thought are not exclusive. On the contrary, they have tended to adopt ideas and insights from each other and responded by offering composite syntheses. So, for example, Poulantzas's (1973) theory of the 'relative autonomy' of the state may be regarded as a synthesis of structural-functionalist and pluralist theories with Marxism. At the same time, the ambiguities of the 'relative autonomy' thesis have focused attention on the problematic of institutional adaptation, giving rise to sociological institutionalism. Similarly, Skocpol (1979) and Mann (1984) adopt a statist approach which shows evidence of an incorporation of Marxist insight into methodological individualism.

Unfortunately, none of these syntheses has proved wholly successful. They remain, by and large, theoretical pastiche: the relative autonomy thesis of Poulantzas and the derivation school (Holloway and Picciotto, 1978) have failed to explain fully the relationship between class and state. Similarly, institutionalism has largely failed to take account of group and class interests. This section outlines the intellectual journey from methodological individualism to Marxism to institutionalism. It is not meant as an exhaustive literature review, but rather as a brief outline of the main characteristics of the debate.

'The state' is a political organization; on that everyone agrees. The meaning of 'politics', however, is hotly debated. In the approach taken in this chapter, politics is understood at the level of an instance of social reality. As Lévi-Strauss notes, a society:

> consists of individuals and groups which communicate with one another ... In any society, communication operates on three levels: communication of women, communication of goods and services, communication of messages. Therefore, kinship studies, economics, and linguistics approach the same problem on different strategic levels and really pertain to the same field. (Lévi-Strauss, 1953: 536)

There is a fourth level of communication, and that is the level of the formal ordering of society, or the political level. The political process is the process by which societies organise themselves by *formal* means (Clasters, 1977).

I would like to emphasize the idea that politics is a formal ordering of society. Politics is only one of the processes contributing to a structured pattern of social life. Sociologists habitually distinguish between two sets of power relations, integral and intercursive power (Mayntz, 1969). Integral power is the material and moral power of the collectivity over its members, the constraints exercised 'by all against all'. 'The individual is placed under observation and surveillance and appreciation of those around it; the result is collective constraint; anonymous, but infinitely more enveloping and powerful than the one placed by a despot' (Claval, 1978: 42, author's translation). Intercursive power draws on Weber's notion of power constraining action by others. The political is intercursive power, which includes premeditated forms of 'agenda control'.

All societies are therefore 'political' in the sense that all evolve formal or semi-formal procedures for self-organization. Here, in contrast to Weber, I define the state as *a specific political organization characterized by the separation and differentiation of a governing apparatus from the governed.* Whereas tribes or clans are governed by elders and chiefs, the state is governed by 'the state'. Within the state, therefore, procedures of self-organization are formally demarcated from other social processes. The term 'state' here denotes two distinct phenomena: it is simultaneously an aggregation of people normally residing within a given territorial space, and the governing set of institutions of that people. Historically the two terms have collapsed into one during the period when a plethora of different political systems was drastically reduced and replaced by one overarching model. This was perceived by contemporaries to resemble the Roman *status respublicae* or, in short, *status*, the state.[3]

Methodological individualism: state versus globalization

One tradition of state theory attributes the 'governing apparatus' of the state to independence of will. The state in this restrictive sense is characterized as a social actor in its own right. There are two primary routes by which this theory has evolved. One strand originated in the anti-reformation tradition of the 'reason of the state' (Botero, 1598/1956), which asserts the ethical calling of the state. This tradition then found echoes in nineteenth-century romantic and idealistic thought to produce a concept of the state as personality. In this tradition the state is believed to be a 'real' person endowed with its own historical logic, or the 'reason of state'. I have argued elsewhere that this tradition formed the backbone of realist thought, from Treitschke through Morgenthau to Hedley Bull (Palan and Blair, 1993).

Today the theory of the state as personality is all but defunct, replaced by the so-called neo-Weberian theory of the state. Methodologically speaking, action theory assigns different action-orientations to different arenas so that in the modern world economically-oriented action takes place primarily in the marketplace, while politically-oriented action takes place in the state.[4] Politically-oriented action implies a separation between Us and Them. Weber (Roth and Wittich, 1978: 54) defines a political or ruling organization 'insofar as its existence and order is continuously safeguarded within a given territorial area by the threat and application of physical force on the part of the administrative staff'. Economically-oriented action is 'concerned with the satisfaction of a desire for "utilities". "Economic action" is any peaceful exercise of an actor's control over resources which is in its main impulse oriented towards economic needs' (Roth and Wittich, 1978: 63).

Weber's classification was grounded in a historicist position. It has, however, been adopted uncritically in the service of ahistorical thought which informs much of the latest research into the relationships between state and market, perceived as a relationship between specifically organized arenas of activity. This has generated a political economy grounded in the separation between politics and economics. The market is perceived in this view as an arena in which individuals and companies are allowed to pursue their interests. Adam Smith introduced the notion of the 'invisible hand', pointing out that the market serves as the best mechanism for the co-ordination of the collective pursuit of individuals' desires. Towards the end of the nineteenth century the concept of the market underwent a dramatic change and became an 'abstract concept that acquired tremendous analytical interest as a price-making and resource allocating mechanism' (Swedberg, 1994: 259).

The marginalist revolution conceived of the market as a mechanism of resource allocation. States and markets are viewed in this tradition as two alternative and competing modes of 'resource allocation' so that the increasing scope of one implies by necessity a reduced scope for the other. In this way a conceptual separation of politics from economics has become a presumed political conflict between state and market. This presumed conflict serves as the underlying model for the study of the state and globalization. I would like to emphasize that there is no logical necessity in either action-theory or neo-classical economics to warrant such an interpretation: both methodologies are sufficiently broad and flexible to accommodate different perspectives. In practice, however, they have given rise to the view that globalization is driven inexorably forward by market forces and that the state, as a unified structure, is reacting to this external force.

Although 'state versus globalization' theories present a plausible viewpoint, they contain a number of shortcomings which are indicative of a deeper conceptual difficulty. First, the entire analysis is predicated on the assumption that we are examining objective conditions 'out there' (i.e., empirically verifiable action-orientation phenomena). Since the debate is about 'getting your facts right', the literature is trapped in what may be described as a 'binocular' debate whereby each side accuses the other of blindness, myopia and biases, while congratulating itself on having in its possession superior binoculars with which they are able to see developments in the 'real' world. Perversely, this results in subjective analysis in which the prestige and academic standing of the observer is the crucial factor. Academic journals, therefore, permit only academics of the highest standing to pontificate on the future role of the state.

The binocular debate is sustained by a second characteristic of this literature, the prevalence of what I call a 'realist' scheme of social change. This scheme takes its cue from the biological metaphor in which the body, the unity, is understood to react to outside stimuli, the environment. This scheme tends to ignore cognitive processes (hence its affinity with the less sophisticated strands of structuralism) and assumes an automatic response embedded in the organic structure of the entity. In this view 'the state', as a social entity, is inherently limited in its capacity to react to what is understood as an external process called globalization. Globalization is therefore depicted as a structural-teleological process that is external to politics, and indeed prior to the state. Globalization is narrated as if it were impacting on the state, which is conceived in functionalist and structuralist terms as an adaptive system. Globalization and the state are represented therefore as conflicting tendencies.[5]

As a result of this double-bind, methodological individualism provides no indication as to how change in state structure comes about: certainly there is no indication that the state may play a constitutive role in defining the process of globalization. In that sense methodological individualism reproduces in subtle ways an ideological argument. By representing globalization as if it takes place 'outside' politics, it reaffirms the *political* message that the role of the state is not to reject market forces, but to take account of changing circumstances and try and take advantage of them. This is clearly a status quo position rightly suspected to be an ideology.

Marxism: globalization as capitalism

State autonomy theories argue that the governing apparatus which they have labelled 'the state' enters into struggle over the distribution of resources with other social forces. The problem, however, is that in asserting this, state autonomy theories abandon a great portion of what state theory needs to explain, such as inquiry into the dynamics of those *prior* processes which define the social forces that participate in redistributive battles; the institutions and norms that define the matrix of such struggles; the processes that change over time; and so on. Instead, they must assume a complementary theory of social process, which normally goes under terms such as civil society and so on. The problem, however, is that in so doing, civil society is taken as a discrete social entity in its own right, external to politics. Such state theory, in other words, underestimates the role of politics in social ordering and provides little insight into the dynamics of state formation.

Society-based state theories, of which Marxism perhaps is the strongest, seek to understand politics and the nature of political authority in a broader social context. Whereas for methodological individualism the separation between politics and economics is constitutive, for Marxism it is constituted: it is the result of the historical processes which are associated with the rise of capitalism. Marxism offers a different sociology, a sociology of exploitation (Casanova, 1971) , and it is grounded in the belief that exploitation of one human being by another is the motor force of history. This is not to imply that everything can be reduced to class or that class can explain the totality of social relationships. The Marxist argument, properly understood, is limited to the contention that processes of exploitation are central to the dynamics of societal order and change. In other words, processes of exploitation *overdetermine,* to use a term borrowed from psychoanalysis, other aspects of social life.

The stress on processes of exploitation largely define the Marxist approach to the problem of political authority. In Marxist thought there is no separation between politics and economics so that the state is inseparable from the process of accumulation. This idea is a necessary precondition of a sociology which places the stress on exploitation. After all, exploitation has to be organized concomitantly at an economic, political and ideological level, otherwise it does not work. But that is the crux of the problem! If there is no separation between politics and economics then how are we to interpret empirical developments?

One is left with one of two possible interpretations: either treat concrete change in state structure as evidence of the changing nature of the economic base, so that a political analysis is taken *ipso facto* to be economic analysis; or, alternatively, treat the changing nature of capitalism as the cause of observable change in the state so that the development of the state is interpreted *a priori* as serving the functional needs of capitalism. From such a position Marxists have no other recourse but to view globalization as a liberal capitalist agenda and maintain that the state does not negate globalization but embraces it. Not only does the state system promote globalization, but the very structure of political authority is internationalized to accommodate the functional needs of capitalism (Piccioto, 1990). In other words, globalization is a reaffirmation and entrenchment of exploitative relations. Even if this is the case, however, this approach still does not tell us *how* these processes have taken place. Rather, it tends to demonstrate that observable change does not affect the fundamentals of organized social life. Here, explanation of how social classes – whose main political struggles occur within states – are able to impose incredibly complex and intricate sets of changes upon the entire world is notably absent.

This last point serves as a hidden central paradox in recent Marxist thinking. The two 'simple' solutions to this puzzle reproduce, in effect, the methodological individualist premise of the separation between politics and economics. In one approach emphasis is placed on the 'hegemonic' designs of the USA. The complexity of state and class is then reduced to the activities of the USA – a much simpler problem, no doubt. The other solution assigns 'global capitalism' a certain independence, and sees the state as a mere servile instrument of capitalism. 'The state' (or, more accurately, social and political relations) does not impinge therefore on the underlying dynamics of capitalist development.

Such oversimplifications are unsatisfactory. Marxist state theory had therefore to develop a methodology capable of handling concrete conditions – the institutional and normative structures of the modern state – which means, ironically, incorporating insights brought from so-called 'positivist' studies of the state in order to avoid falling into the positivist trap. While methodological individualism stresses the separateness and autonomous dynamics of the political and the economic 'systems', Marxism places the emphasis on their interrelationship. Combine the two together and we end up with a concept of an inherent interrelationship between political authority and the economy; yet, due to their separate dynamics, they are conceived to be 'relatively autonomous' from one another.

This was of course Althusser's great contribution to knowledge. Put in this way, however, his concept of complex structure does not seem to amount to much. Indeed Althusser's 'solution' raised more questions then he was prepared to answer. The concept of the relative autonomy of the state unwittingly opened the door for the incorporation of institutionalist thought into Marxism. Despite what many consider to be its impoverished theoretical status (albeit not without certain insights), scholars have nevertheless attempted to make sense of the concept of relative autonomy by condensing a number of separate arguments together.

The 'Gramscian' problematic: here the state is a mode of class control. Its unity is contradictory because it represents itself as a universal, all-encompassing institution serving the general interest of the 'nation' even though it is a servant of class interest. The ruling class, however, is not a homogeneous group and has to make concessions to other classes. At the same time, universalizing ideology imposes its own rules. A king, for instance, cannot lay claim to be the 'first servant of the nation' (as did Frederick II of Prussia, for example) without voluntarily restricting his actions. These two tendencies produce a distance which can be interpreted as 'relative autonomy'. The idea here is that any form of political authority is ensnared by the logic of its own legitimizing language. Such language places obstacles in the way of class interests being pursued within the state in an open-ended fashion.

The 'Lockean' problematic: Locke argued that the competitive interests of capitalist factions require a mediating structure so that conflicting short-term interests do not degenerate into permanent civil war. In the Marxist tradition a distinction is made between the short and the long-term interest of capital (van der Pijl, 1984). The state operates as mediator and achieves 'relative autonomy' *vis-à-vis* the ruling class in order to play this role. States that do not achieve 'relative autonomy' (such as some African neo-patrimonial regimes) fail to succeed in the modern world (Clapham, 1986; Bayart, 1993).

The 'institutional' problematic: social classes seek to institutionalize their gains. The modern conception of private property, the removal of internal barriers and traditional privileges are all outcomes of past class struggles. A given institutional structure and norm consists therefore of layers of sedimentation of past struggles or, as Braudel puts it, societies embedded in one another. This historical edifice informs the parameters of political agenda and hence constrains the nature of the struggle. Due to past sedimentation the state appears at any historical moment as 'given' and external to any one class or group interest. The state is in a relation of 'relative autonomy' to any given class.

The 'Hegelian' problematic: here a 'relatively autonomous' class order comes about as a product of the 'dialectics of history'. Hegel and Marx argued that powerful or successful states, from Venice and Genoa in the middle ages, to Spain and Holland in the seventeenth century, Britain in the nineteenth century or (in the case of Marx) the USA in the twentieth century are successful because they embody, in the words of Hegel, the perfect rationality of their time. Through struggle and competition these perfect embodiments of rationality diffuse their institutional arrangements and social structures to other states.[6]

It is easy to poke holes in the relative autonomy thesis. Skocpol typifies the widespread exasperation with this theory when she asks to what extent is the state autonomous (meaning, is this theory open to counter-arguments and verification)? And yet, typically, she ends up with her own similarly flawed theory of the relative autonomy of the state. For our purposes, the significance of the relative autonomy thesis here is that it increasingly places the stress on the logistical and discursive constraints that are represented by the state. It confirms Poulantzas's notion of the 'relational state' as an historical creation: that is, that procedures and forms of political authority are able to evolve according to circumstance (Poulantzas, 1973). It also alerts us to what an incredibly flexible type of social organization the state is, and that it is capable of extraordinary transformations.

Institutionalism: intercursive power and institutional change

The relative autonomy thesis places the stress on the historical journey by which the state changes and adapts. It offers a non-teleological historical interpretation in the sense that it represents states as 'political experiments' (Lipietz, 1987). Such political experiments do not take place in a vacuum, but, as the new sociological institutionalists point out, within a historical context of institutional change. The institutionalist scheme of social change develops ideas derived from historical sociology, Marxism and discourse analysis. In this approach, the state as 'unity' is a hierarchical and logically interrelated set of institutions and structures, including governing or 'political' institutions which provide the 'unity' with instruments of adaptation and change. As a 'unity' it is not 'ontologically' but socially constructed, so that it comes about, maintains and reproduces itself as a result of identifiable social processes.

Governing or political institutions are 'thinking' or 'policy-making' bodies and react to events (sometimes by refusing to act). They exist and reproduce themselves within formal and informal procedural frameworks and are limited in their ability to react by their formal and informal social structures. They are knowledge-based interpretive and discursive institutions, in which discourse is not an open-ended possibility but is contained by the concretely evolving institutional framework. The 'environment' is 'not an abstracted 'social structure' but considered to be an aggregation of institutions as well (Tool, 1994). The institutional unity generates knowledge of its environment and of its relationship to that environment. Indeed, the very processes of knowledge generation work in a particular way: the formal structure of the unity is taken to be separate from the process of knowledge accumulation and reproduction so that 'knowledge' can then act as a basis for 're-action'.

The conventional or 'realist' interpretation of the relationship between unity and environment (see above) is thus not false; rather it reproduces uncritically the epistemological assumptions upon which knowledge is gathered. Here the policy process tends to treat globalization as an external, objective force to which it is supposed to respond. The 'reality' of the situation, however, is that presentation of an objective condition is an *objectification,* so that the 'knowledge' of the environment constitutes both the environment and the unity. And while there are clearly difficulties with this approach, not least because intercursive power relationships grounded in socio-economic interests are, by and large, abandoned, it is none the less a scheme of social change which offers better insight into the concrete processes of change and reform.

The nation-state

With this in mind, we can now continue our discussion of the state. I defined the state as a mode of social organization distinguished from other modes of social organizations in that it possesses a formal governing apparatus legally defined as 'the state'. Such an 'inclusive' definition of the state can be criticized for associating everything that takes place within a given territory with the state. My understanding of the state is that it is a *specific* type of social organization which, in the words of Braudel (1979: 519), 'shaped itself around pre-existing political structures, inserting itself among them, forcing upon them whenever it could, its authority, its currency, taxation, justice and language of command. This was a process both of infiltration and superimposition, of conquest and accommodation.'

My interpretation of Braudel is that the state is not only a relationship between rulers and ruled, but also a specific 'logic' or theory of government which then infiltrates and transforms the entire social scene. It follows that it is not enough to examine the activities and structure of the 'governing apparatus', just as it is insufficient to examine the socio-economic structure in which the state is embedded. A more complete study of the state must contain an analysis of the matrix of ideologies that define historically the nature of the social collectivity and political rule. It is this third aspect which is commonly missing in the debates on the state and globalization, and this is the aspect I now examine.

Transition points and discursive links

The historical entity we identify as 'the state' is in fact a very specific concept of 'government' which has evolved from the early nineteenth century. Commonly described as the nation-state, its underlying theory of government is a relationship between political authority and territoriality, represented normally by the three different concepts of state, society and nation. There is, however, a particular set of internally and logically coherent dynamics to these 'conceptual' relationships. In what follows, I select and narrate what I consider to be critical transition points and discursive links in the transformation from the absolutist state to the 'nation-state'. I highlight those aspects which have proved important retrospectively in the establishment of the modern flexible structure which is currently bracing itself to adapt to 'globalization'. Broadly, my argument is that from the early nineteenth century, the principle of nationality is deployed as a new principle of territorial rationalization.

Transition points: centralization and homogenization

Absolutist rulers sought to homogenize and rationalize their territories in the belief that diversity encourages factionalism and conflict. Thus the expulsion of the Moors and the Jews from Spain in 1492, the Thirty Years War concluding with the Westphalian compromise, and the expulsion of the Huguenots from France, all fall within this broad trend of political homogenization. In order to raise revenues, rulers learned from each other about institutional and fiscal policies and then sought to impose a standard administrative rule over their territories. More often than not, they employed local traditions which proved successful in raising revenues and then sought to impose such practices on other territories. Rulers have failed spectacularly on many occasions. When Carlos V went to Spain from the Netherlands he brought with him his court and sought to impose the sophisticated administrative structure which was inherited from Burgundy and passed to the Netherlands. His failure led to the division of the Habsburg lands. Similarly in 1494 France was divided into four administrative regions, so beginning the process of the dissolution of traditional feudal privileges. The Holy Roman Emperor unsuccessfully sought in 1496 to introduced similar administrative rationality in Germany, contributing to the tension that exploded in the Thirty Years War.

The breakdown of self-enclosed communities

The slow process of homogenization, the enclosure movement, and the rise of the market encouraged the breakdown of the self-enclosed or spontaneous communities which largely defined the real living experience of most of the population. Economic slowdown from the

1630s (Hamilton, 1934) and the disastrous pan-European wars all led to the appearance of a mass of vagabonds. This rendered problematic both the issue of social control and the reproduction of social order (Bauman, 1992a). Combined, these developments raised the stakes of social order. Louis XIV's edict to place all the homeless in workhouses was a significant development in social control, both in getting the state directly involved and in educating the cadres of capitalist labour.

Mechanical order

The breakdown of spontaneous communities brought, as Bauman (1992a: 6) notes, 'The heretofore invisible, "natural" flow of things ... into relief as a "mechanism" – something to be designed, administered and monitored, something not functioning, or not functioning properly, unless attended to and operated skilfully.' Statist order drew on a number of techniques to penetrate and dominate ever more comprehensively every aspect of social life. As Foucault (1977) pointed out, the establishment of the new *grand écoles* for administration and engineering in the early nineteenth century served to diffuse techniques of control learned from military barracks to the hospital and the prison.

Decline of natural law

Natural law theories of universal and unchanging hierarchical order are replaced by dynamic and evolutionary theories of social order. Kant and Hegel are key historical figures, spokespersons of the transition to this new 'episteme'. Social theory shifts from questions of justice and ethics to a question of logistics: from theories of the cause of order and change, to more pragmatic discussions of procedures and the organization of the body politic. Comparativists like de Tocqueville thus expound on the merit of the American federal system of checks and balances.

The modern concept of space

The breakdown of spontaneous communities, combined with the rise of the bourgeoisie, or post-Renaissance conception of the 'individual', produced a novel perception of social space as consisting of aggregation of individuals. In effect this entailed an abstracted concept of space. As Liverani notes, the 'notion of a homogenous, qualitatively indifferent space, viewed as the locus of the relations of reciprocal positions among objects, therefore unchanging whatever point is selected for observation, is an abstraction – not only a modern one, not only "our" abstraction, but certainly fitting only to particular fields of analysis' (Liverani, 1990: 33).

The individual and society

Individualization meant that for the first time, 'man isolated and as part of a group became an object of scientific inquiry' (Foucault, 1966: 356). The very atomization of the body politic places the state in a privileged position of being the organizer of 'the people'. The state is the political manifestation of the unity of the people; it is a mechanical structure superimposed, as we will see, upon an organic or spiritual unity. Michael Mann (1984) depicts these changes as the rise of the 'infrastructural state', a type of social organization with diffused power patterns. In his later work Mann (1994) identifies the historical link between nationalism and class in the development of the modern state. Lacking Foucault's theory of governance, however, Mann fails to note the discursive logical relationships that links them all together.

Discursive links: the concept of shared destiny

Nationalism is essentially predicated on the assumption of a shared destiny of a group of people. The nation is no mere aggregation of people which happen to reside within territorial confines, rather it is a spiritual unity linking each individual's inner selves in primordial or pre-political ways. Conceptually differentiated from the state, the nation is based, therefore, not on domination and hierarchy but on feelings of love and a deep sense of history. The nation is a great journey of discovery and spiritual renewal. The concept of the 'people,' the *volk* (Fichte, 1981), discovers *en route* great historical experiences. So France had discovered its origins in the misty days of the destruction of Troy no less, and the German Romantics discovered their medieval past in 'Germanic' attributes.

The concept of shared responsibility

The presumption of shared destiny begets an assumption of responsibility: each individual has a responsibility towards the collective for, in assuming a responsibility towards the 'constitutive absence', as Debray (1981) calls the nation, nationalism is predicated on the assumption of a shared responsibility to the inherited culture of the forebears. This implies, in turn, both a shared responsibility towards one's descendants (hence 'national' education is so central to nationalist theory) as well as a responsibility of individuals towards each other. Responsibility here is a double-edged sword: it is responsibility for your fellow citizen's general well-being, but also a responsibility for their spiritual well-being so that in practice they learn to toe the line. The nation becomes a huge machine of surveillance and control. Because of the location of the primacy of the social whole at the ontological level (whether this was a real ontology, i.e., definition of being, or not, is here irrelevant), this implies by necessity that individuals, legally and morally constituted as 'members', must subordinate themselves to the common good. It is incumbent upon the nation, for instance, to educate its people 'to substitute from the egotism and self-love another love, a love to the common good, for the nation' (Fichte, 1981: 80; author's translation).

The role of collective choice

The pursuit of the 'common good', however, is a matter of choice. Since the imaginary absence, in this case the 'nation', is unlike the previous imaginary absence, God, immanent to itself, by implication, it must take control over its shared destiny. God-fearing people are likely to entrust their destiny to God and therefore to His emissaries on earth so that political choices are seen as moral choices about following His injunctions or not. A God-fearing collectivity such as medieval states or modern Iran is a hierarchical entity, subordinating itself to eternal laws. God's emissaries, the ruler and his associates, merely interpret this eternal law for the benefit of the community, much as modern law continues to work on a similar principle of original truth and judicial interpretation. A national community, however, cannot rely on eternal laws and must make choices as a community. Consequently, as members of the nation, not only do people have responsibility towards the nation, but the nation has to organize itself so that its spiritual aims are fulfilled. The nation must evolve procedures of choice-making.

The nation as a self-organizing organic unity

Since members of the nation share a destiny, states are viewed as mechanisms for the organization of these mutual care societies. Indeed the notion of 'organic' and 'organization' share an etymology because the original concept of social organization reflected the notion that nation-states were 'organic' entities. The state emerged from the French Revolution as an organization which was supposed to respond to the 'needs' of the people who inhabited that territorial space. The state is given the task of maintaining peace and harmony at home, and defending the territorial integrity of the nation. There are, naturally, diverging interpretations as to the mechanisms that will ensure such beneficial outcome. Whereas conservatives are happy to leave such practical matters to the government, liberals prefer to place their hopes in a democratic process which requires constant communication between rulers and ruled. Nationalism suggests that ruler and ruled are locked in a systemic relationship and that their mutual relationship has an ulterior motive: the spiritual and material well-being of the people.

Social classes

It did not take long to figure out that the unity of people does not carry any guarantees about uniform experiences. On the contrary, the people can have divergent opportunities which may identify them as belonging to different classes. Indeed, the advance of one class implies the retreat of another. It is not therefore by accident that Marx represents a Left Hegelian trend. The point is quite simple: a unity must be presupposed for the class struggle to be discovered.

The 'nation-state' is therefore not an accidental coupling of two marginally related concepts, but a reference to a historically specific form of what Foucault defines as 'governance', for it was only during this phase of territorial rationalization that a unique and uncompromising relationship between political authority and territory could be postulated. Equally, only during this phase could the state be seen as a historical entity, or a social body representing the 'will of the people'. The state sought to symbolize this merged relationship (which is captured by the nineteenth-century concept of society) not only in its institutions, but also by investing its geography and architecture with meaning so that the state became a 'living map', able to symbolize the spirit of its people.

While the form of governance of the nation-state lingers on, in practice nationality proved impossible to implement. National self-determination proved non-operational until it was reinterpreted in the early twentieth century away from the ethnic principle to the idea that self-determination is the democratic wish of persons inhabiting a given territory (Rigo-Sureda, 1973). The 'national' side of the bargain has become simply an abstracted legitimizing principle so that, from the 1920s onwards, the principle of 'national self-determination' stands for the delineation of the political process within territorial boundaries. As the state progressively sheds the metaphysical values associated with its territorial boundaries, it becomes institutionally a 'political process', defining the boundaries of the mechanisms of representation. In this way the second, 'metaphysical' phase of territorial rationalization gave rise to a loose and flexible type of institutional structure which accommodated with ease the behemoths such as the Soviet Union or Canada and minute entities such as the Cayman Islands or Vanuatu. The great flexibility produced during this era played a constitutive role as the third phase got under way (see also Chapters 4 and 9 in this volume).

The thesis of the demise of the state narrates in fact not the end of the state, but the demise of these sets of connections between the concepts of politics, the nation and society which lay at the heart of the nation-state. Concomitantly, the sequences of public debates which go under titles such as 'reinventing the state', the 'new politics' and 'new social movements', which elicit thorough examination of traditional state functions and the place of individual in society are, in this interpretation, aspects of what may be described as the constructive motion of the third phase.

The competitive state

Following from the above, there is no particular reason why globalization should adversely affect the institutional framework of representation which is the state. The significance of globalization lies in how it undermines the nation-state theory of government and replaces it with a new concept of governance. For example, it is noteworthy that globalization is always accompanied in policy discourse by an adjunct: that it implies heightened international competition. International competitiveness, in other words, has become a broad guide to policy. The trade and business literature has replaced the notion of comparative advantage with competitive advantage: states are now placed on the sliding scale of a world competitive indicator on the basis of their supposed 'competitiveness'.

Superficially, the notion of competitive advantage may appear as a mere reformulation of comparative advantage. There is, however, a profound difference: comparative advantage is a 'passive' concept. It suggests that states are endowed with certain resources and characteristics and that international trade is advantageous because it links countries which possess different endowments. This reflects, in turn, the nationalist conviction that each nation is unique. In other words, comparative advantage assumes diversity. 'Competitive advantage', on the other hand, implies a notion of sameness: that natural endowment and culture, let alone the 'national spirit', are either unimportant or can be overcome. All states and territories are therefore considered to be in principle the same. Once this principle is accepted, then nationalist theories of government cannot be grounded on the notion of some underlying spiritual unity of the people. This implies, in turn, that ideas about the shared destiny of the nation, about mutual responsibility and so on, cannot be sustained. Competitive advantage is therefore the quintessential ideology of globalization, for it reinforces the notion of 'global' sameness. Two implications follow.

First, since all countries are in principle the same, geographical location is immaterial. This reinforces a particular notion of the global as a common, undifferentiated and shared space, *artificially* divided into national spaces. The artificiality of political boundaries suggests further that the underlying theory upon which the democratic edifice has been constructed is damaged. Since all countries are the same, individuals and companies increasingly feel comfortable in choosing their country of residence instrumentally. And they do so on the basis of the tax regime, 'friendliness' to business, climate and so on. Conversely, states consider it part of their job to go aggressively in search of those more valuable types of corporate personality. The state is shaping its citizens through the operation of the market.

Second, since all countries are deemed to be in principle the same, they are forced to compete with each other by offering better packages of legislation to corporate citizens. By implication, the state is seen no longer as the political voice of the people but as a provider of the means of accumulation. The state is detached and is perceived increasingly as a separate body which needs to justify itself functionally; in other words, a new theory of governance comes into being. The 'national space' is perceived as an artificial space carved out of the more 'natural' global space; national space is a political act and requires political rationalization for its continuing existence.[7]

The new theory of governance and the state

It is too soon to pronounce on the exact nature of the new theory of governance. There are, however, some indications as to how it might develop. On an institutional level, in the name of this new competitive rationalization governments are advised to develop a closer relationship to business. The territorial space is organized according to principles of the internal market and internal auditing.[8] Tasks are broken down and examined and then it is decided which arm, the public or private, is better able to pursue goals within specific budgetary limits. The surprising effect of all this is that the distinction between public and private is increasingly blurred. Whereas previously the state represented a growing chunk of society, the language of current politics cannot differentiate any more between state and non-state. In this discourse, the entire social realm is mobilized as a competitive unit and it is this overall competitive goal which defines the division of labour.

As a 'commercial enterprise' the governing apparatus is streamlined and organized into a lean and competitive machine. Entire societies are perceived as 'models' of accumulation such as the 'developmental state', the 'Anglo-Saxon model', the 'Alpine model' and so on. But here we come to see a conflict between discursive practices and the structural characteristics of the state inherited from the previous phase. In 'intent' the state has transcended its class and social structure, and become a lean and competitive machine, but in 'content' the nature of this machinery, the strategic dimensions, are defined not in the abstract, but by sectoral and class interests. The effect of this is to create what I described in my opening statement as a variety of experiments in political forms. Since the modern principle of territorial rationalization is phrased explicitly in reference to other states – competition – the impact is felt primarily at the international level. There are three developments to note here.

Regionalism

Fierce competition in high value-added industries throughout the 1970s encouraged the argument that a large, competitive and vibrant market was necessary for modern industry to compete in the world market (Dumont, 1990: Franko, 1990). These ideas helped to bring about the second phase of European integration and the Maastricht Treaty. In Palan & Abbott (1996) we came to the conclusion that the economic argument for regionalism is too weak and insignificant to sustain such a difficult process (even optimists argued that the Maastricht Treaty or the North American Free Trade Agreement, NAFTA, would only raise respective Gross Domestic Product (GDP) in the next few years by 1 or 2 per cent). In the case of NAFTA, it appears that its principal backers in the USA were driven by fear of resurgent EU industries (Palan & Abbott, 1996). Some suggest that similar anxieties are behind the move towards the formation of the Asia Pacific Economic Community, or APEC (Higgott and Stubbs, 1995). It appears therefore that regionalism has become the preferred defensive competitive strategy of those countries that wish to compete in high-tech industries. Of course, such a primary competitive agenda has allied itself with a number of secondary agendas as each member state brings with it a distinct set of reasons to join (Palan and Abbott, 1996). None the less, regionalism may be seen as the primary concrete effect of the new phase of territorial rationalization (see Chapter 9 in this volume).

The dominance of such economic giants may be interpreted as the institutionalization of multilateral regimes and, indeed, what we call globalization. The regionalist strategy, however, ensures that market rule is by no means a foregone conclusion. Rather than view the issue in terms of 'states versus markets', it is the politics of regionalism, and the dynamics of interregionalist competition, which are going to determine this issue. More specifically, I see the significance of regionalism on three counts.

First, with the entire Organization for Economic Cooperation and Development (OECD) area controlling over 70 per cent of global GDP organized into regional blocs, regionalism (or, rather, large political formations) flourishes. It appears that for the foreseeable future the world economy is going to be dominated by *hybrid* political giants: an expanding NAFTA and EU, together with APEC, joined possibly by India, China, Mercosur (unless Mercosur joins with NAFTA to produce the American Free Trade Association) and perhaps an alliance of states centred on Russia. I call these giants 'hybrids', because they represent diverse experiments in a political association and in state-market relationships (Lipietz, 1997). It is impossible to say whether one or two of these experiments will come out on top. Furthermore there are reciprocal dynamics so that the direction the EU takes must affect the future of NAFTA and China, and vice versa. The point is that the evolutionary dynamics of these hybrids will define the future relationship between political authority and the market.

Second, as experiments in political association and state-market relationships, these hybrids are currently defining the central political battles of our era. The core of their political struggles is conducted neither between these hybrids, as realists tend to assume, nor at the level of the state, as traditional political theory persists in assuming, but rather within these hybrids. In this sense, politics in the era of globalization is shifting not from a national to a global basis, but from a national to a regional basis. One cannot underestimate the significance of this. These hybrids are experiments in political institutions, but also, more crucially, they are experimenting with the degree of social protection they are prepared to offer their citizens. One of the important advantages of such huge hybrids is that they are political organizations that can credibly make claims to offer a certain degree of social protection against the vagaries of the market.

Finally, it currently appears that one of the attractive aspects to these hybrids is that they are, on the whole, economically very powerful yet militarily incapacitated. This gives credence to claims about the end of war as a central aspect of international relations (Strange, 1988).

Low-wage strategies

The competition in low value-added mass consumer goods is directing the emergence of different state forms. The giant hybrids are locked in a close and interdependent set of relationships with a great number of states that seek to take advantage of their plentiful supply of cheap labour. Such low-wage strategies are producing a combination of spectacular effects in the world economy.

One strategy which has attracted a lot of attention points towards an activist government engaged in defining the developmental trajectory of its economy. Here, talk about the demise of the state is greeted with derision. This, however, is proving to be a transitory strategy, because some states (e.g., Japan, South Korea and Taiwan) have managed to upgrade themselves into the next stage of development and in doing so have tended to get embroiled inevitably in a regionalist framework. Others, less fortunate, are heading in the opposite direction. Low-wage strategies and dependent relationships can lead to the utter collapse of centralised political authority. A great number of African states have never achieved proper statehood in the Western sense and have produced political structures that are mixtures of traditional rule combined surreptitiously with modern techniques of governance. This type of political authority, following Weber's famous scheme, can be designated as neo-patrimonialism.

The new competitive geography

The third aspect of contemporary territorial rationalization is a new political geography. The literature on international competitiveness tends to assume that international competition is about macro- and micro-economic conditions that foster economic growth. However, in conditions of increased mobility, competitiveness may evolve in entirely different directions. Since the independence of state power is expressed in the dual capacity of the state to devise both policies and laws, the two are normally considered to be one and the same. In the confusion that has ensued in the era of globalization they have, however, achieved a certain autonomy. Indeed, it appears that two have given rise to separate competitive games. The first, which attracts much attention, is the competitive game in state policies as exemplified in 'strategic trade theory' and 'new trade theory'. The second, which has attracted less attention, is the perverse game of competition in regulatory laxity. As Johns (1983: 6) notes: 'Given that some countries adopt a permissive regulatory environment and others a stringent one, gaps and differentials arise in national systems of regulation. These differences can lead to perverse competition in regulatory laxity and a gravitation by some institutions to the least regulated financial centres.'

The 50-odd tax haven states are the paradigmatic examples of this trend. These states are aggressively embarking on the search for corporate citizens and seek to attract them into their territory. By now it is estimated that over half of the global stock of money goes through these havens. At the same time, an increasing number of low-wage states are experimenting with special economic zones or export processing zones, areas in which they suspend most of their laws and regulations. I have argued elsewhere (Palan, 1996) that in conjunction with the 'offshorization' of finance, the 'offshorization' of production is creating a new political realm which is supported and maintained by the state system, but in which market forces can develop almost unhindered.

Conclusion

The present is dominated by a new and spectacular political geography, one obscured by the state versus market debate. This political geography consists of large political hybrids, fed by low-wage states, and supported by the parallel realm of 'offshore'. Globalization is characterized therefore by a voluntary bifurcation of the space under the 'sovereign' power of the state. This brings me to my last point. None of these developments is 'structural', if by structural we mean that such processes are embedded in the very dynamic of the situation and are therefore separated from individual will. Regionalism is not the only solution but the preferred and, indeed, a contested solution to a situation; offshore did not emerge 'structurally' but in a series of policy decisions, perhaps unconscious of their ultimate effect, but policy decisions none the less carried for very specific reasons. It is important therefore that we bear in mind that the changing nature of authority is not unmediated, but mediated: mediation means contestation, interpretation and political battles. The global effect of all this is to produce a new concept of governance and a heterogeneity of state forms which, in combination, will ensure the continuation of the process of globalization.

Notes

1. An earlier version of this chapter was presented to the 'Globalization and its Critics' workshop. In addition to the points raised by participants at that workshop, I have gained enormously from the comments provided by Angus Cameron and Randall Germain.
2. The French language does not distinguish between politics and policies. Similarly, it does not distinguish between government and governance.
3. "The state" is a neologism ... The word derived from the Latin *status* (signifying) a condition or mode of existence ... *Status* was used as *status respublicae* or *regni,* or *ecclesiae* or *populi christiani*. In the 13th century the concept of the "juridical structure" of a community emerged. Only at the end of the 15th and beginning of the 16th centuries did the concept of "state" emerge in its contemporary meaning' (Fédou, 1971: 6, author's translation).
4. As Weber states: 'we shall speak of "action" insofar as the acting individual attaches a subjective meaning to his behaviour' (Roth and Wittich, 1978: 4).
5. Scholars are increasingly attracted to an 'empirical' variant of this theoretical model, paying close attention to (national) statistics and 'factual' evidence in their quest for answers. The state and globalization are here perceived as two opposing sets of empirical data. By arbitrarily differentiating between nationally-oriented and globally-oriented social and economic activities, 'analysis' comes down to a quantitative assessment of the dominant social orientation of this data. So data which is deemed to belong to the state is taken as evidence which undermines the globalization thesis, and vice versa.
6. This is an evolutionary, if not necessarily a progressive perspective. The evolutionary perspective does not mean that the current institutional arrangement is the best so far, but that it is the one most adequate to current conditions.
7. The instrumental approach to rationalization is to represent the national space as a platform for competitiveness. Another approach, which I would label as fundamentalist (but which I will not discuss here), being disappointed with mere nationalism, seeks to re-embed the state in the spirituality not of the nation, but of the religious sect.
8. 'Germany is too big and the Netherlands is too small. Hence the intriguing suggestion from a Dutch politician, This Woeltegens, that his country should gain economic and political weight by merging with its German neighbour: the giant federal state of North Rhine-Westphalia.' As reported in *The Economist,* 31 August 1996: 36.

6
What are Global Markets: The Significance of Networks of Trade?[1]

Jonathan Perraton

Economic globalization is often seen simply as the emergence of global markets. This is problematic for two main reasons. First, economic globalization also includes non-market organization of economic activity, notably MNCs' international organization of production within firms. Some accounts point out that non-market organization is rising relative to market operations though globalization (Dunning, 1993b; Ruggie, 1995). Second, it assumes that the concept of a global market is itself self-explanatory. This chapter examines what the globalization of product markets through international trade entails and thereby examines the nature of global markets and their importance relative to other forms of global economic activity.

The view of the global market as an unproblematic concept derives from the standard vision that once protection has been removed and transport costs have fallen sufficiently such markets will emerge which producers and consumers can readily access. Although this vision derives from neo-classical economics, it remains implicit to many approaches to globalization which may acknowledge the market as a social institution, thereby obscuring how and why the actual operation of a global market might vary from the standard account. This chapter differs from such accounts by considering not just the institutional framework within which global markets, like any other, are embedded, but also the institutional nature of these markets themselves. The institutional nature of markets varies over time and space, necessitating that the operations of global markets be investigated directly rather than read off from a standard account.

Trade is pre-eminently action at a distance. We can therefore characterize global trade as the stretching and deepening of product markets in time and space. This still begs the question as to what a global market is and whether the shift to a global scale affects the nature of market operations. The perspective offered here regards markets as social institutions which require human agency to construct and maintain them. Understood as such, it is clear that, if the nature of markets as institutions matters, it must make a difference to their operations in practice. To pursue my argument, I first consider general approaches to globalization and then review the historical growth of trade. The operation of markets for internationally traded goods is considered next in terms of recent literature which indicates that the nature of global product markets does significantly affect the nature of global economic processes. I close the chapter with a broader consideration of the constitution of global markets.

Globalization, markets and institutions

Globalization here refers to a shift in the spatial form and extent of human organization and interaction from a local or national to an intercontinental or interregional level (Held *et al.*, 1999). Historical forms of globalization can be distinguished in six principal ways: first, the geographical extensity of its processes; second, the intensity of these processes and the degree of their enmeshment with domestic social relations; third, the impact of global flows and interactions on the activities and power of local and national actors; fourth, the development of infrastructures to facilitate these processes and institutions to manage and regulate them; fifth, the patterns of hierarchy and unevenness of access to global networks and sensitivity to their impacts between different countries and groups; and sixth, the mode of interaction, whether broadly co-operative, competitive or confrontational.

Taking the last point first, organizing international production within a firm represents substituting co-operative internal transactions for using competitive external markets. Firms may also co-operate internationally, either informally or formally through joint ventures and strategic alliances. Furthermore, creating, developing and sustaining international institutional structures to regulate international markets requires co-operation between national authorities. Although this chapter concentrates on the emergence of global markets through trade in the post-war period, the framework deployed here is able to provide a basis for comparing contemporary developments to other historical episodes of intercontinental trade.

This conception of globalization emphasizes shifts in the scale of human organization. As such it stands in contrast to approaches that hypothesize a globalized end-state and either claim that this state has essentially been reached (Ohmae, 1990; Redwood, 1993) or, by testing such claims, find that reality falls some way short (Hirst and Thompson, 1996). Even on its own terms, positing a single end-state is problematic since multiple equilibria, rather than a unique end-state, are not merely possible but highly probable.[2] Analysing globalization as a process can be justified simply because it is a multicausal phenomenon with multiple possible end-points determined by the process of response to the causes (but see Chapter 2 in this volume). But, more than this, globalization is the outcome of purposive human agency, both working within the parameters set by existing institutions and attempting to modify these institutions and create new ones.

This conception of globalization affects the analysis of global markets. Analysing economic globalization in terms of a unique end-state presupposes – implicitly or explicitly – that markets are a natural, uniform phenomenon, so that once restrictions on them have been removed they will emerge at the global scale in essentially the same form as at the national or local level. In this conception any variations in markets are due to exogenous restrictions on their operations, not the nature of the markets themselves. In the case of trade this refers particularly to protection, transport costs and the legal framework governing cross-border transactions. As such the end-state approach has no conception of processes of the emergence and operation of markets; the only process is the adjustment of market operations to changes in exogenous imperfections. Rather than seeing global markets as emerging from automatic adjustment to falls in barriers to trade, this chapter examines the processes whereby such markets have been actively created and the consequences of this for their operation.

Seeing markets as institutions begs the question of what is an institution. North (1990: 3) defines institutions as 'the rules of the game in a society or, more formally, ... the humanly devised constraints that shape human interaction. In consequence they structure incentives in human exchange, whether political, social, or economic.' However, institutional constraints do not simply limit actions, they provide the frameworks that enable regularized and systematic activity to be conducted (cf. Hodgson, 1988). As Hodgson (1993: 253) points out, they 'enable ordered thought and action by imposing form and consistency on the activities of human beings'. In this view markets can be seen not only as embedded in a set of institutions that frame their operation, but are themselves institutions whose operations vary. This is in contrast to the standard view of markets as a pure uniform type whose operations are constrained merely in the sense of being limited by exogenous institutional factors.

The 'new institutionalist economics' provides a variant of this approach (North, 1990). It emphasizes the importance of legal structures for securing property rights in exchange over physical barriers to market development, the development of these structures and the importance of variations in them for market operations. However, whilst this approach provides valuable historical insights, it typically regards problems of securing property rights as having been solved for contemporary international trade, a perspective that is misleading for trade in some goods and for an even greater proportion of trade in services. By retaining the view that markets will operate in accordance with the standard vision once legal restrictions have been removed, this perspective can offer only a limited account.

Seeing markets as one economic institution amongst several provides a stronger basis for examining the growth of markets relative to other economic institutions for organizing international transactions. In the now standard transaction costs literature of why firms exist, the market is taken as given and the theory accounts for why firms exist to organize transactions through internal hierarchies rather than through the market in terms of economizing on transaction costs. Recognizing that markets are not of one uniform type illuminates the choice between market and hierarchy in the organization of international economic transactions. Dunning (1993b) argues that not only has globalization (and other economic changes) increased the importance of private economic activity relative to government organization of economic activity, but also that organizing economic activity through hierarchies has risen relative to organizing economic activity through markets compared with earlier in the post-war period or past phases of high international economic activity, such as the classical Gold Standard.

Why have transactions become increasingly organized through hierarchies as opposed to markets? As production processes have become more complex their organization has entailed a greater number of transactions, whilst the falling costs of undertaking international transactions have increased the international dispersion of production. Alongside this, created assets, often intangible and unique to the firm, have become increasingly important in production processes. The incompleteness of markets for these assets and the difficulties of securing the property rights associated with them act to increase the level of hierarchical transactions relative to market transactions in international (and national) economic activity. I will now examine trends in post-war international trade in order to assess competing explanations of this shift from markets to hierarchies.

The emergence of global trade

Except during the early 1980s, trade grew rapidly throughout the post-war period – more rapidly than income – as protectionism fell under the General Agreement on Tariffs and Trade (GATT) regime and transport costs also fell.[3] Trade continued to grow even after tariff protection had been reduced to negligible levels and the falls in transport costs had largely ceased, or even, in some cases, been reversed (Hufbauer, 1991). The growth of trade, therefore, is easily analysed in terms of the perspective on globalization outlined above. The extensity of the trading system has been transformed since the war so that there is now a much denser network of world trade than before: Nierop (1994: ch. 3) finds that by 1990 the majority of countries traded with the majority of other countries. Table 6.1 shows this rising density, giving the trade flows between countries as a percentage of the maximum possible of every country trading with every other. The first row is for a constant sample of 68 countries, including the developed countries and established developing country exporters, the second for an increasing sample as more data becomes available. Other evidence also indicates that the density of trading networks was lower in the interwar and classical Gold Standard periods (Irwin, 1993). Whilst it is often claimed that trade is breaking down into relatively self-contained regional blocs, this is not borne out

Table 6.1 Density of trade links as percentage of maximum possible

	1928	*1938*	*1950*	*1960*	*1970*	*1980*	*1990*
Constant sample	–	–	64.4	74.4	83.8	89.6	95.3
Non-constant sample	55.4	53.5	64.4	62.2	55.5	56.2	66.2

Sources: 1928 and 1938 calculated for 54 territories from League of Nations (1942); 1950–90, Nierop (1994: 41).

either by this evidence or by other studies which fail to find marked regional biases and show that interregional trade has been growing alongside trade within regions (Anderson and Norheim, 1993).

Alongside the growing extensity of trade, the intensity of trading relations has grown so that trade: GDP ratios are higher globally and nationally than ever before, in contradiction to the view that comparable levels were reached during the classical Gold Standard (e.g., Hirst and Thompson, 1996: ch. 2).[4] Even using current price data, trade: GDP ratios are higher now at around 20 per cent than during earlier periods (Krugman, 1995). Using constant price data, as reported in Table 6.2, gives a clearer picture since traded goods' prices tend to rise less rapidly than non-traded. On this basis trade: GDP ratios are higher than ever before and have been at least since the early 1970s. Subtracting government activity from GDP indicates that industrialized countries now typically export around one-third of private GDP, a ratio that surpassed classical Gold Standard levels in the 1970s and has been significantly higher since.

It is not, however, simply a question of the rising quantitative importance of trade. The intensity of trade has risen as a wider range of goods and services have become tradable, and therefore subject to international competition. International trade has grown alongside the development of market relations domestically, particularly in developing countries, so that international markets have become increasingly enmeshed with domestic ones. This is in contrast to the classical Gold Standard period, when there were marked variations amongst developing countries in the levels of trade, the degree of development of domestic market relations, and interactions between the two (Morris and Adelman, 1988: chs 3 and 6).

Table 6.2 Trade: GDP ratios for developed countries in constant prices (percentages)

			1913		*1950*		*1973*		*1985*
Exports: GDP			11.2		8.3		18.0		23.1
	1880–1900	1901–1913		1948–1958		1959–1972		1973–1987	
Imports: GDP	12.4	13.3		10.1		15.4		21.7	

Sources: Maddison (1991: 327); McKeown (1991: 158).

Prima facie this growing extensity and intensity of international trade has linked national markets for traded goods so that global markets for them have emerged. Although space precludes detailed analysis of the impact of this trade, it clearly plays a key role in determining the distribution of international production and the way in which competitive pressures force national firms to operate at the global productivity frontier (Baily and Gersbach, 1995). In this chapter I focus primarily on the nature and development of the infrastructures that have allowed global markets to emerge and the institutional bases of these markets. By the late nineteenth century, at least amongst the major established trading nations, a basic legal structure for securing property rights in international exchange had developed, together with a range of agreements over transport, communications and product standards (Murphy, 1994: chs 2–4). After the Second World War the GATT provided an effective framework for ensuring international exchange and reducing tariffs on trade in industrial products, even with the many ambiguities of its operation and application in national law (cf. Jackson, 1989).

The emergence and sustenance of any system of markets requires a set of supporting social and institutional arrangements, but international trading markets require a particular set of such arrangements since exposing national markets to international competition through trade can have a profound impact on the fortunes of different social groups. Whilst the initial post-war framework for freer trade might be attributed to US hegemonic power and a collective desire to avoid the tariff wars of the 1930s, subsequent developments cannot be accounted for so easily. Whereas classical Gold Standard trade largely consisted of the exchange of different products between countries with dissimilar factor conditions, trade between developed countries since the war has increasingly been intra-industry, the exchange of similar products between countries with similar conditions. The impact of these types of trade can be quite different: whereas increased 'classical' trade raises the income of relatively abundant factors in the trading nation and reduces the income of relatively scarce factors, with intra-industry trade it is possible for all factors to gain from increased trade. This may provide a partial explanation for the trend and pattern of trade policy since the war: not only was there a general shift to freer trade, but as a policy this was much less politically contentious than in earlier periods. Alongside this, individual industry lobbyists, often both employers and employees, periodically succeeded in gaining piecemeal protectionism for particular industries.[5]

Three cases of market operations

This section considers three examples highlighted in the recent literature where the nature of markets for internationally traded goods can be seen to affect their operation. There are two obvious examples where significant volumes of international trade are conducted through consciously designed institutions. First, estimates suggest that between a quarter and a third of world trade in goods takes place between branches of the same firm (Bonturi and Fukasaku, 1993; UNCTAD, 1995: 37). This is clearly a case of substituting transactions through internal hierarchies for using markets. Second, on current definitions much trade in services is necessarily conducted through multinational networks and therefore such international transactions are organized by firms. Trade in services has grown rapidly over the past twenty years and is now conservatively estimated at one-fifth of world trade. While these cases are significant, however, they still fail to capture much of what is meant by global markets.

Multinational corporations as trading companies

Recently a number of MNCs have responded to increased international competition – itself a reflection of global markets – by reducing their direct organization of production and contracting it out instead.[6] This is often described as 'hollowing out', but rather than simply viewing it as a reduction in a firm's operations it can be seen as a strategic reconfiguration by the firm of its use of markets and hierarchies. In terms of transaction costs theory, contracting out is indeed a reduction in the firm's role as it substitutes market processes for internal organization. However, this perspective ignores what firms are actually doing here. A firm is not just an institution for organizing production, but operates as a strategic locus of control. As such, firms do not simply organize production, but organize their operations within input and output markets. Further, they do not just respond passively to market conditions, but actively seek to modify existing markets for inputs and use their outputs and to create new ones. With the rise of flexible low-cost producers of inputs, in some areas multinationals' advantage as processors of market information and organizers of markets may have increased relative to their advantage as organizers of production. Here MNCs are linking and creating markets precisely because of the particular knowledge of international conditions.

How far these developments result in a fall in estimated levels of intra-firm trade depends on how close a relationship between the trading partners is defined as constituting an intra-firm transaction. What this example demonstrates is that rather than a trend shift from markets to hierarchies, international market conditions sometimes lead to markets expanding at the expense of hierarchies. The ability of firms to operate in markets internationally and to shift the risks of production on to lower-cost producers means that the advantages of hierarchically organizing transactions are not inexorably rising relative to market trade, an observation consistent with evidence that intra-firm trade remained constant as a proportion of total trade over 1984–93 (UNCTAD, 1995: 37).

There are significant parallels here with the great trading companies of the seventeenth and eighteenth centuries. Rather than the cumbersome beasts early MNC theory portrayed them as, recent research has highlighted their sophisticated structures for the internal organization of transactions (Carlos and Nicholas, 1988). Further, these companies sought out new customers and suppliers, and thereby created new markets. Similarly, it is modern multinationals' expertise and organization that enables them to establish and run low-cost trading networks that link buyers with suppliers. The comparison is significant here because new institutionalist theorists (e.g., North, 1991) explain the success of the great trading companies in terms of how they internalize transactions in order to secure contracts in an era of minimal international trade law. This perspective downplays the infrastructural role of multinationals, both contemporary and historical, in creating new markets and linking distant ones to create international markets.

Marketing arrangements for developing country exports

One of the major shifts in the world economy over the past twenty years has been the emergence of developing country exporters of manufactures. This is typically portrayed as a competitive thrust, implicitly or explicitly on the assumption that if these producers supply their products at or below the ruling world price they will automatically find a market. However, recent research shows that developing country exporters do not simply turn up to world markets with their wares, and neither are their exports simply the result of MNC production: the proportion of manufactures exports accounted for by MNCs varies widely between developing countries (Blomström, 1990), but probably the majority, at least from established less developed country (LDC) exporters, is produced by domestic firms (Keesing and Lall, 1992).

Nevertheless, it is important to note that only a few of these firms have developed their own marketing networks. Most have had to negotiate marketing arrangements for their exports in order to gain access to their main markets in developed countries (Keesing and Lall, 1992; Egan and Mody, 1992). Some of these arrangements are contracting out by purchasing firms in the manner described above. Typically the buyer seeks out the supplier, followed by extensive negotiations over price, quantity, quality and delivery. Amongst established LDC exporters at least, standardized manufactures are a small and declining proportion of their trade (Keesing and Lall, 1992). Furthermore, once these arrangements have been initiated, frequent renegotiations take place between the parties on these conditions, which often provide a valuable source of information for the producers on incremental technical improvements and tailoring their products to the demands of final consumers.

So far this research has been largely descriptive, but some conclusions can be drawn. One corollary of assuming that developing countries can simply turn up to the world market at a given price is the assumption that they are small countries in the trade theory sense: that is, they face infinitely elastic demand for their exports. This assumption has been rejected by direct econometric testing,[7] and although there are several possible explanations for such results (Perraton, 1994), these arrangements may partly be responsible. For exporters wanting to gain access to world markets these arrangements may present significant barriers to entry (Egan and Mody, 1992). For those producers that have negotiated such arrangements these will determine, at least in the short run, the quantities they export. This may approximate to the maximum the firm could profitably produce at a given world price, and thus approximate to the open market vision,[8] but it may also fall well short. To the extent that the arrangements link exporters to specific ultimate buyers they may act to limit exporters' access to developed country markets as a whole. In this case they would not face the total demand curve for their produce and this would tend to restrict their exports to below that in the hypothetical case of facing the whole global market.

Exchange rate volatility and marketing arrangements

If the previous example considered the importance of marketing arrangements for access to global product markets, this example illustrates their importance in creating and shaping such markets. Krugman (1989: ch. 2), in a characteristically elegant model, notes that, although the dollar first appreciated sharply and then fell heavily against other currencies during the 1980s, this did not lead to catastrophic declines in first American and then other countries' export industries, as might have been expected if the exchange rate changes were fully reflected in the prices of exports. Moreover, declines in the dollar in the latter half of the 1980s did lead to significant improvements in the US balance of payments, indicating that currency movements do still have important effects and that the US deficit is not structural in the sense of being not amenable to adjustment through (nominal) price movements.

Krugman's explanation for this is that trading infrastructures require significant investment in resources. Exporting to distant markets often requires the establishment of marketing capacity and networks: there are sunk costs to exporting (although I argue below that this is a slightly misleading term). The services provided by these networks often play an important role in the non-price competitiveness of exports, which, in turn, is often important in determining their sales. Firms make decisions on the prices of exports and the quantity produced based on expectations of exchange rate levels; thus in an environment of fluctuating exchange rates they do not necessarily change prices and enter or vacate the market with each movement in exchange rates. This carries with it two key implications. The first is that in global markets at any one time prices for the same goods will differ between countries when expressed in a common currency: purchasing power parity does not hold at the individual commodity level. Whereas exchange rate movements might be expected in global markets to induce offsetting movements in prices, adjustment may take place in firms' profits instead.

Second, it emphasizes that global product markets are actively created by firms establishing marketing networks overseas. Exchange rate changes can induce entry and exit into foreign markets that may not be reversed if the exchange rate reverts to the original level. Krugman's modelling of this assumes that there are one-off sunk costs to entering markets and the recurrent costs of operating them are simply part of the variable costs of production. Although this makes the model more tractable, in practice the costs of maintaining overseas networks are recurrent and often only weakly related to the level of sales. Firms thus incur costs in establishing and maintaining export markets and, by extension, there are costs in the establishment and maintenance of global product markets. This evidence suggests that the costs are sufficiently high to be of significance in affecting the response to exchange rate changes whilst having been low enough to enable the emergence of global networks of trade.

Krugman's model is part of a wider literature explaining how far prices in different markets change in response to exchange rate changes (e.g., Menon, 1995). Space precludes a detailed analysis of this literature, but it has emphasized both these arrangements and the strategic decisions by firms facing oligopolistic competition in different national markets. Thus, the key point here is that international markets develop and are maintained not costlessly and automatically, but through the active decisions of firms based on projected pay-offs of the gains from doing so as a strategic decision in an oligopolistic industry. Thus rather than prices necessarily being equalized between countries through trade, firms respond to international price differences only if they judge it to be in their strategic interest.

Despite the importance of these market features in determining the effects of exchange rate movements on prices and sales, so far there is little direct work on estimating the costs of marketing networks or indirect work on their implied magnitude to account for exchange rate movements. Similarly, although it can be shown that domestic market structure, demand and supply elasticities, and the level of foreign competition affect the degree of price response to exchange rate changes, most studies have been indirect estimates of price responsiveness to exchange rate changes rather than direct studies of the strategic behaviour of exporting firms.

So what are 'global' markets?

The three examples in the previous section illustrate ways in which international trade is conducted and show that the operation of these markets cannot simply be read off from the standard account. Since 1945 firms in different countries have entered foreign markets at the same time as foreign firms have entered their national markets, so that the resulting networks of trade have produced global markets for traded goods. This can be characterized as globalization in terms of the scheme above: not only has the extensity of these markets spread beyond just the industrialized economies, but this process has also led to international markets becoming increasingly enmeshed with national ones. The global markets that have emerged are not of one uniform type; on the contrary, the process of market formation has affected the type of markets that have emerged and the nature of their operations.

This still begs the question of what is a market. Curiously the economics literature offers little guide. As noted above, much of the literature explaining why firms (and other economic institutions) exist effectively takes the market as datum and asks why economic institutions besides markets exist. Early neo-classical definitions of markets tend to be deceptively commonsensical, such as Cournot's definition as 'a region in which buyers and sellers are in such frequent intercourse with each other that the prices of the same goods tend to equality easily and quickly'.[9] Defining a market in terms of the equalization of price is implicit or explicit in much of the analysis since. By invoking such a definition economists such as Milton Friedman[10] can deny globalization simply by pointing to the continued dispersion of prices in the world economy. It is well-known that price levels (adjusted for exchange rates) are not systematically equalized between countries, and this holds for the prices of individual traded commodities (Ceglowski, 1994), but the models of price adjustment in response to exchange rate movements noted above can explain contemporary price dispersion even with extensive trade and minimal protectionism.

It is not just that there is a strong degree of circularity in defining a market in terms of price equalization and then defining non-equalization as implying the absence of an integrated market. In practice for many products, even when there are significant numbers of buyers and sellers rather than a single ruling market price, individual buyers and sellers may negotiate prices between themselves. Austrian economics (e.g., Kirzner, 1992) is more helpful in examining the processes of market operations, since it views markets in terms of their dynamic adjustment to continually changing conditions, but it too fails to provide an adequate definition of a market.

For slightly different reasons, the business studies literature also offers little guide. Often the formulations here are vague or implicit, but the general conception of global markets in this literature is that a global market emerges when there is sufficient convergence in demand conditions across countries that firms can sell essentially identical products in different national markets (Levitt, 1983; Ghemawat and Spence, 1986). Again, markets are conceived as a homogeneous type and global markets are then only said to emerge when national markets can be replicated on an international scale. Whilst even with free international trade demand conditions may diverge sufficiently between countries to ensure that markets are essentially discrete national entities, requiring global homogenization of demand before one can talk about global markets is too limiting, with the apparent rigour gaining little in insight.

A more sustainable definition of a market is offered by Hodgson (1988: 174):

> We shall here define the market as a set of social institutions in which a large number of commodity exchanges of a specific type regularly take place, and to some extent are facilitated and structured by those institutions. Exchange ... involves contractual agreement and the exchange of property rights, and the market consists in part of mechanisms to structure, organize, and legitimate these activities. Markets, in short, are organized and institutionalized exchange. Stress is placed on those market institutions which help to both regulate and establish a consensus over prices and, more generally, to communicate information regarding products, prices, quantities, potential buyers and potential sellers.

This definition emphasizes markets as the regularized contractual exchange of property rights, distinguishing them from various near-market institutions, although it may still retain greater emphasis on price equalization than is necessary or appropriate. Dietrich (1994: 7) extends this definition to characterize a market as involving:

- the exchange of goods and services and the associated property and contractual commitments;
- communication to inform potential consumers that goods or services, with their associated prices, qualities and quantities are available for sale;
- informing suppliers that there is a demand for their products.

A global market therefore implies that this institution of regularized exchange operates at the intercontinental level. During the major phases of intercontinental trade before the Industrial Revolution, these markets were either operated by trading companies or by merchant traders (Chaudhuri, 1985; A. K. Smith, 1991). Trading companies, as noted above, were able to create international markets by linking up existing markets and creating new ones, as well as surmounting the legal difficulties of securing property rights in international trade by conducting it within the firm. Merchants operated to arbitrage between different markets and therefore their activities approximated to the standard vision of equalizing prices through trade. In both cases intercontinental markets were effectively created by traders linking discrete markets at different points in the world.

By the time of the classical Gold Standard period, basic legal structures had emerged to ensure property rights in international exchange. For some primary commodities, global markets were established as their trade was physically concentrated in a handful of locations, if not just one: bulk trading of produce from around the globe took place in specific institutionalized markets. Even where significant proportions of the product were not physically traded through these markets, they fulfilled the function of collecting and disseminating information about demand and supply conditions and setting benchmark prices. It seems probable that, as with international financial markets, there were important economies of scale encouraging the centralization and collection of market information in a few locations (cf. Germain, 1997: ch. 2). However, for other commodities the networks of trade were less extensive than today and often followed the flag of empire or past historical association. Partly as a result of this, even with high levels of trade and a stable exchange rate system, price levels only converged slowly between countries over this period and remained significantly affected by domestic factors (Wallace and Choudhry, 1995). This is indicative of the limited number of global markets at the time.

Some organized international markets persist today, such as the Rotterdam spot market for oil, but they are basically confined to certain primary commodities and are therefore responsible for a declining proportion of international trade. Neither do they necessarily operate as perfect markets: some have periodically been subject to intervention through commodity agreements, some of them have been manipulated by key players, and some have been cartelized. As shown above, global markets have primarily emerged in the post-war period not through the direct institutionalization of organized international markets, but through the interpenetration of foreign markets by firms as dense networks of trade were created. National markets became interlinked through both increased foreign competition in each market and national companies competing abroad. Firms thus both created global markets and were subject to their pressures. These global markets therefore have been created largely by firms themselves. Much of the collection and dissemination of information is done within the firms themselves. The costs to firms of creating and maintaining these markets are simultaneously high enough to have real effects and low enough to enable these global market networks to emerge.

Drawing on the definitions of a market above, a global market would not necessarily lead to price equalization, but it would be expected to have a common institutional structure. Whilst the pre-existing legal structures and the skeleton GATT framework provided the basis for post-war trade growth, the growth and deepening of global markets has led to increasing pressure for institutional harmonization. Firms operating through global markets played a key role over the post-war period in opposing protectionism and lobbying for freer trade (Milner, 1989). More recently the patchwork nature of global markets through networks of trade has led to increasing demands for both a harmonization of national standards for trade in products and services, and for an agreed framework for securing intellectual property rights in exchange. This pressure is evident in the drafting and implementation of the Single European Market and NAFTA, and in the negotiations over these issues in the WTO. Indeed, the founding of the WTO itself is a recognition that the GATT provides an inadequate framework for addressing these issues. Thus the emergence of global markets is leading to an institutional harmonization that goes beyond the shallow legal integration of the GATT regime to a deeper integration of harmonized standards of competition policy, health and safety, labour and environmental standards, trade in services and in intellectual property rights.

Thus the creation of global markets has preceded the emergence of common institutional structures in which they can operate. In this sense, far from the issues highlighted by the new institutionalist literature having been solved by the post-war trade regime, they remain up for negotiation. At present the operation of trade policy in these areas is emerging from piecemeal negotiation rather than agreement over a consistent set of rules. Negotiations are proceeding at the bilateral and regional level, as well as at the world level, again tending to lead to the slow development of an international regime rather than a consistent global framework, even though this is the WTO's goal. Neither does the pressure from business, let alone other interest groups, necessarily lead to agreement on a single framework. Different firms and industries have different interests, leading to continued negotiation with national and international authorities rather than – to take the obvious case – a 'race to the bottom' of minimal regulation (Vogel, 1995).

That the emergence of global markets highlights the absence of a common institutional framework for trading markets might be expected to lead to an increased use of hierarchies rather than markets for organizing international exchange, as various authorities have claimed is happening. Whilst the issues arise with final consumer sales, which obviously cannot be conducted within firms, the evidence is not consistent with a general response of firms substituting hierarchies for markets. Two points can be made. First, as global markets have emerged, firms have pushed for a global institutional structure, indicating that they do not regard hierarchies as a simple or optimal solution to the difficulties of using existing global markets. And second, as emphasized in this chapter, the nature of markets matters. Whilst there may be important failures in markets around, in particular, the transfer of technology and the securing of related property rights, not only is this strongly related to the legal framework of international exchange but it varies between types of markets.

The market types involved in contracting out and for developing countries exports highlighted above represent structures that allow purchasing firms to take advantage of the flexibility markets offer whilst ensuring technology transfer and securing intellectual property rights. The contractual arrangements and levels of communication between the parties partially address these difficulties. Although it might be objected that these markets often involve exchange in less technologically advanced products, where the intellectual property rights are no longer the exclusive property of the purchasing firm, it cannot simply be assumed that these problems are absent or unimportant. Instead, it is more accurate to argue that firms have constructed global markets in particular ways to manage these problems. Thus paradoxically, although firm and market organization are typically counter-posed in the transaction costs (and other) literature, here it is firms that provide the trading markets between countries that link them together into global market networks.

Finally, this discussion enables us to clarify some of the issues of hierarchy and unevenness in global markets. Power operates in these markets, but is not necessarily intrinsic to their operations. Developing countries' access to export markets, as highlighted above, may be dependent on them negotiating marketing arrangements with importing firms. As with other markets, poorer consumers often pay more, as the case of African countries paying higher prices for their imports than other countries shows (Yeats, 1990). Again, this demonstrates that a market does not necessarily lead to price equality. However, whilst its operations may be affected by the power of different agents, firms do not make their money in these markets by systematically overcharging or underpaying developing countries. The issue of control over intellectual property rights in a range of goods and services is more complicated. To the extent that firms' business is dependent on them earning monopoly profits, at least temporarily, it can be seen in terms of the exercise of market power. This, however, is a vast issue which cannot be dealt with satisfactorily here.

Conclusion

Although this chapter has examined what global markets for traded goods are, it has only begun to scratch the surface of a question virtually unasked by those who examine globalization today. The emergence of global markets in goods over the post-war period has been largely constructed by firms establishing export networks abroad so that domestic markets have become linked to other domestic markets through chains of market relations. Global markets do not simply emerge with falling barriers; they are actively built and maintained with significant costs being incurred to do so. In terms of the approach to globalization outlined at the start of this chapter, the growing extensity of the emerging world trading system has entailed a growing intensity of global trading relations as international markets have become increasingly enmeshed with national ones. Moreover, markets vary in the nature of their operation and this makes a significant difference to the outcome, especially in comparison to standard visions of how global markets operate. If it is clear that global markets have emerged in association with a limited institutional framework, and that this has led to increased pressure for some kind of global institutional convergence, it is also fairly certain that these pressures continue so long as these markets are in operation. On this basis, it is safe to assume that this underresearched area will become more salient in the near future.

Notes

1. I wish to thank participants at the 'Globalization and its Critics' workshop and Michael Dietrich for comments on an early draft. I remain solely responsible for the contents. This paper draws on work from the 'Globalisation and the Advanced Industrial State' Project at the Open University, funded by ESRC Research Grant R000233391.
2. Held *et al.* (1999) provides a critique of the theoretical bases and empirical claims of these approaches.
3. This section (and, to a lesser extent, the rest of the chapter) draws heavily on both the general work and my chapter on trade in Perraton *et al.* (1997).
4. The classical Gold Standard refers to the period from about 1870 to 1914. It should be noted here that the figures used are for goods trade; including services trade would increase them still further and heighten the comparison with the period of the classical Gold Standard.
5. Some of these points are made in Midford (1993).
6. This section draws on Casson (1995).

7. Faini *et al.* (1992), Muscatelli *et al.* (1994) and Perraton (1994).
8. Even here the situation would not be identical to the small country case since the differentiated nature of these exports implies that they face less than perfectly elastic demand.
9. Quoted in Hodgson (1988: 173).
10. For example, as quoted in Ruggie (1995: 516).

Part III

Problematizing Globalization: Knowledge and Technology

7

Deficit Discourse: The Social Construction of Fiscal Rectitude[1]

Timothy J. Sinclair

> The budget has been to our era what civil rights, communism, the depression, industrialization, and slavery were at other times.[2]

Budget deficits are bad, very bad indeed. Creating them was indulgent; tolerating their continued existence, insufferable; reigning them in, imperative. Or so we are led to believe. The 1990s has been a decade of budget-cutting austerity and restructuring in most advanced industrialized countries. Great attention is directed to competitiveness as the liberalization of trade rules is extended further, and as governments seek to attract scarce financial capital (Gill and Law, 1989; Sinclair, 1992; Cerny, 1993; Krugman, 1994b). In many countries, government budget deficits have been identified by neo-liberal policy intellectuals as one of the leading causes of relatively lower growth rates and persistent unemployment (Williamson, 1994: 26). Deficit reduction has become a major priority for governments, and strategically important elements within many civil societies seem to support this objective.

As this chapter demonstrates, however, the social and financial impacts of budget deficits are debatable, and the costs and benefits they generate vary for different social interests. The 'common sense' of deficit discourse actually tells us little about what is really at stake in public finance. The more compelling observation about the deficit discourse of the 1990s is the degree to which its real significance lies in areas beyond the strictly fiscal. To properly understand the deficit discourse we must adopt a 'lens that is wider' than that usually deployed (Murphy, 1994: 10). That is to say, we must view the deficit discourse as a mechanism of social and political hegemony construction and maintenance, rather than the usual liberal orthodox account of it as an exogenous set of policy ideas. In structural terms, the deficit discourse must be considered in terms of broad processes of making sense of the world we live in under conditions of increasing uncertainty (Beck, 1992; Beck, Giddens and Lash, 1994; Bernstein, 1996). Within this context, deficit discourse can be linked to the particular interests of globalizing elites, which seek to shape it to their purpose of developing strategies of wealth-creation and political control (Gill, 1994: 179). The deficit discourse, therefore, can be thought of as an important element of what Gramsci saw as the intellectual and political leadership necessary to the maintenance and reconstruction of world order (Murphy, 1994: 11).

The argument to be made here is that the deficit discourse is best understood as a product of a set of conditions which bring into question many of the core ideas, institutions and material capacities that have been at the centre of the dominant system of wealth-creation and social control since the Second World War. These conditions include low growth, a perceived failure of state activism to solve poverty and crime, hyper-competitiveness, and a disenchantment with elite political administration. An important strategic initiative in response to this set of conditions (or threats) on the part of globalizing elites has been to generate what Gill has identified as 'new constitutional' governance devices. This new constitutionalism can be understood as 'the political project of attempting to make liberal democratic capitalism the sole model for future development', through the creation of a defensive system for the new spatially-extended relationships that comprise an increasingly global economic system (Gill, 1992: 159; Sinclair, 1995: 5–8). I argue that the deficit discourse is closely related to this development, and operates as a way, mentally and in practice, of closing off sets of practices from contestation, or at least of greatly narrowing the parameters of the public debate in ways that sustain a globalizing hegemony. An important feature of the discourse has been the propagation of a framework of thought centring around what are called synchronic assumptions, in which policy issues are increasingly interpreted in elite circles (Cox with Sinclair, 1996: 179–83; Sinclair, 1997). Synchronic assumptions, which dominate financial markets, are short-term in nature, and are at odds with the planning, research and development logic required of diachronic or productive processes that underpin the maintenance of social cohesion and growth (Cox with Sinclair, 1996: 181). The propagation of this infrastructure of thought and practice by means of the deficit discourse may be the discourse's most important impact in the long run.

The argument of this chapter is developed in three sections. In the first, the broader context or set of conditions which makes the deficit discourse possible is considered. This includes both the material and discursive conditions of possibility. The second element of the chapter looks at the social construction of the discourse itself. Here attention is given to examining the literature on budget deficits. The purpose of this discussion is to undermine the idea that there is actually unanimity on deficit matters, despite appearances that suggest there is, by providing a sense of the main lines of contestation. This is followed by a brief discussion of the production of the discourse itself, the processes which are central here, and an outline of the way power is exercised in this production. The last part of the chapter considers a series of implications that follow from the emergence of deficit discourse. Some arguments related to investment, knowledge and governance issues are made here.

Conditions of possibility

Five conditions of possibility have allowed for the development of what I term deficit discourse. They each in their own way relate to the transactional volatility, authority reallocation and transformations of work which seem to lie at the heart of the phenomenon called globalization (Mittelman, 1996a; Sassen, 1996). These conditions have enabled the creation of the deficit discourse, although none of them has made it inevitable. How the discourse seems to have been socially constructed is considered in the subsequent section. The five conditions of possibility comprise an absence of prosperity; the perceived failure of state activism; hyper-competitiveness and its effects on individual consciousness; intra-elite conflict and disciplinary social regulation, and the much more entrenched condition of patriarchy.

Absence of prosperity

An absence of prosperity has undermined the basis of the established ensemble of hegemonic relationships which underpinned the post-war world order. This order was premised on critical side-payments between hegemonic social forces (the antecedents of the contemporary globalizing elites), and subordinate social forces which had been brought into alliance with them, such as privileged or semi-skilled industrial workers. These side payments were premised on growth and constant productivity improvement. Mass production (and thus mass consumption) systems grew out of this set of social arrangements, organized around highly rationalized work processes (Amin, 1994).

However, with the onset of inflation in the late 1960s, this system became less able to deliver the sort of growth that was necessary for its own maintenance. Rising unemployment challenged the welfarist norms that had been enshrined in this set of social alliances, by raising the costs of the system, just as the capacity to support the existing level of transfers fell (Pierson, 1994). The effect of these circumstances was the gradual development of a sense of crisis and a demand for new solutions. However, because of the wide popularity of many of the tax transfers created in the post-war prosperity amongst OECD nations, this search was more problematic than it had been previously. There was great reluctance amongst subordinate social forces to go along with policy change of this sort. The crisis would require more infrastructural strategies to develop lasting solutions in most countries, although anti-labour campaigns were effectively deployed in some places, such as Britain.

Perceived failure of state activism

If the first condition created a sense of ongoing crisis that would, on the whole, not find any ready solution in the strategies of the past, the second condition destroyed the idea that solutions were actually possible or desirable. A crisis of confidence developed in the perceived effectiveness of state intervention in the Western economies. Possible causes for this scepticism about the social utility of the state lie in the stubbornness of low growth, despite repeated efforts to refire the post-war growth dynamic through corporatist wage arrangements, large infrastructure and energy projects, and the nationalization of 'strategic' industrial assets. The reversal of many of these initiatives in the second half of the 1980s only reinforced the sense that states were impotent. More recently, the re-emergence of international capital mobility has made states behave in ways which demonstrate to hegemonic and subordinate social forces alike that states no longer preside as supreme sources of effective authority (Ferguson and Mansbach, 1991; Cohen, 1996).

Although states retain legitimate legal power, the substance of their actions demonstrates a diminution of their capacity to act in ways which can effectively refocus social organization towards collective goals. The reassertion of economics in a non-Keynesian, marketized form, which has characterized the period since the mid-1980s, has further strengthened this diminution process by arguing that states do not possess the capacity to make effective choices in markets, because they lack full information and are driven by political imperatives which are not conducive to sound business decisions (Rhoads, 1985). This has now become the point of departure for policy initiatives in the central bureaucratic institutions of Western societies, although this norm varies in intensity, and is at times challenged in the less salient departments which are responsible for maintaining the social safety net. On the whole, however, we can say that it is no longer possible to make convincing arguments about state action in ways that were commonplace in the post-war era.

Hyper-competitiveness and consciousness

The third condition which supports the deficit discourse relates directly to the individual's sense of personal survival. Hyper-competitivesss has become a central feature of everyday life in the West, and increasingly in what was the communist bloc too. This perception relates to what we might typically think of as globalization: plant closures and relocation to low-wage countries, increased trade flows, investment mobility, quickened turnover times, and so forth. But these material developments are matched by a new intersubjective understanding that the old regime of expectations is no longer operative. The 40-hour working week, clear work rules, neat demarcation lines, mass production and large numbers of cheap, standard goods for consumption: these have a core logic which to a degree valued the individual's reproduction, at least as an economic agent. But this set of expectations, broadly protective of the individual's well-being, has now been replaced by fierce competition of a zero-sum kind, often between workers (Gill, 1995).

At the level of consciousness, this means that in the West the individual increasingly views his or her workplace as a danger zone, in which the career failure of fellow employees is considered necessary to maintaining a semblance of one's personal security. Features of hyper-competitiveness include this collective moral instrumentalism about work relationships (intensive hyper-competitiveness), and the extensive hyper-competitiveness of the longer working day. Importantly, hyper-competitiveness reduces the propensity of individuals to place themselves empathetically in the situation of others, thus reducing their tolerance for taxation and having others act as their representatives. Individualization is greatly enhanced, and forms of collectivization are increasingly less possible.

Intra-elite conflict and disciplinary social regulation

Intra-hegemonic conflict is also an important condition of possibility for the deficit discourse. This condition speaks to the issue of leadership, and its necessity in a well-functioning system of social trade-offs between diverging and converging interests, and at the world order level, amongst states. Although certain policy options seem to have been effectively ruled out in these globalized conditions, there is an absence of agreement amongst elites on solutions to large-scale problems of the biosphere, of financial volatility and market panics, and of development in peripheral parts of the world system such as Africa. Gill has also identified the simultaneous development of a more narrow, disciplinary mode of social regulation of non-hegemonic social forces (Gill, 1995). This reflects the inability on many issues to establish a genuine and lasting set of trade-offs between interests. Differences over economic policy, say, which have been generated by business and industrial decline, increasingly come to be 'solved' by the imposition of new frameworks which have very particular benefits (e.g., for the City of London). This way of solving intra-elite differences of view has had a chilling effect on the nature of public debate. The range of what can be contested has significantly diminished. The crucial feature of this environment is to present a picture of ongoing consensus to subordinate social forces, and to conceal this absence of lasting agreement at the core of social co-ordination.

Patriarchy

The last condition of possibility that will be mentioned is patriarchy. This is a broader and much more pervasive condition than the others we have considered. Workman has suggested that ideas about courage and sacrifice, fears of loss of control, abstract representations of policy choices, and the determination of authoritative speech, amongst other things, which are at the centre of the construction of maleness, have helped lay the groundwork for the development of deficit discourse (Workman, 1996: 55–69). For example, he notes that discussions of public finance are typically shrouded in a scientific language which obscures the concrete nature of productive activity. Because our daily lives are real experiences and not abstract, the representations of these issues in symbolic form helps to 'insulate the discussants from considering the human side effects of their policy recommendations, and inure them to criticism' (Workman, 1996: 64). Discussions of budget deficits, and of budget-cutting, can be undertaken without any consideration of consequences (and thus of their meaning for most people), freeing those who engage in these discussions to pursue elite agendas, because the accepted language employed by participants desocializes and technicizes the organization of state funds.

These five conditions have not in themselves brought about the deficit discourse (and neither are they an exclusive list). They are not agents of change. Instead, they represent transformation in the limits on agents, providing motive and opportunity for the transformation of previously coherent and seemingly fixed social relationships (Braudel, 1980: 31).

Social construction of the deficit discourse

So much for the conditions which have made the deficit discourse possible. Let us now examine the processes of social creation or construction of the deficit discourse. A key assumption in this interpretation is that particular accounts of the world go on to shape lived experience, because our social action reflects the norms and expectations we share as if these were material or 'real' structures (Wendt, 1992). Getting control over the process of discourse creation is therefore a significant question of power. Because 'discourses are assets' of power in the hegemonic struggle, it is important to treat these discourses sceptically rather than as direct, true accounts of the world (Shapiro, 1996: xviii). This requires the investigator to adopt a genealogical approach, which seeks to historicize knowledge as reflective of particular interests, times and places (Devetak, 1996: 185). In the long run, the goal of our investigation should be to isolate a 'core logic' – a more fundamental discourse – comprising 'describable sets of formally related assumptions and procedures' which construct social phenomena, and organize initiatives for change, such as public policy (Patten, 1996: 366–7). This chapter is a preliminary contribution to this objective.

Since the early 1980s, there has been an internal and external attack on the magnitude and purposes of government financing. Most recently, in a context of steady or falling tax rates, criticism has focused on budget deficits. Contrary to seemingly informed understandings, there is a debate of sorts surrounding government budget deficits (Savage, 1994: 100). However, this is not a mass, public debate; it is for the most part an internal, closed discussion amongst experts. The most striking characteristic of this debate is what appears to be an implicit agreement amongst the professionals involved that the conversation remain an internal one amongst themselves. The external face, which is familiar from television news, lacks qualification about deficits. Equivocation has been strikingly absent here, where a chorus of commentators from think tanks, corporations and other representatives of elite opinion have called for a fundamental revision of governmental utilization of deficit financing across the developed countries (Republican National Committee, 1994: 23–6). Over time, we might say that the sheer repetition of this call has become a 'dull background noise, a kind of invisible yet inescapable fact of life ... [an alternative view] then comes to sound like a curious, off key whine' (McQuaig, 1995: 13).

Gradually, a restructuring of the parameters of acceptable speech surrounding governmental finance and action has occurred in the OECD. The rhetoric of this campaign has been remarkable in character, volume and frequency, perhaps in an effort to communicate clear messages about arcane matters of economic and financial deliberation through the vehicle of tabloid journalism. This effort to generate public crises in the developed countries around budget deficits is best understood as a way of securing mass support for the reconstitution of hegemony. The immediate consequences of this struggle for influence over mass society are subtle but important changes in the bundles of mental schemata of perception and action which prefigure social relations by defining situations and providing interpretive procedures to us all (Bourdieu and Wacquant, 1992: 18). The best historical parallel to draw is with the campaign waged against inflation in the 1980s. Over time, this very successful effort to influence consciousness cemented into mass thinking the idea that inflation was universally bad, even when it was generally more favourable to wage earners and debtors than to ownership interests and creditors.

Data on budget deficits do not support the idea of crisis. The federal government of the USA, for example, has run a deficit more or less continuously since 1970, and had an accumulated national debt in fiscal 1995 of about $5 trillion, $3.6 trillion of which was held outside government trust funds (Galbraith and Darity, 1995: 5–6). This sum is equal to about 52 per cent of GDP, which is a proportion that has changed very little since 1939, when US Government debt as a percentage of GDP was around 47 per cent (Eisner, 1994: 95). There are many rich countries, such as Canada, that have what are perceived to be high deficits and accumulated debt, but which have nevertheless demonstrated solid growth in the post-recession years of the 1990s. Indeed, some very rich countries such as Belgium top the league tables in accumulated debt, at around 130 per cent of GDP in fiscal 1995 (*The Economist*, 3 February 1996: 105).

This data suggests there is no obvious or automatic link between fiscal rectitude in budgeting terms and economic success. Looking at the analytical supports, it starts to become clear why this link is not found. Oddly perhaps, given the absolutist nature of the deficit discourse, there is no numerical criteria of what is a good deficit and what a bad one (other than the assumption that larger deficits are worse than smaller ones). Inconveniently, public finance and economics do not provide criteria of rectitude. Any figures, therefore, have to be interpreted and considered in light of the macro-economic circumstances surrounding them before arriving at a reasonable view of the current state of affairs.

Precisely this point about the qualification required in the interpretation of numbers is lacking in the deficit discourse. The reason for this, in the first instance, is that anti-deficit thinking has its origins in the historical experience, political theory and adjustment by globalizing elites of what Bourdieu calls habitus, and not in the supposedly technical output of economic or financial analysis.[3] As Savage (1988: 1) has noted, in the USA the issue of balanced budgets ultimately refers to the debate about the appropriate role of the federal government in American society: it 'serves as an organizing principle that guides public policy and public discourse and acts as a symbol for competing visions'. This context for US fiscal policy developed as a response to the aversion to European 'corruption' that was important in the founding of the American republic.[4] A balanced budget symbolizes restraint of federal government authority. This represents, argues Savage, the triumph of Jeffersonian ideas about government, in which decentralization, restrictions on federal power and states' rights are emphasized over the (more European) Hamiltonian model, which values enhanced federal authority, reduced state competence and federal promotion of the economy. Van der Pijl (1994: 100) allows us to recast the US debate globally by connecting Lockeian premises to the Jeffersonian ideas, and Hobbesian ones to those of Hamilton.

The strong linkage of deficit politics to thinking about contemporary morality is evident in much of the anti-deficit writing. The most eloquent articulator of the relationship of moral constraints and deficits is Buchanan (1995: 347–55). Others have noted a 'norm' of budgetary balance, and how this suffered erosion under Keynesian influence in most parts of the world between 1933 and 1979 (Kettl, 1992: 17 and 21). Buchanan argues that the moral discipline (at least in public) that characterized the British Treasury and parliamentary elites in Keynes's era, and allowed for a regime of implicit norms to govern public finance there, could not be successfully translated to the American (or other) contexts, as Keynes's ideas about fiscal policy grew in popularity around the world. The greater number of self-seeking actors, and the decentralized nature of constitutional arrangements, meant that once Keynesian ideas had given the US Government the new role of economic manager, moral constraints were removed from deficit spending, and public expenditure could grow without moral hindrance (Buchanan, 1985: 1–6).

The problem with Buchanan's argument, however, is that if it is moral constraints which have been lost, why then have deficits only consistently characterized the period since 1970? What of the first 40 years or so after the Second World War, when Keynesian ideas were hegemonic in the USA and elsewhere, and yet deficits were still largely creatures of war (cf. Stern, 1964; Chamberlain, 1996)? The more probable explanation for recent growth in deficit figures, as Eisner argues, is that the relative lack of economic growth in recent times is at fault. He cites, for example, the Congressional Budget Office estimate that each 1 per cent of additional unemployment adds around $50 billion to the US federal budget deficit (Eisner, 1994: 94).

What of the other arguments made by the promoters of deficit discourse? Here it should be stressed that the purpose of this chapter is not to defend budget deficits as an optimal policy choice; rather, it is to peel back the 'common sense' propagated by deficit discourse, to relativize it, and to demonstrate that this mechanism of hegemony actually rests on an unsure footing in the sense that it is, in fact, a mechanism for the promotion of particular interests, and not just a 'technical' matter. The main arguments made against deficits are, first, that deficits 'crowd out' efficient private investment because the government soaks up all available cash; second, that deficits lower long-term savings rates; and third, that they cause inflation. To the extent that these issues are discussed outside policy-making circles they are presented in an unsophisticated way by using analogies to our own private incomes and expenditures. Just as one must manage one's personal finances with an eye to income and be aware of the opportunity cost of purchases, so, this view contends, governments face the same choices.

The assumption of an individual unit in isolation, upon which much of the deficit discourse is founded, must of course be rejected. Governments do not face similar constraints to individuals. For example, there is not a finite stock of financial resources awaiting investment in either private or public forms, as confirmed by evidence of falling interest rates in high deficit periods (Belton et al. 1995; Savage, 1994: 104). Neither can discrete national quantities of monetary resources be identified. Similarly, with savings rates, Eisner argues convincingly that they only exist in a circuit in relation to other activities. By reducing governmental outlays, pressures are brought to bear elsewhere. Mass layoffs of government employees, for example, might impose costs in terms of increased welfare expenses. The rapid increase in expenditure on private security in recent years in the USA is one example of flow-on effects, where private spending now overshadows public by 73 per cent, up from 57 per cent a decade ago (Blumenthal, 1993).

The implication of Eisner's view is that the orthodox economic arguments about deficits lack consideration of diachronic factors: the actual conditions of resource use themselves. The primary issue here, according to Eisner, is whether there are actually slack resources or not. If there are, then deficits are more likely than not to raise savings rates and assist output, employment and consumption (Eisner, 1994: 119). It follows that deficits do not necessarily bring inflation. It all depends on the state of things – the diachronic conditions – and if deficits generate purchasing power that would otherwise be lacking, they can mobilize economic life. On this logic, deficits can be 'too small' as well as 'too big' (Eisner, 1994: 102).

At its core, what jumps out from the economic literature on deficits is the low valuation placed on governmental activities as a feature of wealth-creation. Krugman, for instance, distinguishes governmental activity from 'real investment' that could have been used to raise productivity, and this seems to be a widely held view (Krugman, 1994b: 159; Rhoads, 1985). The very centre of the deficit discourse should therefore be more accurately understood as an attempt to transform the guiding set of norms generated by the Keynesian welfare state rather than a concern with changing narrow fiscal matters. In political terms, what is interesting about this discourse is that it both represents itself as being a question of necessity rather than considered judgement – judgement being supposedly unnecessary in such a situation – and acknowledges no distributional impacts between social forces as a consequence of its implementation.

While an in-depth account of the mechanisms through which the deficit discourse is produced and distributed is beyond the scope of this chapter, three important processes are identified here. The first of these focuses upon public, legally-constituted authority, or institutions of the state. Pre-eminent amongst government departments everywhere is the Treasury or Ministry of Finance. The budget process, which is usually secret, is the main means through which the Treasury establishes its view of what are appropriate and inappropriate policy choices. Budgetary responsibility provides a point of entry for the Treasury to review existing arrangements of all kinds in its own terms. Assets can be sold and governance patterns altered in ways that would otherwise not be possible through the normal policy-making machinery of government. Constant references to deficit problems vastly empower the policy effectiveness of the Treasury in encounters with officials from other agencies who do not have this strategic financial oversight. The community then, is likely to see Treasury officials as those 'in authority', and to inflate the importance of their discourse accordingly (Lincoln, 1994: 4).

A second means through which deficit discourse appears to be generated relates to expertise and professional knowledge, and the judgemental systems which surround it. This is Lincoln's second sense of authority, where an audience is prepared to listen and follow the counsel of the speaker, because that speaker is 'an authority' in that they possess (or are supposed to possess) understanding, insight or experience which has made them of eminence, to be deferred to. Academics fall into this category, especially in the natural sciences and to the extent that they mimic the Cartesian model in the social sciences. Economics is the most successful social science in this regard. The judgements of economists about what a prudent deficit might be are much weightier than those of politicians, even if the economist in question actually has no understanding of public finance. This characteristic provides an important avenue in which neo-liberal ideas about appropriate (and inappropriate) types of state intervention can influence deficit discourse. A more institutionalized form of these judgements can be found in the bond rating agencies which publish credit ratings on major securities issues (Sinclair, 1994). Their views on appropriate financial arrangements are eagerly followed by potential bond issuers, who have a strong interest in altering their own activities to secure a better rating and lower their costs of borrowing. Ratings may also have crucial public impacts on voters and on stockholders, who treat the agencies as important authorities (Hayward and Salvaris, 1994).

The final means of discourse construction to highlight here is market behaviour, principally in the financial sector, where the value of currencies and of bonds, stocks and other assets can fluctuate significantly with great consequences for governments, corporations and society (Woodward, 1994). In mainstream accounts, markets are perceived typically as eminently rational and thus excellent means of judgement about matters such as deficits. However, research is increasingly highlighting the short-termism and less than rational character of financial behaviour (Heisler, 1994). Markets are not, in fact, an unquestionable source of value-free opinion, but simply the most developed (and well-resourced) form of the short-termist, speculative mentality I referred to above as synchronic (Cox with Sinclair, 1996: 174–88). The fear of financial market judgement, which has developed with the re-emergence of international capital mobility, has promoted the validity of market conceptions, and is an important element promoting deficit discourse.

Prognoses for investment, knowledge and governance

What follows from this identification of a deficit discourse? The important questions which emerge from this discussion of the conditions and construction of the deficit discourse relate to its likely future impact on the world we live in. A series of prognoses are considered below, organized in three broad fields: investment, knowledge and governance.[5]

Investment

Three arguments about investment and fiscal rectitude are made here. The first is what can be called the deflection argument, which is essentially about a self-defence mechanism for synchronic investment norms. These norms seek to legitimate speculation in the non-real economy as worthy, socially-valid and respectable activities. However, since what Susan Strange has called casino capitalism took off after the collapse of the Bretton Woods order, average real wages have remained flat in the West, and especially in the USA (Strange, 1986; Reich, 1991: 206). Given the dominance within the nascent hegemony of synchronic norms, this mental schemata excludes distinctions amongst the types of investment being pursued. In this system of thinking, all investment has utility, and the real economy has no privilege over others. Accordingly, there must be some exogenous force, outside the framework of investment itself, which acts as a drag on wage growth. In the 1970s and 1980s, this exogenous force was understood to be labour unions, who could be blamed for the onset of inflation. In the 1990s, these unions were in retreat. Deficit spending has now become the perfect target for deflecting concern away from persistent problems of low growth. The most attractive thing about this for globalizing elites is the fact that the flat real wages of workers can be blamed on the demands of these same people as voters for all manner of pork barrel policies. That most of the US deficit is in fact due to demographically-driven entitlement programmes, which reflect the cyclic nature of a more synchronic economy, is not, of course, widely appreciated (Peterson, 1993).

The second argument suggests that concerns with efficiency in the narrow or 'allocative' sense have given the synchronic hegemony a new militancy. This new militancy, which is actually a reflection of pervasive economic insecurity even within globalizing elite circles, opposes the maintenance of socialized risk in a context of re-emergent international capital mobility (Thomas and Sinclair, forthcoming). This harder edge can be seen in the venom reserved for welfare mothers, the roll-back of affirmative action in California, and heightened expectations on the part of employers concerning working hours and labour intensity.[6] The anxiety amongst elites is revealing of their own understanding of the budget discourse and what it means. The new militancy is not just an external development: it reflects a struggle inside the leading edge of the hegemony itself. White and Wildavsky have argued that in Washington, the deficit is seen as a sign of ineptitude. The deficit became a 'symbol of order', and its persistence seems to have generated the view amongst elites, especially those in the political regime itself, that they were 'failing to govern the nation' (White and Wildavsky, 1990: 428). Focusing on the deficit through rhetoric that demonizes welfare mothers perhaps acts as a salve for the wounded confidence of these globalizing elites. Increasingly, this new militancy is being transmitted in professionalized form, through the agency of bond rating agencies and the other surveillance and judgemental systems (Sinclair, 1994; Pauly, 1997).

The third argument concerns policy autonomy. The more obvious claim here is that OECD nations are seeking to lower their deficits so as to avoid leaving themselves open to political influence by their creditors. This is the implication of the work on the institutionalization of credit undertaken by Epstein and Gintis, which identifies a world of uncertain, reluctant lenders and borrowers, and thus qualified capital mobility (Epstein and Gintis, 1995: 698–9). A less intuitive argument, but perhaps a more feasible one, focuses on the effects of making a crisis out of budget deficits, so as to generate external sources of fiscal and more general policy discipline. External sources, not being subject to the same constraints as those coming from internal elite sources, might be understood to 'tell it how it is', with no equivocation or qualification. My view, then, is that rather than wanting to see governments escape external constraints to a world of autonomy, globalizing elites are actually endeavouring to terminate national policy autonomy by attracting these sort of negative judgements. So, for example, McQuaig (1995: 44) found that financial market elites in Toronto actually sought a downgrade of Government of Canada bonds by the New York credit rating agencies. Policy autonomy was the last thing they wanted to reinforce.

Knowledge

Three arguments about the knowledge or ideas implications of deficit discourse are proposed. The first of these evaluates the reductive intellectual impact of the deficit discourse on how problems are conceived. A central feature of the impact of the deficit mantra is the effect it has on the way problems are considered. Not only does the discourse potentially limit the schemata for thinking about the deficit problem itself, as discussed above, but it also reduces how other problems may be conceived. These limits emerge from the orthodoxy of economic and financial analysis, which is fast becoming one of the most important modes of contemporary human judgement and expression.

Since the deficit discourse has emphasized the strategic role of deficit reduction in cross-national competition, perhaps as a means of popularizing the agenda, the tools used to make judgements about deficits – the schematic tools – have acquired a new salience. We can discern a 'financialization of knowledge' and an exclusion of 'soft' variables in progress. The society where financialization and empiricization is most developed is the USA, but the importation of American accounting standards and the internationalization of business practices is increasing the salience of this form of knowledge outside the USA at a rapid pace. This process is linked to the hegemony of professional knowledge over local or situational knowledge, and the denigration of experience and institutional memory that are the results of successive efforts to 're-engineer' organizations (Hammer and Champy, 1993). Within the deficit discourse itself, discussions of the savings 'rate' reflect this mentality, in which financial indicators, rather than diachronic considerations about organically-planned and executed productivity improvement, are held to be key (Gramlich, 1995: 171).

The second argument looks again at the private analogy in deficit thinking. Western culture places a very high value on pragmatic knowledge focused, ostensibly, on solving immediate social problems. Discourse, or attempts to make real what is said to be meaningful, tends to be organized in ways which disguise the contested nature of its own assumptions through appeals to seemingly everyday problems with which we are all familiar. This appeal to common sense is the reverse of what we might see as the epistemic authority strategy, which utilizes agents of high repute and is also a crucial aspect of the social construction of fiscal rectitude (Lincoln, 1994: 3). In the deficit context, as we have seen, the way this appeal to common sense is achieved is by invoking an analogy between the individual's own bank account and the government's expenditure. 'We can't spend more than we earn, because if we do, our checks will bounce', seems to go this refrain. 'If it makes sense for us, then it does for the (profligate/wanton/immoral/sinful) government too.' This is an enormously powerful mechanism for the articulators of the discourse to bring into play, as we have discussed, because it avoids having to explain how government finances actually work (or, indeed, to come to an understanding of them). It appeals to the most resourceless part of the population who do not have access to credit, and it has an intergenerational appeal, perhaps along the lines of the 'Four Yorkshiremen' sketch.[7] The falseness of it needs little reiteration. Governments are agents of collective action, and enjoy the most superior creditworthiness because of their unlimited taxing powers.[8] The rhetorical effect of this argument in delegitimizing anti-neo-liberal social criticism, however, cannot be discounted.

The final argument about the knowledge implications of the nascent hegemony concerns its effect on changing norms and values. Of all neo-liberal policy platforms, deficit cutting is perhaps closest to common prejudice. It provides an entry point for globalizing elites in different parts of the world to pursue the full range of their agenda. As the most intuitively obvious, it is also the easiest to sell to a wary community. If done convincingly, if it is a 'good sell', then other aspects of the synchronic orthodoxy might be experimented with. There is a very subtle process of re-education of both local elites and hegemonized communities taking place here. To understand it more clearly will require extensive research on business schools, on patterns of foreign student recruitment and so on. Possibly the most interesting line for further research is the relationship between the deficit discourse 'Trojan horse' and privatization of governmental services. What is apparent without further work is that deficits provide a crisis context for the insertion and acceptance of otherwise negatively perceived positions.

Governance

Three arguments are also made about the governance implications of the nascent deficit hegemony. The first suggests that deficit cutting, the US balanced budget amendment proposal and fiscal responsibility legislation are all features of the new constitutionalism project. The new constitutionalist dimension of the deficit discourse has two aspects. The first is the more obvious, and concerns proposals such as balanced budget amendments or fiscal responsibility acts, which attempt to tie the hands of subsequent administrations should they perhaps become motivated to use fiscal policy as an electoral tool. Parallels can be seen here with initiatives to give central banks formal independence from executive agencies that serve ministers, the origins of which can be found in the aftermath of the subjugation of the Federal Reserve to the US Treasury during the Second World War.[9] More subtly, we can also discern a new constitutionalist agenda to allow the financial markets to have more leverage over government policy, by introducing commercial debt management and by freeing government pension funds to invest where they see fit rather than just in government assets. The agenda is to reduce progressively the advantages which governments enjoy in the market, thereby increasing the costs of future deficit finance and reducing its attractiveness as a policy option.

The second argument is that deficit cutting is actually a more effective form of new constitutionalism because it generates less opposition, and thus is more likely to succeed than other forms. From a global governance point of view, where the focus is on diffuse forms of control, deficit discourse can be seen as a low cost and thus potentially more effective option than many alternatives. The argument is that deficit cutting is infrastructural and incremental – when done well – and thus likely to encounter less direct opposition. Over time it can build up an understanding, and thus a basis for governance, within the hegemonized population about new ways of doing things (and not doing them). But not all deficit discourse is created equal, and some will be less effective than others in generating opposition. The most effective forms will use attrition, productivity gains and professionalization strategies (such as citizens' or consumers' charters) to demobilize opposition. On the other hand, short sharp shock strategies may also work.[10] Strategies are likely to be based on the circumstances actually encountered.

The final argument about the governance implications of the nascent hegemony of deficit discourse is that it is hard for elites to maintain public focus on this matter over time, as the 1996 US presidential election demonstrated. However, as might be argued from the British experience, strategies focused on adjusting schemata of perception and practice can be pursued without mass support. Indeed, the absence of a high profile campaign – such as those pursued by the British Prime Minister Margaret Thatcher, for instance – might be a source of governance strength over the long haul if it limits the potential for organized, effective opposition.

Conclusion

The foregoing discussion was a first cut at the issues raised by the advent of the deficit discourse. It barely considers the varying degrees to which this discourse operates or does not work in different parts of the world order. Ideally, it has suggested some useful lines of thought for further research and conceptual development. What follows is a series of preliminary conclusions. The first is that deficit cutting is actually only properly understood as a political development, and not the objective or neutral process of technical correction it is represented to be. It is a process (or processes) pursued by elite interests; it can be thought of as a covert space of interelite competition, and one in which a synchronic social hegemony is in the process of being constructed.

It also seems reasonable to say at this point that deficit balancing norms and the *degree* and *form* of fiscal rectitude are likely to vary in influence, even as some sort of broad orthodoxy amongst globalizing elites is established across space. Although deficit elimination appeals to common-sense notions of financial management, mass publics seem unlikely to maintain the attention required to secure them within an explicit balanced budget hegemony over the long run. This in turn suggests the probable recourse to infrastructural and incremental strategies. Moreover, small increases in prosperity may blunt the short-run motivation for deficit-cutting when new, unexpected revenues improve the fiscal position, as seems to be the case currently in the USA.

A crucial feature which this chapter has only started to consider is the nature of global processes of promulgation, modification and adoption of deficit discourse. As in other areas of contemporary economic and financial life, there seems to be a transnationalization tendency at work here, which is linked to the spread of American business and policy norms. Given this, and likely future resistance to this development in other parts of the world order, research also needs to be focused on alternative public finance agendas, such as those in the rapidly developing societies of East Asia, where diachronic norms have been hegemonic in recent years. Here we might anticipate resistance to the mental orthodoxy of deficit discourse.

Notes

1. This chapter was first presented at the 1996 annual meeting of the International Studies Association in San Diego. Subsequently, it was also given at the 'Globalization and its Critics' workshop at the University of Sheffield, and in revised form to departmental seminars at the University of Sussex and the University of Arizona. For useful comments, I thank Bill Dixon, Bud Duvall, Randall Germain, David Gibbs, Roger Haydon, Martin Hewson, Paulette Kurzer, John MacLean, Cary Nederman, Rob O'Brien, Ronen Palan, Jonathan Perraton, Herman Schwartz and Lord Skidelsky. Responsibility for the arguments remains mine.
2. See White and Wildavsky (1990: xv–xvi, cited in Wildavsky, 1992: 462).
3. Lury defines habitus as a set 'of dispositions, a system which organizes the individual's capacity to act' (Lury, 1996: 83). It can also be thought of as a framework of taste and preference.
4. Savage (1988: 94) notes that post-colonial Americans thought:

   > Corruption was most easily achieved when unscrupulous ministers took advantage of speculative opportunities offered by a large public debt and the government's need for revenues. The presence of a substantial public debt, or an abundance of excess revenues, justified a minister's claim that his agency required additional employees to administer the government's finances, thus enlarging his ability to offer graft and patronage.

5. The ontology I incorporate here is adapted from Cox's essay, 'Social Forces, States, and World Orders: Beyond International Relations Theory' (Cox with Sinclair, 1996).
6. This new militancy has strong links with Stephen Gill's (1995: 411) discussion of disciplinary neo-liberalism.
7. A Monty Python comedy sketch in which four self-made men discuss the hardships of their youth, trying to outdo each other in describing the extent of their privations.
8. Even that bastion of deficit discourse, *The Economist*, has repudiated the private analogy (*The Economist*, 10 February 1996: 90).
9. Caner Bakir helped me make this connection. See Clifford (1965).
10. This is the view taken by former New Zealand Minister of Finance, Sir Roger Douglas (Douglas, 1994).

8
Technology and Globalization: Assessing Patterns of Interaction[1]

Michael Talalay

> Two vectors shape the world – technology and globalization.
>
> Theodore Levitt (1983: 102)

Open any scholarly book or popular article on the shape of the future and two ideas leap out: technology and globalization. Despite their evident importance, little agreement exists on what they mean, how they interact, and whether they work for good or for ill. The only certainty is a lack of consensus. Start with globalization. Some commentators laud it as a beneficial process, leading to increased wealth and a peaceful world community. Others view it as regrettable, eroding national sovereignty, destroying local culture and marginalizing much of the world's population. Analysts equally disagree on the influence of technology. Some hail it as the primrose path to leisure and prosperity, while others damn it as socially divisive and the road to an environmental hell on earth. The one area of agreement seems to be that globalization and technology will continue to exert a major influence on all our lives.

Technology and globalization do shape the world. They also shape each other. This chapter examines some key aspects of this interaction and then asks what are some of its likely consequences for the issues of IPE.

Globalization as practice

The term globalization has been used and misused in a wide variety of ways. It has become a buzzword and a polemic, and it has been appropriated by different academic disciplines in ways that suit themselves. Some scholars, notably economists and business theorists, define it in terms of global markets, the transnational corporation (TNC), and the internationalization of production (e.g., Dicken, 1992; Dunning, 1993a). Others, among them students of international relations, conceive of globalization in terms of the future of the nation-state, be it the creation of a global system of states or alternatively the eclipse of the sovereign state (McGrew 1992b; M. Smith, 1992). Still others (Harvey, 1989; Giddens, 1990) relate globalization to modernity and post-modernity, terms that are themselves contentious.

Through all these different views runs a common strand. It is based on the erosion of what has been called 'the tyranny of distance' (Blainey 1983; Henderson 1992). This is simply the idea that traditional geographic constraints have lost much of their potency in the face of modern technologies of transportation and communication. This is certainly the view of Anthony Giddens (1990: 64) who writes that globalization is 'the intensification of world-wide social relations which link distant localities in such a way that local happenings are shaped by events occurring many miles away and vice versa'. And Malcolm Waters (1995: 3) interprets globalization similarly as 'a social process in which the constraints of geography on social and cultural arrangements recede'. The essence of globalization lies in this changing nature of geographical relations.

Equally important, as both Waters and Giddens emphasize, is the reflexive nature of this process. In the concluding part of the sentence just quoted, Waters goes on to say that not only are the constraints of geography receding but also that the actors themselves perceive this to be happening. Businessmen, politicians, journalists, environmental activists: all are aware of the growing irrelevance of traditional geographical restrictions. The intellectual debate over the meaning of globalization has itself become part of globalization. This reflexivity makes it possible to conceive of globalization not merely as process but more interestingly as practice: as something that is consciously pursued (see Chapter 2 in this volume).

This view of globalization as practice puts the emphasis on agency. It focuses attention on the actions of individuals and organizations. It implies that globalization is 'something' to be chosen or worked towards (or against) rather than merely a state of affairs or an impersonal process. As Ruigrok and van Tulder (1995: 9) emphasize, 'Globalization is best considered as a strategy and not an obtained reality.' It is subject – as is any practice – to politics, where different interests compete and co-operate in an attempt to further their own, often parochial objectives. Globalization may be a buzzword, but it nevertheless reflects a real phenomenon where the traditional constraints of geography are receding and where individuals and organizations increasingly base their actions on this erosion of the tyranny of distance.

Technology and economic growth

Technological innovation lies at the heart of economic growth. It is the prime factor behind Joseph Schumpeter's (1950: 81–6) 'gales of creative destruction' that are the essence of capitalism, distinguishing it from traditional societies and giving it such a dynamic force. Though this approach is not the orthodoxy of conventional, neo-classical economics, there is growing recognition that technology and technological change are the key factors in growth and the generation of wealth.[2]

There are three different types of technological change: incremental change, new products or processes, and paradigm shifts.[3] Incremental improvement is by far the most common type. Adding another cycle to the washing machine; putting disc or anti-locking brakes on cars; making the manufacture of widgets more efficient: these are all examples of incremental improvement. The second type of technological change is the development of a new product or process. The invention of the video cassette recorder and the compact disc, the creation of financial derivatives and the world-wide markets for them, the use of advanced manufacturing techniques such as statistical process control or manufacturing resource planning: all are examples of technological change in the sense of new products and processes. Far more so than incremental improvement, these can have profound implications for wealth and power, within industries, between industries, and on a global basis. This is particularly so if, as in the case of information technology (IT), the new technology becomes generic: an enabling factor in virtually every sector from heavy manufacturing to personal services.

The third type of technological change is what can be called a paradigm shift.[4] This is a change in technology so fundamental that it alters the very nature of society. The steam engine and electricity are two historical examples of such a shift, as was the invention of movable type (Diebert, 1996). A move from fossil fuels to hydrogen as the main source of energy could signal a similar shift in the near future (Talalay, 1996). However, despite its undisputed benefits in terms of reducing pollution and ushering in an era of renewable energy, the shift from a hydro-carbon to a hydrogen society may well never happen. The fact that a technology is possible does not mean that it will be adopted. Technological change is of profound importance, but it is not external to the global political economy. It is not something that takes place in isolation in an ivory tower or a research institute. Neither is the course of technological development 'deterministic' or inevitable in any sense. Its nature, its direction and its effects are governed by the complex interplay of social, political, economic and cultural influences.

There have been numerous attempts to explain how these influences work (e.g., Dosi, 1988). Perhaps the most useful approach is to view technological change as being driven by the attempt to overcome perceived problems. These need not be by themselves technological. They can be economic, as in the need to reduce costs. They can be social, as in the need to overcome labour shortages. They can be military, as in the need to develop lighter, stronger materials for aircraft performance. They can be political and legislative, as in the impetus to develop electric cars as a result of emissions regulations in California. This is the approach Thomas Hughes (1983) puts forward in his analysis of the development of systems of electrification in the USA, Germany and Britain. The key to his argument lies in the recognition that innovation and technological change are 'problem driven' as opposed to 'science pushed'. A number of other writers have arrived at a similar conclusion. The authors of the MIT study of the world automotive industry state quite definitely that it was a number of social and economic problems in post-war Japan that gave rise to those technological changes that they termed 'lean production' (Womack *et al.*, 1990). The same phenomenon was recorded by Tracy Kidder (1982) in his immensely readable story of how Data General developed its 32-bit super minicomputer in response to the knowledge that its main rival, DEC, had just brought its own offering, the VAX, to the market place. More generally, Michael Porter (1990), in his identification of those factors that lead to competitive advantage, emphasizes that the presence of problems (and of course the *recognition of their existence*) is crucial for the continued success of firms, to the extent that they need to anticipate problems and perhaps even create them.

Patterns of interaction

Globalization increasingly dominates political, economic and social practice. Technology acts as the main driver of economic change and wealth creation. How do they interact? The answer depends, of course, upon the purposes and the inventiveness of the writer. Scope exists for volumes on this subject. I propose merely to touch upon four different patterns of interaction:

1. technology as the key enabling factor in the practice of globalization;
2. technology and the globalization of culture;
3. the globalization of technology as a political issue;
4. the global spread of technology itself.

Technology as an enabling factor

Modern technologies of communications and transportation have allowed information, goods and people to move around the globe as previously they may have moved around their neighbourhood and river valley, shrinking distances both physically and psychologically, spreading knowledge and ideas far more rapidly than ever before, and confounding the definition of the local. Technology is therefore the *sine qua non* for globalization. Without technology, globalization could not exist.

Physical distance is a function of time and cost. The length in crow-flying miles from New York to London or Paris to Tokyo has remained much the same over the years, but in practical terms these cities are closer to each other than even 20 years ago, considerably closer than 100 or 200 years ago, and unimaginably closer than on the eve of the last millennium. This contraction of distance is due to the increased speed and decreased cost of transportation and communications made possible by technological innovation. Whereas the pilgrims took weeks to get from Plymouth to Massachusetts, a modern ocean liner would take only just over four days, a jet plane can whisk you across in about seven hours, and with Concorde it is possible (in a certain sense) to land in New York before taking off from London. Where a passage to India would have lasted several weeks around the time of the mutiny in 1857, today British Airways or Air India can get you there in less than half a day.

Land transport has seen similar shrinking of distances. First the canals, then the railroads, then the motor car and the highway have all made for a much smaller world. The same is taking place with communications. The telegraph, the telephone, the radio and the television have now made global communications virtually instantaneous. All of this has been accompanied by a reduction of cost. The erosion of the tyranny of distance is not only possible but affordable. To those on the Internet, sending messages around the world is the price of a local phone call, and where local calls are free global communications can be costless as well as instantaneous.

Not only have these developments made the world a smaller place, but they have also enabled globalization as *practice* to develop. The recognition – on the part say of a London businessman – that Manchester in New Hampshire is not much farther away in time and money than Manchester in the UK makes globalization possible as a strategy. Japanese and American companies set up electronic component assembly operations in the countries of South-East Asia in order to take advantage of large pools of low-cost, semi-skilled labour. Even local authorities or town councils, hardly exemplars of globalization one would have thought, now find themselves faced with a global marketplace. They compete to attract industry not against an adjacent county or nearby city but rather against locations scattered half-way around the world. The same happens culturally and socially. Holidays increasingly involve overseas travel, and wherever tourists travel they are likely to recognize many of the periodicals displayed on the kiosks. Newspapers such as the *International Herald Tribune* and the *Financial Times* print editions around the globe, allowing readers all over the world to share the same information.

It is of fundamental importance to recognize that technology enables globalization to be practised in almost every aspect of social existence. What Giddens (1990: 108) calls 'the primacy of place' has been largely destroyed by what he terms 'time-space distanciation', or what Harvey (1989: 240), in more intuitively appropriate language calls 'time-space compression' (but see Chapter 2 in this volume). While it would be stretching reality somewhat to describe the entire planet as one's back yard,[5] technology in the form of cheaper and faster transportation and communications is certainly leading in that direction.

The erosion of the tyranny of distance also contains a large psychological element. The 'foreign' is becoming less so. From my house in west London, I can comfortably stroll to Indian, Nepalese, Chinese, Italian, Greek, English, French, American, Thai, Polish, Caribbean, Japanese, Korean and Mexican restaurants. At my local newsagent's, I can find an even greater babel of papers and periodicals. On television every evening, I can see what is happening half-way around the world as clearly as if it were next door. Even more pronounced, my physical territory – that part of the world which to me is *local* – consists of a number of separate areas neither contiguous nor necessarily close to where I live. I feel equally at home in Toronto and in London. Val d'Isére in the French Alps is more familiar to me than Wandsworth across the Thames, and I can communicate in English as easily in the one as in the other. Here again, technology plays a critical enabling role. Because 'strangeness' or 'foreigness' works as a bar to much of social interaction, technology encourages the practice of globalization by helping to foster a wider feeling of familiarity and a less geographically bound conception of the local.

If, as Waters (1995: 136 and 164) says, globalization 'implies greater connectedness and de-territorialization' and may be defined as 'a reduction in the geographical constraints on social arrangements', then technology is central to globalization in reducing the physical tyranny of distance and breaking the psychological connection between geography and foreignness. Only because of faster, better, cheaper and more comprehensive systems of transportation and communications can globalization be 'practised'. Only because technology removes the constraints of geography can strategy and tactics – be they national, corporate or individual – be hinged upon an increasingly globalized world.

Technology and culture

As an old man in 1898, when asked what he viewed as the decisive factor in modern history, Bismarck was said to have replied, 'The fact that the North Americans speak English.'[6] He was right. Given that Britain and the USA have been the leading political and economic powers for the past 250 years and given their dominance of science and technology, it is hardly surprising that Anglo-American products, values, pop music and media as well as the English language have become the basis of a global culture.

This development has, of course, led to charges of 'cultural imperialism'. No doubt the practice of globalization – facilitated by technology in the guise of Hollywood, CNN, BBC, Sky, MTV and so on – can be motivated intentionally by a desire to spread a particular set of cultural values (see Chapter 3 in this volume). Charlene Barshefsky, at the time the Deputy United States Trade Representative (the second highest ranking American trade official) was quoted in a *New Yorker* profile as saying that trade agreements 'become vehicles for the spread of democracy and American values' (Walsh, 1996: 88). This desire to promote American values is of course hardly novel. The messianic strand in US foreign policy has been commented upon many times by scholars of IR and can be traced back at least to Woodrow Wilson. What is new, however, is the way in which technology enables cultural influences to spread faster and wider than ever before as a consequence of the global movement of information and people. Moreover, this will happen without any intent on the part of governments either to disseminate or to block any particular ideology or set of values. What may often appear to be cultural imperialism is in many cases merely the apparently unstoppable influence of technology. With the growth of the Internet and the World Wide Web, Bismarck's prediction is coming true. On the back of modern technology and the consequent spread of English as the global language, the entire world is heading for a common culture.

This globalization of culture is a far more complex and multidirectional process than critics of 'cultural imperialism' would have us believe (see, e.g., Tomlinson, 1991 and Chapter 3 in this volume). If you are listening in Nairobi to the Rolling Stones version of the Mississippi delta blues classic 'Little Red Rooster', just whose culture is having what done to it? Technology, by enabling the free flow of ideas and of people and of goods, opens up all societies to a multiplicity of cultural influences and enables the individuals in those societies to chose what elements they want. The result is not homogeneity but rather pluralism and cultural diversity, the enrichment of all cultures by their being fertilized by the challenges posed by others. Of course, this is a process of change and can be threatening. Moreover, some customs and ways of life will probably disappear (as they have in the past under other pressures such as conquest). What is inevitable about the influence of technology is neither cultural imperialism nor any particular brand of global culture but rather cultural competition, resulting in a world culture continuously enriched by multiple and diverse influences. Technology certainly enables the English language and Anglo-American values and lifestyles to set a global cultural baseline, but it equally facilitates this base being constantly influenced from other cultures and societies and being moderated everywhere by local variations.

A second and more subtle way in which technology is leading to the spread of a global culture starts with the proposition that technology is the key factor in economic development, or in other words that technological innovation lies at the heart of the creation of wealth. Some very compelling evidence in support of this thesis comes from the historical analyses of global levels of growth and industrialization put forward by Angus Maddison (1995) and Paul Bairoch (1982, 1996). Maddison has shown how the rate of growth in wealth after the industrial revolution far exceeded that prior to it (see Table 8.1).

Table 8.1 Levels of world economic performance, 1500–1992

	1500	*1820*	*1992*
World population (millions)	425	1068	5441
GDP per capita (1990 $)	565	651	5145
World GDP (1990 $billions)	240	695	27 995
World exports (1990 $billions)	N/A	7	3786

N/A: not applicable.
Source: Maddison (1995: 19). Reproduced with the permission of Development Centre Studies, *Monitoring the World Economy*, 1820/1992, copyright OECD, 1995.

From 1820 onwards, just after the Napoleonic era and at more or less the beginning of the industrial revolution in Western Europe (except for Britain where it had begun around the middle of the eighteenth century), the rate of growth skyrocketed. From 1820 to 1992, world GDP increased at an annual rate over six times greater than during the period from 1500 to 1820. However, as population was growing three times more rapidly during this later period, faster GDP growth was only to be expected. What is astonishing, however, is the increase in the rate of growth of GDP per capita. From 1500 to 1820, it averaged (at an annual compound rate) 0.04 per cent, whereas from 1820 to 1992 it was 1.21 per cent. In other words, the annual rate of world per capita GDP growth since the Industrial Revolution has been *30 times greater* than it was in the 300 years before that revolution (Maddison, 1995: 20).

This growth, as Maddison also points out, was not evenly distributed. It took place primarily in North America and Western Europe: precisely those areas which Bairoch identifies as having most successfully industrialized. Taking the period from 1750 to 1980, Bairoch has calculated the level of industrialization (relative to Britain in 1900) of most of the world. The gross figures are interesting in themselves, but what paints a remarkably clear picture are these numbers adjusted for population growth to show changes in per capita levels of industrialization over this period. This pattern (summarized in Table 8.2) closely matches the growth of wealth as measured by per capita GNP.

Moreover, as Bairoch makes clear, this lead in industry and unparalleled growth in wealth correspond not merely with technology but with technological innovation. Bairoch emphasizes the essential role in this process of 'new technologies', ranging from the mechanization of the cotton mills to the new steel-making processes to the rise of the chemical industry. It was the ability of the major industrial powers in

Table 8.2 Per capita levels of industrialization (UK in 1900 = 100)

	1750	*1800*	*1860*	*1913*	*1928*	*1953*	*1980*
EUROPE	8	8	17	45	52	90	267
United Kingdom	10	16	64	115	122	210	325
France	9	9	20	59	78	90	265
Germany	8	8	15	85	101	138	393
Switzerland	7	10	26	87	90	167	354
Russia/USSR	6	6	8	20	20	73	252
Canada	n/a	5	7	46	82	185	379
USA	4	9	21	126	182	354	629
Japan	7	7	7	20	30	40	353
THIRD WORLD	7	6	4	2	3	5	17
China	8	6	4	3	4	5	24
Indian sub-continent	7	6	3	2	3	5	16
Brazil	n/a	n/a	4	7	10	13	55
Mexico	n/a	n/a	5	7	9	12	41
WORLD	7	6	7	21	28	48	103

Source: Bairoch (1982: 281).
n/a: not available.

the nineteenth century to develop and exploit these new areas of technology that largely accounted for their rise. Simply put, over the last 250 years technological innovation underlay the successful pursuit of that industrialization which correlated very closely with increased growth.

The question now becomes, why did technological innovation lead to successful industrialization in these parts of the world? Why not elsewhere, where technology was equally if not more advanced just prior to the Industrial Revolution? The answer lies in the apparent necessity of a particular culture as the essential precondition for exploiting technology. This is the culture of the Enlightenment, which is essentially that of modernity. It led to the rise of Europe, allowing a poor and backward part of the globe – one that was technologically behind both the Chinese and Ottoman empires around the year 1500 – to overtake them both and literally conquer the earth (McNeill, 1982; Kennedy, 1989). The example of the one non-Western nation that has become a major economic power is the exception that proves the point. Japan has seen two major spurts of growth since the middle of the nineteenth century, both coinciding with and due to periods of dramatic Westernization. The first of these took place after the Meiji restoration in 1861; the second during the American occupation at the end of the Second World War. Not only is this clearly supported by Bairoch's figures, but it has recently been confirmed by a leading Japanese opposition politician who has called for a third dose of Westernization in order for Japan to be able to continue to compete economically with the West (as reported in *The Economist*, March 9, 1996).

As the per capita GDP figures demonstrate, with the exception of those fortunate few countries sitting on a large pool of oil, Westernization is the essential ingredient for growth and development. The conscious adoption of the culture of the Enlightenment by a society is the central prerequisite for achieving a sustainable level of wealth. Only thereby is it possible to capitalize upon technology, the single most important factor for economic success. There is only so far that technology can develop without a broader 'scientific' base (Pacey, 1990: 44–5);[7] and it was this base, essentially the rationalism and modernism of the Enlightenment, that accounted for the triumph of the West.

Technology is central to the globalization of culture. On the one hand, technology 'pushes' a global culture through the ubiquity of the English language and Anglo-American media and pop culture. Arguably far more interesting and less obvious, however, is the 'pull' argument: that is, the conscious choice of modernity in order to reap the benefits of wealth that only technology can give.[8] The point here is not that technology leads to modernity but rather the very opposite: without adopting modernity a society is in no position to take advantage of technology to prosper. In both ways, technology and the globalization of culture go hand in hand.

Technology and international politics

Technology has increasingly become globalized as a political issue. Where in the past only military technology had been discussed at the international level, now all aspects of technology have become the focus of multilateral conferences and of bilateral (dis)agreements. Trade negotiations between China and the US have recently revolved around compact disc and software piracy (Walsh, 1996). The Uruguay round of trade negotiations extended the GATT rules to services and intellectual property. Fierce battles rage over copyright, patent protection, and the issue of intellectual property rights. The use of satellite-based global positioning systems for international air traffic control (Hayward,

1997) promises to solve the problem of controlling increasingly congested air routes, but the US military have set up and currently control this Global Navigation Satellite System (GNSS), with implications that are both commercial (limited contracts for non-US companies compared with the microwave alternatives?) and political (will the USA give military users priority at the expense of commercial airlines?). The whole issue of access to, and exploitation of, the global commons has become highly politicized and subject to numerous international conferences, arguments and agreements (Vogler, 1992).

In the globalization of the politics of technology, three distinctly different practices are going on. The first is increased co-operation. Examples are the Montreal agreement on chloro-flouro-carbons and increased co-operation on the Arctic by the countries around the littoral. All of these initiatives demonstrate how technology has brought to the fore issues that cross state boundaries. The problems have become global, and consequently the solutions require a response that is itself global.

The second type of practice has to do with what Susan Strange (1988) calls structural power, the ability to determine the rules of the game, be it the Bretton Woods agreement and the international monetary system or the global standards for high definition television. In any arena, being able to set the standards and regulations allows one to do so in a manner favourable to one's own interests. What we see here is an attempt to shape in various areas the global rules by which technology works. The law of the sea provides a good example of this with the argument over who has the right to mine manganese nodules from the deep sea bed. The USA, with its ability actually to get at these nodules, wanted unrestricted access and exploitation; Third World countries, on the other hand, lobbied for control over access and sharing out the proceeds. A similar argument is currently under way on the subject of intellectual property rights: who has access to technology and at what cost?

The third type of practice in the globalization of technology is contention as opposed to co-operation or rule-making. A prime example here is the existence of cultural content strictures in national media. Both the French and the Canadians have notably come into conflict with the USA over this issue. Access to the limited number of prime geo-stationary satellite orbits is another contender, as indeed is access to broadcast frequencies. Global pollution quotas, were they to be attempted, would probably provide another area of conflict in the practice of globalization.

The principal actors in these examples have tended to be states. This is not accidental. States increasingly find it difficult to regulate events in their own territories. Monetary and cultural policy, air and water quality, and access to information are only a few examples of issues that have escaped national control. Increasing globalization has turned many previously domestic issues into international ones. As it is technology that is largely responsible for this globalization, it follows logically that technology itself has become a main subject of the politics of globalization. Because it is recognized that technology is central to political power and economic wealth – as well as to social and cultural traditions and global survival – technology has become too important to ignore. The ability to gain and to restrict access to technology has turned into an urgent matter of diplomatic negotiation and threats on the part of the state. The globalization of technology politics is an attempt by the state to counter the globalizing influence of technology itself.

Globalization of technology

Technology is not spread evenly around the world. This is true in aggregate terms, with some states or regions being much more technologically intensive than others. It is also true in terms of specific technologies, where even between high-tech regions there are vast differences in which technologies are sited where. What accounts for this apparent non-globalization of technology?

On one level, technology is inherently global, and becomes ever more so as it increasingly rests on science rather than craft. An internal combustion engine or a laptop computer operates identically in Istanbul, in Hanoi and in Omaha. Unlike social systems or customs, unlike culture, unlike political arrangements, technology works the same way regardless of where you are.

Nevertheless, despite its inherently global nature, technology is very obviously not spread evenly around the world, and never has been. The reason why not is simply that both the development of technology and its exploitation are influenced by a wide range of factors not themselves technological. In his study of electrification, Hughes (1983) focuses on the systems that developed in Berlin, Chicago and London. He makes it very clear that the knowledge and technology were common to all. The same engineers were often involved in all three, ensuring that any developments in one were known to the others. Despite this commonality of knowledge and persons, the systems that were created in these three cities and the process of setting them up differed substantially. What explains these distinctions were the social, cultural, political, economic and physical differences among the three situations. Similarly, products and processes are often invented in one place by one group of individuals and then successfully exploited elsewhere. Gunpowder may provide the best known example, penirillin another. The course of technological innovation is charted by factors outside the realm of technology itself.

Consequently, there is no reason to expect that technology should be spread evenly around the world, either in terms of development or application. Certainly, firms themselves have become globalized. The well known passage from Robert Reich's (1991: 113) *The Work of Nations* gives a fair indication of this:

> When an American buys a Pontiac le Mans from General Motors he or she unwittingly engages in an international transaction. Of the $20,000 paid to GM about $6,000 goes to South Korea for routine labour and assembly operations, $3,500 goes to Japan for advanced components (engines, transaxles, electronics), $1,500 to West Germany for styling and design engineering, $800 to Taiwan, Singapore and Japan for small components, $500 to Britain for advertising, $100 to Ireland and Barbados for data processing. The rest – $8000 – goes to strategists in Detroit, lawyers and bankers in New York, lobbyists in Washington, insurance and health care workers all over the country and General Motors' shareholders – most of whom live in the US but an increasing number of whom are foreign nationals.

However, while industry may be globalized, 'new' technology and innovation are most definitely not. There are a number of very good reasons for this. First, innovation tends to flourish within communities of innovators. Human contact – often the informal kind over a cup of coffee or in the local bar or café after work – is essential for the emergence of ideas. With respect to the development of foam rubber, for example, while the patents tend to be in the separate names of my grandfather (Joseph Talalay) and two of my uncles (Leon and Anselm Talalay), in fact much of the work took place around the dinner table in the evening when the three would have long discussions on the ins and outs of the subject (no doubt boring my grandmother to tears). Who was exactly responsible for what is impossible to say. The point is that the act of discussion was itself essential for the development of foam rubber. Similarly, rivalry among firms combined with the active movement of staff between them leads to a ferment of innovation that would be, if not impossible, certainly much less common in isolation. As a matter of practice, any company is likely to set its research and development (R&D) function in an area where this is already going on, and success breeds spin-offs and further success. The end result is clustering, as in Route 128 or Silicon Valley (Piore and Sabel, 1984; Saxenian, 1994).

Second, as the patenting statistics suggest (see Table 8.3), most TNCs concentrate their R&D functions in their home countries. Again, this is perfectly logical. As R&D is usually key to the success of the firm and as it is intimately related to marketing and to corporate strategy, there is a strong case for centralizing that function. The third reason for the uneven spread of technology is that it is not free. It comes with a high price tag in terms of opportunity costs. To put resources into one technology means, in a world of limited time, money and skilled workers, to forgo pursuing another technology. Hence, there is an inevitable tendency to focus on those areas in which some competitive advantage is known to exist. Again this leads to national, regional or local specialization, working against a more even spread of technology and innovation.

In addition to this opportunity cost, technology has a very high social cost. Here I am thinking not of externalities such as pollution but rather of the requirement to be able exploit technology. Much of the international political argument over technology has centred around access to and transfer of technology (basically from the rich to the poor). Unfortunately, this line of reasoning ignores the requirement for the resources to exploit technology. These include an edu-

Table 8.3 Geographic location of large firms' patenting, 1981–88: percentage distribution by country of origin and home base of firms

Home country	*Country of origin of patenting of large firms*							
	USA	*Japan*	*France*	*W. Germany*	*Netherlands*	*Belgium*	*Sweden*	*UK*
USA	91.9	0.7	0.5	2.3	0.2	0.3	0.0	1.8
Japan	0.7	99.1	0.0	0.1	0.0	0.0	0.0	0.1
France	3.4	0.2	90.9	2.5	0.2	0.3	0.0	0.5
W. Germany	8.3	0.2	1.2	87.1	0.1	0.8	0.3	0.4
Netherlands	25.0	0.4	6.0	13.3	43.4	0.6	0.6	7.7
Belgium	27.0	0.0	1.2	16.7	11.7	39.4	0.0	1.9
Sweden	5.1	0.3	1.2	13.5	2.8	0.3	71.2	1.7
UK	21.5	0.1	2.4	3.8	0.9	0.4	0.3	65.9

Sources: Sharp (1997) from Patel and Pavitt (1991).

cated work force, a developed infrastructure, secure property rights, and market access. As Arnold Pacey (1990: 44) has written in his history of technology in world civilization, 'People cannot adopt technologies from other cultures unless they have the skills necessary to modify, adapt and develop them to suit their own purposes.' Given global, and even regional differences in levels of skill and education and infrastructure, it is hardly surprising that technology itself is far from evenly spread around the globe.

Technology, globalization and the international political economy

The Prime Minister of Canada (Chretien, 1996: 1) recently said, 'We cannot stop globalization, we need to adjust to it.' While there is nothing inevitable about globalization, Chretien is assuredly correct in the assumption that it will increase. The same applies to technological innovation. The accelerating pace of change is unlikely to slow down. Moreover, the interaction between globalization and technological innovation creates a dynamic, self-reinforcing spiral. As increased globalization is perceived to provide competitive advantage, there is more commercial opportunity for those companies that provide the technology of globalization. This further increases the opportunities to gain competitive advantage from the practice of globalization, which again leads to more opportunities for the providers of globalization technology. For example, as companies perceive that the Internet enables them to compete more effectively, so use of the Internet increases. This provides an opportunity for more ISPs (Internet Service Providers) to start up. As this happens, more companies jump on the bandwagon of electronic commerce, leading in turn to still further opportunity for ISPs, and so on; a dynamic spiral most certainly.

Technological innovation functions as the continuing cause and consequence of globalization. The actors that will fare best are those that can most successfully adapt to this situation. This trend has implications for states and firms, for global society and culture, and for economic and social inequality.

The firms that will do best will be those that can do one of two things. Either they can set the standards (i.e., they have the structural power to define the rules of the game) or they can organize themselves to be simultaneously global and local corporations. An example of the former is Microsoft, with its ability to be able to define IT standards. An example of the latter would be BTR, the English engineering and materials conglomerate, where a small head office sets high-level strategy and imposes financial controls and reporting requirements but where operational matters are devolved down to the local level. ABB, the very successful Swiss–Swedish engineering firm, is another company often heralded as the ideal global corporation.

These trends of increased globalization and faster technological innovation mean that the sovereignty of the nation-state will continue to erode. States are not independent because they are sovereign. The very opposite is the case. They are sovereign only because they are independent, because they are able to regulate events within their borders and to control what crosses those borders. Autarky is an essential pre-condition for sovereignty. However, in a world where technological change meets globalizing practice, autarky is becoming impossible. States are increasingly penetrated from the outside and often, as with information, entertainment and pollution, in ways that they cannot avoid.

The nation-state thus confronts a trade-off. It may well have to forgo notional ideas of sovereignty in exchange for real methods of effectiveness: to sacrifice the overall sovereignty of the state as a general principle in return for certain concrete goals. Under technological pressures, the nature, the function and the power of the state are all changing. The international system is a system of states, but it is no longer a system merely of states. In 100 years' time, it will probably still be a system of what we will call states, but those entities are likely to be so dramatically different from the European nation-states of the nineteenth century, that all the arguments among realists, neo-realists, liberal-idealists and Marxists will seem pointless. While we are perhaps not witnessing the nation-state's last stand, we are equally probably witnessing its transformation into a very different entity from the one that economic and political theory posits (see Chapters 4 and 5 in this volume).

Fuelled by this interaction of globalization and technology, a global society is developing. Based on English as its *lingua franca* and on the rise of the internationally mobile knowledge worker, a type of international citizenry is appearing. In the office of one of my consultancy clients in Switzerland, the native languages of the staff include Italian, Croatian, Russian, Serbian, Portuguese, Hindi, French, Greek and German. The working language, however, is English. This is the official policy of the company, not merely a *de facto* development. Engineers, scientists, consultants, senior managers, doctors, bankers, all of those who work with intellectual capital, can live and work almost anywhere.

Some interesting questions arise here. Will this international citizenry lead to growing inequality both between states and regions or within them between those with education and those without it? And does it follow from this that the key competitive advantage of a state lies in its education system and in its ability to attract the globally mobile corporations and individuals? Equally interesting, will there be an erosion of the global tax base, with all the consequent implications for social spending? As the global reach of electronic commerce on the Web grows, will VAT and sales tax revenues disappear? And will both corporation tax and income tax be subject to competitive devaluations in order to attract (or at least to avoid losing) firms and skilled employees, both of whom are increasingly mobile? Already we see headlines in the press such as 'French companies flower in the garden of England' (*The Times,* 22 July 1997: 25). Located at the end of the Channel Tunnel, Kent in south-east England provides a convenient location to service France, and French companies are moving there not only because of lower wages and more flexible labour laws but also because of the significantly less onerous tax burden. Whatever the answers to these questions may be, the very fact that it is reasonable to ask them indicates how far the interaction of globalization and technology has gone to alter the nature of global society.

Are these alterations for better or for worse? Is technology a force for good or for evil? Technological change does not take place in a vacuum. It results from the necessity of responding to problems. As these themselves are likely to be political or at least politicized, there is every reason to assume that the course of technological innovation will be conditioned by social, economic, cultural and political factors. Technology can be harmful; it can also bring immeasurable benefits. But to gain from these benefits requires the appropriate social structures plus a satisfactory level of education. As technology is exploited, it becomes easier to enhance these factors, making it easier for those already wealthy to maintain their advantage. The end result is that technology can easily heighten rather than reduce inequality. A world that increasingly depends upon technology will be one in which the rewards go to those able to use and exploit it. Technology most certainly leads to globalization, but the emerging global society, economy and culture do not encompass all equally. Together, globalization and technology threaten established patterns of power and wealth. Schumpeter's gales of creative destruction are now global, and they blow harder all the time.

Notes

1. I would like to thank participants at the 'Globalization and its Critics' workshop for helpful comments on an earlier draft.
2. In addition to Schumpeter, see Boskin and Lau (1992), Krugman (1994b), Rosenberg (1994a), and Solow (1957); for some interesting and conclusive historical evidence see Bairoch (1982).
3. Compare this typology with the four-fold one of Freeman and Perez (1988: 45–7), who use the categories of incremental innovation, radical innovation, new technology systems, and changes of techno-economic paradigms.
4. Thomas Kuhn (1962) refers to the paradigm shift inherent in moving from a Newtonian conception of the universe to an Einsteinian one. The very nature of modern physics changed fundamentally as the assumptions of physicists and the questions that they were trying to answer altered radically. This idea of a paradigm shift has entered the disciplines of economics and political economy. It is associated with a number of scholars interested in long waves and in the role of science and technology in economic growth. See, for example, works by Schumpeter (1950), Freeman and Perez (1988), Dosi (1988), and Rosenberg (1982, 1994a).
5. This possibility is, however, certainly imaginable. In his science fiction series based on the worlds of 'known space', Larry Niven envisions the transfer booth, which is essentially a phone booth where upon dialling the number of another booth you are physically transported to that new location. One of the alien species in this series, Piersons puppeteers, have gone even further and created 'stepping stones' which have a similar effect (the ultimate in seven league boots).
6. Taken from 'Language and Electronics: The coming global tongue', in *The Economist* 21 December 1996: 37–9.
7. Technology does not entail science, and in fact antedates it considerably. However, increasingly in practice technology rests on a scientific base: thus we tend to speak of 'science and technology'. Dosi (1988: 222) argues that one of the major properties of contemporary innovation is 'the increasing reliance of major new technological opportunities on advances in scientific knowledge'.
8. An individual or a culture may of course prefer an alternative future and eschew the wealth offered by technology. Modernity hardly brings unmixed benefits, and it is perfectly rational and possible to reject it. The point, however, is that a rejection of modernity must be seen also as a rejection of the possibility of building a wealthy economy.

9
Beyond 'Techno-globalism' and 'Techno-nationalism': Rearticulating the Sites and Stakes of Technological Competitiveness in East Asia

Ngai-Ling Sum[1]

Faced with the alleged challenges of globalization, various scholars working within the IR and IPE traditions have been advancing competing alternative conceptions of the emerging global (dis)order. In doing so they seek to go beyond inherited approaches based on the familiar global-national distinction. Thus some IR theorists attempt to displace a state-centric interpretation of globalization, narrated mainly in terms of the 'decline of the nation-state' and the prospects for a world state. In its place they offer a more ambivalent but none the less carefully considered view of the political implications of globalization. They see the national state as seeking self-preservation through self-transformation: trapped within an extensive web of international interdependence and beset by transnational forces, it is resorting to new (or reinvigorated) forms of intergovernmental co-operation or coalitions and policies to enhance its own strategic capacities (Rosenau, 1990; Keohane and Milner, 1996).

Conversely, some IPE theorists are attempting to reinvigorate a 'world system' interpretation of capitalist dynamics. They have been prompted in this by the growing economic interdependence among advanced capitalist states, the vitality of certain NICs, and the increasing integration of post-socialist economies into the world economy. They conclude that this provides even more justification for interpreting the global economy as a 'world system'. However, they still tend to see the latter in an unsatisfactory way: that is, as being constituted by the coupling of pre-existing nation-states and the global developmental logic organized around core, peripheral and semiperipheral zones, which may move between the zones only as complete entities (e.g., So and Chiu, 1996; cf. the criticism in Lever-Tracy *et al.*, 1996: 8, 189).

There are other IR and IPE scholars still working with the global-national distinction but who seek to complexify it by introducing new or borrowed concepts.[2] Although these latter accounts may offer good vantage points for viewing globalization, unreconstructed accounts derived from the global-national dichotomy offered by earlier scholars still need to be criticized. For these analyses retain the primacy of the nation-state typical of traditional realist IR theory, thereby producing an 'inside-outside' account whereby globalization is seen as impinging from the 'outside' and so threatening the nation-state (cf. the critical comments in, for example, Agnew, 1994: 87–106; Held and McGrew, 1994: 74–6).

As an exogenous process, globalization is related, somewhat ambiguously, both to extra-political forces grounded in other systems (e.g., technological change) and sometimes to supra-state forces that are inherently rootless (e.g., MNCs and transnational banks or TNBs). In both cases globalization is regarded as a complex source of turbulence in the nation-state's environment; it challenges the sovereign identity of nation-states, their traditional *modus operandi*, and their security, thereby threatening their structural coherence.[3] This chapter is not the place to undertake an extended critique of the 'inside-outside' model so dominant in traditional IR and IPE (Walker, 1988b). Instead it merely seeks to demonstrate how this 'inside-outside' distinction is deployed in the study of globalization and technology, and to argue that this distinction limits our understanding of globalization as simultaneously a process, a practice and a structure.

This chapter proposes a *critical* approach towards globalization based on its relation to technological change. Thus I will critique both the 'placeless' understanding of globalization which ignores its varying regional and national manifestations, and the 'statist' model which seeks to understand global-national relations in terms of place-based notions such as national sovereignty or territorial states. While the former approach abstracts from space, the latter has too concrete (and statist) an understanding of place. My own approach favours a more complex perspective which allows for the variability of time, space, and their articulation in the process of globalization. It stresses the relativization and rearticulation of spatial scales (such as global, regional, national and local), and adopts the dynamic 'time-space' language of technological flows. I focus on the reordering of the global system in terms of the complex, tangled dialectic of changes on the macro-regional, meso-regional, national, regional, and local scales; and I consider the implications of technological change on this process with special reference to its time-space flows.

Tendencies towards 'techno-globalism' (interpreted here in a 'techno-economic' rather than 'military' sense) and time-based competition have led to more complex patterns of value creation, especially in R&D. Both 'placeless' and 'place-centred' accounts of globalization oversimplify the complexities of these tangled hierarchies. This chapter argues that countries tend to co-operate on a regional basis to create or maintain a competitive edge. It is here that 'techno-regionalism' becomes one specific form of globalization: a form that co-ordinates the flows and interconnections across global-regional-national, time-space, and private-public forces for global competitiveness. This form also helps to shape the nature of globalization.

To capture the rich multilayered complexity of the reordering of social life, this chapter suggests the concept of 'geo-governance'[4] as a way of studying 'techno-regionalism'. It outlines key aspects of geo-governance capacities and illustrates them with respect to east Asia. It argues that it is inherent in the politics of technology transfer that tendencies towards 'techno-globalism', 'techno-regionalism' and 'techno-nationalism' co-exist in sometimes contradictory, sometimes complementary, forms. This creates dilemmas over the priority to be accorded to co-operation or competition, interdependence or dependence. These dilemmas raise questions concerning 'techno-identities' (the 'who is us?' question) in the politics of competitive synergy associated with regional technological orders. A dialectical interplay of identities may therefore guide actors in their choice among strategies concerned to advance their interests (as defined in terms of one or another identity) through new competitive and/or collaborative initiatives on national, regional and/or global bases. These are complex issues and we begin with critical reflections on the 'placeless' understanding of 'techno-globalism'.

Critical reflections I: a 'placeless' understanding of 'techno-globalism'

From the mid-1980s, some globalization discourses have suggested that the global comprises a space of flows that is both 'placeless' and 'borderless'. This is seen in narratives of the 'end of geography', and is related to technological change, ecological crisis, and the rise of MNCs and TNBs (Camilleri and Falk, 1992; O'Brien, 1992). More specifically, in relating globalization and technology, two kinds of drives behind 'techno-globalism' are identified. First, there are problems of the global commons, such as resource exploitation, communication regimes, climate change, and pollution. The search for collective solutions has stimulated cross-border technology-related activities. The second set of drives involves R&D, as more MNCs are attempting to exploit their own technology globally and access new technology, leading to global diffusion of R&D and strategic alliances (Ostry and Nelson, 1995: 25; Simon, 1997: 8; but see Chapter 8 in this volume).

Here I focus on the second kind of 'techno-globalism'. Its rhetoric can be related to: (i) the end of the Cold War, which has reoriented international competition from geo-political concerns structured around the capitalism-communism cleavage to geo-economic concerns about the competitive advantage of different forms of capitalism (e.g., the challenge of the East Asian models to North American and European ones and the emergence of the 'triadic world': Ohmae, 1990); (ii) the rise of knowledge-and-capital-intensive core technologies such as telecommunications, microelectronics and robotics, which require collaboration within each part of the triad and among distant competitors in different parts of the triad for cost reduction in sourcing, production, R&D and so on, and/or for rapid cost recovery; (iii) 'time-based' competition more generally, which prompts firms to shorten R&D time by entering into cross-border collaborative research on the basis of strategic alliances, licensing and joint ventures; (iv) the paradigm shift from so-called Fordism to post-Fordism, which suggests that the next long wave of economic growth depends on flexible production, knowledge- and design-intensity, innovation rents, scope economies, and much shortened product lead times (cf. Lipietz, 1987 on Fordism; Ohmae, 1990; Amin and Thrift, 1994; Jessop *et al.*, 1993: 228–31); (v) the information technology revolution (including its cyberspace dimension), which helps to meet the communication and co-ordination requirements involved in the rapid (if not instantaneous) transmission of information, people, and material resources (cf. Castells, 1989); and (vi) the impact of the 1980s neo-liberal turn which introduced deregulation, liberalization, and greater opportunities for cross-border co-operation and alliances.

'Techno-globalism' is sometimes discussed as a mutually beneficial and 'placeless' phenomenon. This occurs both among business strategists and scholars from the liberal tradition, who often interpret 'techno-globalism' as 'borderless' and progressive; and among scholars from more materialist and critical schools, who relate it to the emergence of new accumulation regimes and modes of development with their associated forms of social relations (e.g., transnational class relations). Such understandings tend to disembed globalization from its regional and national contexts. Global and regional nexi are studied separately, as if they were somehow mutually exclusive phenomena. Thus global processes are studied in terms of transnational networks: for example, whilst regional processes are related to 'trading blocs', and so on. Rather than adopting such approaches, the present chapter seeks to show how these processes might be articulated. Before elaborating this approach, however, let us consider another moment of critical reflection.

Critical reflections II: 'techno-globalism', 'techno-nationalism' and the discourse of inside-outside

Globalization and the economic practices it allegedly subsumes are often discussed in terms of their adverse impact on sovereignty and national policies. In this regard, globalization is seen as an exogenous process impinging from the 'outside' on the security of the nation-state. In relation to 'techno-globalism', these dilemmas or challenges are usually conceived in terms of cross-border spillovers, diminished national security, and challenges to political sovereignty (Ostry and Nelson, 1995: xviii–xxii).

First, 'cross-border spillovers' occur when activities in one nation affect other nations. More R&D-relevant spillovers occur as the rapid diffusion of knowledge, science and technology policies in one nation generates knowledge that other nations can use without full reimbursement. Second, as cross-border R&D activities increase, nations find it harder to control formally domestic events. This prompts national states to redefine 'national security', especially in 'techno-security' matters. This involves "not only protecting the integrity of a country's stock of technological knowledge, but also the capacity to enhance a country's capabilities and promote its economic competitiveness and national defence through the use of both domestic and foreign technological know-how" (Simon, 1997: xiv–xv). Third, pressure from cross-border linkages is sometimes deemed to challenge national political sovereignty on the grounds that nation-states allegedly have the sovereign right to organize their property in line with their own preferences and policies (Doty, 1996: 122–3).

Such 'challenges' highlight the utility of the inside/outside distinction (Walker, 1993: 26–7) as a vantage point for observing globalization. Regarding technology, accounts of the challenges by 'global outsiders' are often linked to issues of the 'national interest' and the best policies to reinvigorate the economy. Given the US–Japan trade conflict in the 1980s, two forms of 'techno-nationalist' discourse have emerged: protectionist and competitive. The former promotes a defensive kind of technological protectionism which urges 'bashing Japan' and 'buying American'. It is linked to public debates about increasing protectionism to help US firms wage battle against their global 'enemies', to protect intellectual property rights, and to reorient the Central Intelligence Agency from 'military security' to 'techno-security'.

The techno-nationalist discourse of competitiveness is as much concerned with the welfare of the nation's citizens as with corporate welfare. This is especially clear in Reich's (1991) definition of competitiveness in terms of the skills and productivity of the nation's labour force. This requires the federal government to decide policies in terms of which (emergent) technological capacities can be exploited within their borders. This approach emphasizes the strong interconnections among many different 'stakeholders' in the society. These include new high-tech firms, the academy, public and private research laboratories, venture capital, unions and government agencies (Ostry and Nelson, 1995: 34). This suggests that place still matters in organizing innovative activities. These are consistent with the new body of literature emphasizing the role of national systems of innovations (Porter, 1990; Lundvall, 1992; Nelson, 1993) which link the global flow of technology collaboration to national capacities.

These technology issues are typically framed in global-national terms. Most accounts assume that globalization is an accomplished external fact; and that nation-states are natural containers of technology and policies. Expressed more critically, they adopt a place-centred approach concerned with 'challenges', 'security' and 'national competitiveness'. This approach can be countered by broadening the analysis of globalization to take account of the relativization and rearticulation of scales and stakes across borders. The concept of 'techno-regionalism' is useful here.

A relational approach to 'techno-regionalism': the rearticulation of the sites and stakes of technological competitiveness

This approach builds on work by Harvey (1989), McGrew (1995: 24) and other critical international relations scholars (Agnew, 1994; Campbell, 1996). It stresses: (i) the re-ordering of the global system in terms of the complex, tangled dialectic of changes on the macro-regional, meso-regional, national, regional and local scales; (ii) the relativization and rearticulation of spatial scales (such as global, regional, national and local) and the dynamic 'time-space' flows across borders; (iii) the complex array of time-space flows which reorder social relations across different spatial sites/scales and the identities and reimaginations that are involved; and (iv) a tendency towards 'geo-governance' and its strategic capacities to reproduce regional competitiveness. In this context 'techno-regionalism' offers a more complex approach to understanding globalization. As one form in which globalization occurs, techno-regionalism involves an approach to 'geo-governance' with major implications for the remaking of social space.

'Techno-regionalism': tendencies towards 'geo-governance'

In order to examine this specific form of globalization from the perspective of flows and interconnections, existing work on IPE needs further cross-fertilizing with other disciplines. These will help to overcome binary categories (such as global and national, private and public, state and market, and structure and agency) which block adequate analyses of flows/interconnections. Thus, in developing my arguments, I draw not only on recent work in IPE and IR but also on concepts developed in other disciplinary and post-disciplinary contexts.[5] Useful concepts in this regard include the social construction of regional identities, time-space dimensions, social embeddedness, governance, mode of growth, interorganizational networks, technologies of power, time-space compression, societal steering and organizational learning. Their utility is especially clear in the growing literature on the role of the local embeddedness of industrial and/or producer service agglomerations or innovative milieus (e.g., Emilia-Romagna, Baden-Wurttemberg, central business districts in global cities) in generating institutional networks and practices conducive to post-Fordist growth (Camagni, 1991, 1995). My task here is to transfer this approach to spatial patterns that involve transnational and trans-local forms of regional analyses.

A more abstract conceptual innovation which is none the less useful here is the proposed transcendence of the structure-agency dichotomy in the so-called 'strategic-relational' approach (cf. Jessop, 1990). This introduces 'strategic context' and 'strategic capacities' as mediating categories between structure and agency. This approach has three advantages. First, it emphasizes the structurally-inscribed strategic selectivity characteristic of structures[6] and the scope for structurally-oriented, strategically-calculating activities on the part of social forces. Second, it stresses how spatiality and temporality (both as sites and flows) are inscribed within strategic selectivity, including the role of differential temporal and spatial horizons in shaping strategic behaviour. Finally, it highlights the role of discourses and social identities as constitutive features of social structures and social forces alike. Rather than elaborate these meta-theoretical ideas in abstract terms, I will show how they illuminate the interaction of the economic, political and discursive in shaping regional technological orders. More specifically, I examine the latter in terms of their socially embedded, socially regularized, discursively-mediated and strategically selective character. I also show how they have been formed in and through their articulation with various geo-economic projects oriented to particular spaces as sites for economic growth strategies.[7]

'Geo-governance' and its theoretical contexts

Building upon these insights, this section seeks to capture the complexity of these flows and interconnections at regional sites by developing the concept of 'geo-governance' to transcend some of the dichotomous categories deployed in many IR/IPE studies. Together with the other conceptual innovations noted above, this will enable me to explore the emergence of co-ordinated networks (often themselves a network of networks) of social/economic/political agents that attempt to regularize and 'govern' the flows of cross-border R&D, manufacturing, and even distribution activities. Such strategic networks provide the basis for a new form of what more generally can be termed '*geo-governance*': that is, the governance of social relations *qua* spatial relations.

In the context of regions/sub-regions, this involves recognizing how spatially-specific structure of social co-ordination of border regions (from different national states) more or less coheres into a mode of technological order. The structure of social co-ordination in this context typically involves private-public agents/organizations; and it is typically instantiated through material as well as discursive practices aiming to establish an imagined community of economic interests. The actors involved in the structure of co-ordination are involved in one or more networks (or a network of networks) which typically seek to promote global-regional competitiveness by disciplining/controlling the time-space flows of technological transfer, manufacturing and distribution (Harvey, 1989; Adam, 1994; Gereffi and Korzeniewicz, 1994). For our purposes it is important to realize that these time-space dimensions involve emerging temporal-spatial patterns associated with the reorganization of 'social space' to include 'electronic space' and the compression of social time through new information and communication technologies. This can be developed by examining four key aspects of *'time-space flow'* in the contemporary global, regional, national through to local networks of industrial, financial, commercial and cultural interconnections.

First, industrial/technological time-space flows are shaped by the practices of various global networks of multinational production firms in interaction with regional and more locally based firms which are co-involved in the evolving regional division of labour/knowledge. Their operations are premised on either cost differentials across borders and/or technological complementarities (Simon 1995a: 4). These networks of strategic firms narrate and co-ordinate industrial/technological times and spaces constructed in and through their planning and management of time-bound and/or compressed-time production projects oriented to competitiveness in global/regional markets. Temporally, such networks are driven by their aim to produce goods in time, on time, and every time to customers wherever they may be in the global market. In order to speed up innovation by reducing lead times, and co-ordinate time-bound schedules, firms within and beyond the region enter into strategic partnerships such as sub-contracting activities, joint ventures and strategic alliances in order to produce just-in-time in 'global/regional factories'.

In spatial terms, since production must be closely co-ordinated in a transspatial and time-bound/compressed-time schedules, new institutional and technical forms of integrating activities emerge in both social and 'electronic space'. In social space, we find new spatial forms that cut across borders and are mediated by dense networks of private-to-private and private-to-public alliances based on complex relations of trust, competition and policy support (Jarillo, 1988; Camagni, 1991; Conti, 1993; Mayntz, 1993). These networks are also cross-cut by strategic calculations of how to produce and reproduce labour across borders in the forms of skilled commuter workers, guest and/or migrant labour. Besides social space, these links are reinforced by emerging practices in information highways and 'electronic space' which involve the exchange of relevant industrial/technological information concerned with R&D and stages of the production process from design to manufacturing (Howells, 1995).[8] The sites which emerge in this new discourse/identity are 'regional blocs', 'growth poles', 'competitive regions', growth circles' and 'learning/technological regions', linking the regions globally or with other regional circuits (Ohmae, 1990; Chen, 1995; Florida, 1995).

Second, financial time-space flows are structured by the practices of interconnected networks of multinational banks, other financial intermediaries, and trans-local organizations. Their operations are premised on the denationalization of 'stateless' funds which are pooled and managed in a 'borderless world' (Ohmae 1990). This has obvious spatio-temporal implications which are often explicitly voiced in the discourses and narratives of the financial intermediaries concerned. Specialized networks within and beyond the region co-ordinate their operations and subjectivities virtually instantaneously in and through *electronic space* and *electronic time*. In temporal terms, such networks of transspatialized actors are oriented to the nano-seconds of computer operations as they co-ordinate their decision-making units/operations; in turn, speediness affects profitability and global competitiveness (Adam, 1994: 100–3). In spatial terms, these networks' operations are increasingly mediated through the articulation of practices shaped by information and communications technologies, ranging from the humble fax through electronic data interchange to an ever more mundane Internet and electronic conferencing (Poster, 1995: 26).

In this context the so-called 'information superhighway' (which is still partial and limited) is coming to play an increasingly important role in transmitting urgent data and knowledge that are essential for rapid trading decisions. Share prices, interest rates, stock exchange indices, financial risk of traded instruments, and so on can be exchanged through nodal points (e.g., global cities) fast-in-time and fast-in-place in the highly competitive 'global economic village'. As these practices become consolidated in the future, mastery of 'electronic space' will prove a key dimension of economic and political hegemony. This does not mean that *social space* will become unimportant, of course; on the contrary, it will continue to contribute to the institutional thickness and capacities of the region. Global/regional/national actors from the private-public realms typically need to meet face-to-face to develop trust, establish networks, form partnerships, settle differences and engage in mutual learning and interaction.

Third, commercial time-space flows are influenced by the practices of networks of multinational service firms and their regional/local counterparts located in 'global-gateway' cities (Sassen, 1991, 1996; Shelley, 1993). Their operations are premised on the provision of producer and distributive services and logistics information (i.e., insurance, legal services, consultancies, logistic management, transportation, retail) that "facilitate all economic transactions, and the driving force that stimulates the production of goods" within the 'regional chain' (Riddle, 1986: 26). These networks of service firms co-ordinate and narrate the time and space of global-regional and regional-local nexi of the production and distributive chains. In temporal terms, service firms in the 'supply pipeline' manage information flows that balance cost options and lead- and transit-time in time-bound projects. This is increasingly co-ordinated in 'electronic space' insofar as information is substituted for inventory (i.e., 'virtual' inventory) at the centre so that 'quick responses' can be made directly into the replenishment systems through local outsourcing or procurement (Christopher, 1992: 108–24). Social space is important here in developing trust, forming liaisons with local sub-contractors/management, and tapping local information flows that may enhance customer service management.

Fourth, cultural time-space flows are shaped by social practices embedded in networks of intra- and/or cross-cultural ties. Intra-cultural practices and norms are rooted in common traditions such as linguistic, familial, clan and communal ties; and their operations are premised on the need to 'lubricate the functioning of social networks' through practices such as gift exchange and banqueting in order to generate familial/clan/communal loyalty. The resulting intensification of social space may help to speed up the border-crossing time across the private-public spaces. Cross-cultural subjectivity may involve the consolidation and accumulation of practices and norms that can reduce the border-crossing time between cultural spaces (e.g., global entrepreneurialism, multiculturalism, and even global post-colonialism).

The making of regional 'geo-governance' capacities[9]

The above-mentioned time-space flows embedded in 'geo-governance' combine to produce a regional technological order that can be defined as *a mode and structure of co-ordination that is mediated by a multilayered network of social relations which interconnects global-regional-national, time-space, private-public, and material and discursive dimensions*. These dimensions are mediated by networks of strategic social actors. This allows a consideration of strategic calculation of actors in network formation and the examination of their practice of networking at material and discursive levels of technological production and exchange. As a multilayered network that interconnects these dimensions, its capacities in promoting and reproducing growth/competitiveness are typically influenced by the following components (Jessop, 1990; Fairclough, 1992; Mayntz, 1993; Amin and Thrift, 1994).[10]

Global-regional-national dimensions

1 The (quasi-)hierarchical networks of global-regional-national actors and their specific strategies/mechanisms in co-ordinating their production (such as strategic alliances, joint ventures, subcontracting, and aid-sponsored links) in the region.
2 The strategic selectivity and capacities of this system in consolidating a specific regional division of labour/knowledge, either in terms of cost differentials or technological co-development.
3 The condensation, in this structure of social relations, of certain nodal points (such as global-gateway cities) providing complex services to bridge time-space gaps between global-regional and cross-border production and exchange.
4 The consolidation within this structure of a complementary labour process and labour flow and mode of social reproduction of labour power in and across borders and generations.[11]

Time-space dimensions

1 The consolidation of social and 'electronic space' practices that co-ordinate networks of production firms in planning and managing time-bound and compressed-time projects just-in-time for global competitiveness.
2 The condensation of 'electronic space' and social practices that complement networks of multinational banks and other financial intermediaries involved in pooling and managing trans-spatialized funds fast-in-time and fast-in-space for global competitiveness.
3 The constitution of 'electronic space' and social practices that complement networks of service firms in reducing lead- and transit-time of production and distribution.
4 The accumulation and crystallization of cultural/social practices/norms that can reduce the border-crossing time between cultural and/or private-public spaces.

Private-public dimensions

1 A strong institutional presence and interaction of private-public networks for co-ordinating economic and political resources (e.g., investment, information, knowledge, aids, etc.) at trans-local, (inter-) national, and global level(s).
2 The emergence of new trans-border social blocs which accept, support, and carry the practices and discourse beyond elites.

Material-discursive dimensions

1 The above dimensions are discursively selective[12] and, through the emerging spatial meanings and their symbolism, serve to enhance the realization of the region.
2 The emergence of a unifying discourse in the form of an 'imagined identity'[13] that ascribes and legitimates common purpose(s) for the region as a whole.

Overall, strategic networks of regional 'geo-governance' could enhance the global competitiveness of a region in the following ways: (i) joint decision-making based on information-sharing, strategic alliances and sub-contracting; (ii) capacities to deploy economic and political-bureaucratic resources, such as grants or loans (for infrastructure), authority, organizational intelligence, R&D and manufacturing know-how; (iii) capacities to engage in time-based competition that is related to shortening of lead-time and global technological competitiveness; (iv) the reflexivity and creativity of interactive learning among private-public actors and institutions; and (v) a communication and negotiation system conducive to societal guidance (steering) in the region. None the less, such networks and structures do not arise just because they are needed; and neither, once they have emerged for whatever reason(s), do they always operate beneficially. They develop in quite specific conditions and cannot be created at will through specific policy initiatives. And, once they have developed, they may have difficulties in co-ordination and/or face challenges from within and beyond the networks.[14]

The 'geo-governance' capacities of a regional technological order in east Asia

There are of course many emerging regional networks in east Asia and even more projects to establish such networks. It is impossible within the ambit of this short chapter to list, let alone analyse, all of them. I therefore chose to consider, in a very preliminary way, one of the most important networks, namely the emergence of a 'Japan-centred' network in east Asia since the mid-1980s. Originally, Japanese FDI was largely concentrated in North-East Asian economies, such as Taiwan and South Korea. From 1986, Japan's regional production network also expanded into Hong Kong, Singapore, Malaysia, Indonesia, Thailand and the Philippines. This has occurred against a backdrop of intensifying US moves to correct its trade and employment problems. Under the G5 Plaza Accord in September 1985, the USA has tried to reverse its deteriorating trade relationship with Japan by forcing the appreciation of the yen relative to the dollar. Saddled with uncompetitive prices in its export markets, rising domestic labour costs, and fearing greater protectionism in US and European markets, Japan is seeking to reorganize the region through economic and financial means. These include trade, private FDI, official development assistance (ODA) and technology exports. This process is mediated by a strategic network of private-public actors cross-cutting regional-national and time-space dimensions of production and exchange.

Since the mid-1980s, the Plaza Accord has triggered more sector FDI from Japan and redirected the role of Japanese ODA in the ASEAN (Association of South East Asian Nations) region from securing natural resources to promoting export industries (e.g., improving social and economic infrastructures). Between 1988 and 1990, Japanese ODA amounted to US$6.68 billion and US$6.3 billion in South-East Asia and ASEAN respectively. In Asia in general, this amounts to roughly two-thirds of Japanese ODA stretching from India to China. As for Japanese FDI, some US$41 billion went to the east Asian economies between 1985 and 1993 (Bello and Cunningham, 1994: 453). Unlike Japanese FDI elsewhere in the world, it is largely focused on industry rather than services. In the NICs, manufacturing investments comprised half of all cases of FDI, according to a Toyo Keizai Shimposha survey, and were largely oriented to Japanese innovation in components parts, machinery and sub-assemblies (Bernard and Ravenhill, 1995: 177). For the EU and North America, the comparable figures were 21.2 and 30.2 per cent respectively (Tokunaga, 1992: viii).

The flow of Japanese ODA and FDI to east Asia involves a strategic network of relations embedded in private and public as well as regional-local domains. This multilayered geo-governance network rests on many institutions of different kinds both in Japan and in the region. On the Japanese front, it involves the presence of Japanese public-private actors and institutions co-ordinating aid and trade ties in east Asia. This structural network creates certain strategic advantages for Japanese FDI by fostering regionalization of industrial production centred on Japan. I begin with the network in Japan.

This network is marked by the presence of public-private actors and institutions co-ordinating aid and trade ties in east Asia.[15] Institutionally, it comprises a vertically-segmented bureaucracy of Japanese ministries (e.g., Economic Planning Agency, Ministry of Foreign Affairs, Ministry of Finance, Ministry of International Trade and Industry), aid-implementing agencies (e.g., Export-Import Bank, Overseas Economic Co-operation Fund, Japan International Co-operation Agency, or JICA, Overseas Technical Co-operation Agency), research centres (e.g., Japan External Trade Organization), trade associations and large-scale private multinationals. The strong institutional presence of these bodies is matched by a high level of intra-network interactions, with aid-implementing agencies and trade associations in the middle. Together they constitute a system of communication and negotiation conducive to guiding key Japanese interests in the region. This involves a project-oriented ODA which rests on specific social/bureaucratic practices, thereby privileging certain Japanese economic interests in the overall project cycle. These strategically-selective practices may include request-based procedures; decentralized authority; and case-by-case decision-making (Arase, 1994: 178–89).

First, the Japanese ministries and agencies act officially only after aid requests are transmitted by local Japanese embassies. This enables private Japanese actors, such as trading companies, consulting firms and trade associations, to initiate requests in developing countries. Another variant of this system is project-finding missions. Subsidized by JICA and led by prestigious business leaders sponsored by trade associations, they may send delegations to developing countries to discuss preliminary project proposals and aid requests. Second, the local embassy, on receiving aid requests, sends appraisal reports to relevant main ministries and agencies. Informal bureaucratic rules ensure that the substance of the request determines which ministries and agencies are consulted. Since some 16 ministries and agencies share this caseload, this decentralized authority "is not only important to ensure that the economic ministries retain a central policy-making role, but is also important to the private sector clients of the main ministries and agencies who use bureaucratic sponsorship to gain access to ODA resources" (Arase, 1994: 178).

Alongside these institutional practices, other informal co-ordination mechanisms bring together private and public actors by exchanging personnel between the private sector and aid-implementing agencies and informal study groups between official and business leaders (Arase 1994: 199). This permits a high level of contacts, co-operation and information exchange which may lead, in time, to a certain mutual isomorphism and strategic positioning of the Japanese aid-trade nexus. Overall this strategic network of co-ordination can enhance the following: (i) the reflexivity of interactive learning among private and public actors and institutions, (ii) a system of co-operation, communication and negotiation conducive to socio-economic guidance in the region, (iii) the privileging of business and industrial interests in formulating Japanese ODA policy, and (iv) the capacities to deploy economic and political/bureaucratic resources, such as infrastructure funding, political authority, organizational intelligence, technology and manufacturing know-how, along lines complementing the Japanese economy. Given the reflexivity, selectivity and capacity of this system of geo-governance, it could well consolidate an aid-trade nexus in the region.

Parallel to, and capitalizing on, these structural networks and strategic advantages inherent in the private-public partnership, Japanese FDI tends to foster a form of regionalization of technological production through a layered network in the region (Lim, 1991; Unger, 1993; Kwan, 1994). This imagined network is reinforced discursively by the metaphor of a 'flying geese' region. According to these imaginative constructions, 'economic co-operation with countries in Asia' is carried out through private initiatives assisted by government. This policy enables Japan to organize the industrial integration of east Asia in and through the metaphor of a 'flying geese' region.

This particular model of development has attained some popularity in the region. Given the diverse stages of economic development achieved in the region, the growth model is compared to the delta-shaped formation of 'flying geese'. It portrays Japan as the spearhead of the flock, the four NICs as following close behind, and the six ASEAN economies as poised to take off. The post-socialist bloc is expected to join the flight at a later date. This 'flying geese' metaphor re-presents the NICs' growth trajectory in terms of a movement from a traditional to a modernized economic order. Japan is the pioneer and exemplar of this developmental pattern, and latecomers replicate the experience of the countries ahead of them in the formation. In this sense Japan guides the entire 'flock of geese' on its techno-economic 'flight to success', but each member of the flock makes its way through Japan's staging points under its own independent flight power.

This image of the 'flying geese' reinforces a 'synergistic' division of labour specializing in component procurement. Basically, domestic Japanese operations produce high-value and high-end process products; and off-shore affiliations produce low-value and low-end process products/components. In the electronics industry, for example, Japanese companies concentrate on improving technology through indigenous R&D by supplying leading-edge core components such as active matrix liquid crystal displays and large-screen picture tubes. Affiliates in South Korea and Taiwan engage in original equipment manufacturing arrangements related to intermediate components, parts and moulds (Bernard and Ravenhill, 1995: 191). Low-value products (simple consumer electronics: cassette recorders, headphones, microwave ovens, etc.) come from Malaysia, China and Thailand. The co-ordination of such production networks is enhanced by complex services offered by global cities that help to discipline the time-space gap between regional-national production and exchange. Thus Hong Kong and Singapore are increasingly condensed as nodal points offering services such as financial settlement, finance, insurance, legal, accounting, data processing, engineering services, market research, cargo handling and so on (Tokunaga, 1992: 29; Rodan, 1993: 235).

Although this chapter cannot analyse the time-space moments involved here, the 'social space' is of importance to co-ordinate cross-cultural subjectivity and reduce the border-crossing time between cultural spaces embedded in the network. In addition, both 'social' and 'electronic space' are important arenas for co-ordinating fast-in-time/fast-in-place financial deals as well as time-bound/compressed-time projects requiring intra-company logistics to link the global-regional-national flows of raw materials, inventories, finished goods, and so on. There is an increasing tendency for Japanese FDI to move into the service sectors of Hong Kong and Singapore. In Hong Kong, Japanese FDI has mainly gone into finance, commerce, telecommunication and technical support services: in part to exploit its ready access to, and plentiful knowledge of, China as a cheap production site and consumer market (Steven, 1990: 130–1). Conversely, Singapore acts as regional headquarters of Japanese multinationals (e.g., Sony) as well as providing offshore markets for financing and hedging their FDI in the region (Tokunaga, 1992: 181–8). These patterns suggest how Japanese FDI has given rise to a complementary regional technological order in which Japan is a base for high-tech and R&D development; Hong Kong and Singapore are important for producer services and finance; and other ASEAN countries engage in low-end production.

The Japan-centred network in product/component sourcing is essentially mediated by a constellation of Japanese parent multinationals, their affiliates in east Asia, companies that are part of the parents' group, home suppliers' off-shore affiliates, and complex service firms. As a mode of social co-ordination, its production network predominantly consists of the following interactions in component procurement: (i) between the parent company and its affiliates in east Asia; (ii) among parents' affiliates in east Asia; (iii) among companies that are part of the parent groups and their east Asian affiliates; and (iv) those interactions that parents' east Asian affiliates have established with east Asian subsidiaries of Japanese sub-contractors that participate in parents' domestic sub-contracting systems. The first two interactions constitute intra-firm, the last two intra-group, networks. In other words, interactions are confined within firms/groups with local firms playing a very marginal role. This pattern is sometimes seen as a closed regional production network (Borrus, 1995: 11–12) in which Japan is engaged in 'techno-nationalist' moves to protect its high-tech transfer to the region.

New 'techno-identities' and dilemmas

Japan's techno-nationalist protectionist stance towards east Asia has created tensions in the region's technological domain. These tensions, which are inherent in the politics of technology transfer, are expressed in the dilemmas of co-operation versus competition and interdependence versus dependence (Bello and Cunningham, 1994; Sum, 1996a). They will be expressed in different ways as subordinate partners seek to answer the 'who is us' question in relation to their technological strategies. This search for new *techno-identities* may involve breaking with the earlier taken-for-granted approach to technology transfer (i.e., the product cycle theory). Thus east Asian NICs may seek to leapfrog others and/or catch up with Japan by developing a more competitive rather than follower 'techno-national' identity and/or by redefining and/or reorienting their economic interests towards other spaces and scales.

East Asian NICs, fearing overdependence on Japan, are trying to reposition themselves by developing new 'techno-identities' and associated techno-economic strategies. Since the late 1980s, for example, Taiwan and South Korea have adopted a competitiveness-oriented 'techno-national' identity. They seek to build their technological capacities by innovating, learning to compete with and even 'leapfrogging', Japan (Hobday, 1994; 1995). This is expressed in Taiwan's attempt to develop technological capabilities and to establish market niches in advanced components. Its government has helped to enhance these capabilities by founding the Hsinchu Science and Industry Park, which involves co-ordination and co-operation across the private sector, research institutions and the government. Similarly, in South Korea, government agencies (such as the Ministry of Science and Technology, the Ministry of Industry and Trade, and the Economic Planning Board) are working closely with private firms and research institutes to promote high-tech areas such as micro-electronics and, more recently, aerospace (Simon, 1995a: 21–2).

Making new 'techno-national' identities and practices forms part of the dialectical relationship implicit in the politics of technology transfer in the region. In this particular case, with the continuous appreciation of the yen, the pressure of global competition and the rising technological capabilities of the NICs, Japan, which is still committed to its 'techno-nationalist' strategy, is attempting to deepen regional co-operation by entering into technological-based strategic alliances with prominent MNCs from the NICs. This involves attempts to co-develop technology and to incorporate them as part of the Japanese *keiretsu* system. This is exemplified by the Hitachi-Goldstar agreement for transfer of 1 mega-byte (MB), 4 MB, and 16 MB digital random access memory technology over the last several years. This deepening of regional practices marks the change from a one-way flow of technology transfer (i.e., Japanese sunset industries are relocated to junior partners in east Asia) to two-way flows through the regional co-development of particular products (Simon, 1997: xviii).

Such newly-developed complementarities are accompanied by counter-tendencies towards competitiveness. The latter are evident in the emergence of new 'techno-global' and 'techno-regional' identities on the part of the NICs. For example, some NIC firms are attempting to become less dependent on Japan by developing their own 'techno-global' identity and strategies. They are trying to reposition themselves globally as viable alternatives to Japanese firms for those US and Western European multinationals who are seeking partners for technology-based international strategic alliances (TISAs). This is especially notable for MNCs seeking partners to provide manufacturing process capabilities. Regarding redefined 'techno-regional' identities, some firms from Singapore and Taiwan are initiating an NIC-centred 'techno-regionalism' by entering many TISAs with local firms in neighbouring east Asian countries (Wong, 1997: 181–2).

Japan's drive to open up its closed system through co-development of some high-tech products with NIC partners is coupled with continuation of its defensive 'techno-national' strategy. Despite signs of opening up, Japan still protects its key technologies from the NICs and it is hard for the latter to access Japanese technology-based strategic alliances. Japan is still more interested in entering these types of alliances with American and west European MNCs. This 'techno-global' identity and strategy may continue to marginalize the NICs relative to many of the emerging oligopolistic coalitions.

The preceding discussion has aimed to reveal the dialectical interplay of national-regional-global identities, interests and strategies within the changing regional technological (dis)order. The latter is marked by the co-existence of complementary and contradictory tendencies inherent in the *politics of competitive synergies* emerging in the region. Actors may choose among identities/strategies to advance their redefined interests through new competitive and/or collaborative initiatives. These involve complex choices and dilemmas inherent in the dynamics of this multilayered regional system. More detailed analysis of its geo-governance capacities and the complex dialectics are clearly beyond the scope of this chapter. However, one can try to map two trends: (i) a more complex 'geo-governance' network of social relations that may deepen both competition and synergy in the regional technological orders; and (ii) a thicker system of social and time-space co-ordination which involves a multilayered network organized in terms of public-private as well as global-regional-national-local levels. Mapping these trends should reveal the emergence of a more complex set of dilemmas, since 'techno-regionalism' cannot be divorced from 'techno-nationalism' and 'techno-globalism': they are integral parts of the current dialectic of competitiveness and technology transfer.

Conclusion

This chapter sketches a critical perspective on globalization and technology. It eschews analyses which see globalization as a 'placeless' or supra-territorial phenomenon or which interpret it in terms of a global-national duality. Instead it emphasizes the importance of 'time-space flows' rooted in tendencies towards globalization and cross-border regionalization. Such processes are articulated and mediated through a multilayered network that cross-cuts different sites and involve different stakes.

Regarding 'techno-regionalism', my approach seeks to capture the rearticulation of sites and stakes through the concept of 'geo-governance'. This refers to attempts to co-ordinate the global-regional-national, time-space, private-public and material and discursive dimensions of production and exchange. The preceding discussion has been concerned with the analytical features of geo-governance capacities and tensions in specific historical contexts. Given these specific analytical concerns, we can say that geo-governance can be studied in terms of multilayered networks that mediate these new sites and stakes, creating the material and discursive bases for a shared identity and interests among economic spaces in two or more countries and building the capacities to win a collective competitive edge on a global-regional-national basis.

In this context one can see 'techno-regionalism' as one specific form of globalization with its own distinctive impact on the latter's development. A preliminary case study on recent changes in the east Asian technological order has also been offered to show the key analytical features of geo-governance and to suggest the heuristic possibilities of this perspective. The tendencies towards 'techno-regionalism' shape (and are shaped by) the sometimes contradictory, sometimes complementary, tendencies towards 'techno-nationalism' and 'techno-globalism'. This complex interplay of forces poses questions concerning the techno-identities, interests and strategies involved in the politics of competitive synergy in the current technological race.

Notes

1. This chapter was written while the author was Alec Horsley Research Fellow at the Political Economy Research Centre, University of Sheffield.
2. Other IPE theorists are reintroducing state and/or 'crisis' theories originally developed outside the IPE tradition. These include the rediscovery of Poulantzas's 'relative autonomy' account of the state which stresses its autonomy from transnational capital or the structural requirements of the global capitalist order (Cox, 1987; Gill and Law, 1989) and the reworking of O'Connor's 'fiscal crisis' and 'under-consumption crisis' to understand the 'pressures' on the state in a global era (Palan, 1995: 169–71).
3. This is not true of world-systems theory. This rejects the idea of an 'outside' in the capitalist order (as opposed to pre-capitalist empires). None the less, in deploying another spatial metaphor ('centre-periphery'), it certainly operates with spatial differentiations within the world system and treats the periphery as 'outside' (or beyond) the centre.
4. My conception of 'geo-governance' differs from Falk's (1995) liberal-realist approach on 'geo-governance' and his preferred global ideal of 'humane governance'. My critical-materialist approach is more influenced by institutional economics, new geography, regulation approaches, governance

theories, discourse theory and post-colonial theory. It can be seen as an analysis of the new political economy of cross-border networking: an approach that is more sensitive to the relativization and rearticulation of spatial scales (such as global, regional, national and local) and time horizons (such as industrial, financial, commercial and cultural) across borders.

5. These include critical international relations, institutional economics, organizational sociology, the regulation approach, neo-Gramscian state theory, governance theories, discourse analysis, and radical or post-modern geographies. See, for example, Campbell *et al.* (1991), Jessop (1990), Fairclough (1992), Child *et al.* (1993), Hodgson (1993), Grabher (1993), Kooiman (1993), Amin and Thrift (1994) and Massey (1994).
6. This signifies that structural constraints always operate selectively. They are not absolute and unconditional but are always temporally, spatially, agency- and strategy-specific
7. This approach can be described as integral or inclusive: cf. Jessop's comments on the neo-Gramscian aspects of the regulation approach (with its interest in the integral economy) as well as Gramsci's views on the integral state or the state in its inclusive sense (Gramsci, 1971; Jessop, 1990).
8. Examples include e-mail, video-conferencing, CAD-CAM data interchange, just-in-time production, simultaneous engineering, etc.
9. This schema is partly inspired by Clulow and Teague (1993).
10. This list of components of sub-regional geo-governance is not exhaustive; rather it aims to facilitate the formulation of research questions and discussions.
11. This may involve some kind of articulation between Ricardian and Schumpeterian welfare-workfare policies privileging a mix of public expenditure on housing, education, industrial training and infrastructural development.
12. Discursive selectivity is accessed through (mis)perceptions and representations of the existing context. This may involve actors' perceptions of organization, network, strategy, mutual advantages, etc.
13. A discursive construction that gives a common identity to the sub-region structured around an 'imagined economic community' which the bloc hopes to realize and which provides a basis for co-operation, competition and creative conflict.
14. In relation to the specific conditions and difficulties of constructing and maintaining Japan- and China-centred networks, see Sum (1996a, 1996b).
15. The emergence of this network can be traced back to 1953 and Japan's urgent post-war attempt to organize its international activities to promote rapid industrial recovery and growth (Arase, 1994: 173).

10
Globalization in Perspective[1]

R. J. Barry Jones

This concluding chapter surveys a range of the conceptual issues and arguments that have been raised by the 'globalization debate', within this volume and elsewhere. It argues that contemporary tendencies towards globalization are driven as much by the purposes of pertinent actors as they are by irresistible forces external to human volition and beyond human control. This central dualism within globalization exposes the gross simplicity of many of the more abrupt references to the nature and imperatives of the 'new global economy' made by academics, politicians and business leaders. The contemporary world is characterized by a considerable multiplicity of purposes which highlight the controversial nature of globalization, namely its incomplete condition and the very real possibility of its reversal, in whole or in part, in the foreseeable future.

What might be termed the *strong globalization* thesis contends that the advance of the technologies of communication and travel, the expanding role of TNCs, the progressive opening of many parts of the world to free trade and to free market principles, and the growing interconnectedness of financial systems, has created a world economy that is now highly integrated, subject to common influences and pressures, and increasingly characterized by similarities of practice and taste. In the wake of such economic globalization, opportunities and imperatives have also increased for new global social arrangements and a global culture. The role of states has also been much diminished in the economic realm and by the myriad opportunities for evading 'national' constraints and controls that are now open to firms, groups and individuals alike. Such a view of globalization thus confronts traditional, state-focused views of the world. It also raises questions about change and development that go to the heart of our understanding of the nature, sources and consequences of the processes that are central to the human condition.

In this critical discussion of contemporary globalization, the notions of the purposes and practices of globalization will be employed to tease out some of the forces that are driving this debate. The pertinent purposes are of two kinds: the purposes of those who are promoting the conditions and processes of globalization in practice; and the purposes of those who, for a variety of motives, have sought to propagate the idea of progressive globalization. The former will receive the lion's share of attention within this discussion. Practices then concern the empirical behaviours of actors of many types as they act and interact in a world of complex, and often contradictory, patterns and tendencies. A focus on purposes permits central attention to the subjective bases of human activity; a parallel focus on practices then admits a complex and hybrid methodology that accommodates both 'objectively' and 'subjectively' focused forms of analysis.

Methodological aspects of the globalization debate

Some fundamental methodological issues are involved in the contention that basic human developments are driven by a complex interaction between evolving purposes and established practices and conditions. This also has significant practical implications in that, if global developments are driven by 'objective' forces, then the role for human volition in shaping the basics of the future human condition is severely limited. If, in contrast, developments are driven by the evolving condition of human intersubjectivity, then human beings have the potential of exercising a profound influence upon their common prospects, however problematical such a project might be in practice. The issue of globalization, and its contrary tendencies, thus raises central questions of ontology, methodology and epistemology.

Here we encounter what Hollis and Smith (1994, 1996) term the two 'stories' of explanation, one objectivist and the other subjectivist. A clear comprehension of the complications of moving between these two distinct analytical perspectives is essential if the problems involved in claims about the manner in which 'objective' forces influence the perceptions and cognitions of individual human actors are to be addressed effectively.

Many statements about contemporary globalization resonate with deterministic echoes, particularly those asserting the irresistibility of globalizing forces or the irreversibility of globalized conditions. Such determinism, however, can be defended against the variability of human conditions and the apparent unpredictability of many 'core' developments, through the use of irrefutable metatheory (Castles, 1971), and/or the invocation of the temporally unspecified 'long term'. Such determinism also tends to monocausal explanations of human developments. The embrace of technological determinism is one example of such tendencies within discussions of globalization. Pure voluntarism is also problematical, however, for individual behaviour can rarely be unconstrained by context. The practical constraints upon the individual imagination are substantial, and the restraints upon behaviour are considerable, at all levels of human conduct.

Between the extremes of determinism and voluntarism lie the promising notions of probabilism and possibilism (H. and M. Sprout, 1965: chs 5–6). These suggest a 'path dependent' notion of change and development which can accommodate change at all levels, from the macro-level of global trends to the micro-level of genetic mutation (Monod, 1972; Chapter 4 in this volume). The constraints exercised by prevailing conditions, particularly those of complex aggregations, suggest that the collective framework within which individuals operate thus exerts a profound influence. Such holism, whether *realist* or less ambitiously *empirical* (Jones, 1995: 9–10), by presuming that the *whole* is often greater than the mere sum of the parts, avoids the ontological difficulties, and explanatory poverty, of ultra-individualistic or *atomistic* approaches to human development.

A non-determinist attempt to resolve the holistic-atomistic divide has been attempted by Anthony Giddens (1984) in his concept of structuration. Here, both the collective and individual levels of activity are seen as mutually constitutive, with social formations being the product of the mutually reinforcing intersubjectivity of the contributing and participating individuals. This approach, however, remains severely limited in its capacity to deal with change (Archer, 1988: preface and chs 1–2) and, hence, to address the dynamic of globalization.

A more complex methodology is required for the study of contemporary globalization, in which socially constructed 'realities' are identified as the basis of a constrained possibilism. In particular, a non-deterministic methodology for the study of complex patterns of change is needed, in which the triggers for change may be identified in relatively random happenings, but are more commonly driven by dysfunctional features of existing arrangements. In this sense, all developments are significantly constrained by established conditions. Path dependence, with possibilistic and probabilistic features, is thus seen as a central characteristic of change and development in complex realms of human activity, and remains a vision that is distinct from any notions of predetermination. Such a perspective underlies the observations that are offered within the rest of this chapter.

Purposes

Many of the central questions raised by contemporary debates on globalization can be addressed by considering the purposes of those engaged in the theory and practice of the phenomenon. The purposes of actors and agents can, in terms of the objectivist/subjectivist dichotomy, be viewed as either a matter of 'objectively' identifiable interests and requirements, or as a matter of the subjective determination of aspirations and requirements by participants in any realm of activity.

The ontological and methodological perspective adopted in this chapter envisages a complex relationship between the 'objective' and the 'subjective' in moulding purposes. Subjectively defined purposes are initially generated primarily within the realm of human reflection, debate and discussion. Once defined, however, such purposes will impact upon the multifaceted patterns of established behaviour (practices) and the subjective foundations they rest upon, adding weight to their existing internal tensions and contradictions.

Purposes are not static within the human condition. The antinomy between purposes and practices, so beloved of Michael Oakeshott (1962), is false within the human condition, wherein even highly formalized games might be indulged in to secure general status in life and in which status in life might, in turn, be established by prowess in one or other highly ritualized game. Such interconnections between purposes and practices are manifest in all realms of human activity.

A complex dynamic results from the impact of new subjectively defined purposes upon established practices. This impact in turn stimulates new tensions and incompatibilities, which generate 'objective' pressures for further changes to established practices when the purposes, understandings and expectations of human agents change to accommodate such pressures. Path-dependent complexity thus remains characteristic of the sources and processes of change in human affairs. This complexity, moreover, highlights the inherent indeterminacy and generally non-linear character of change. Path-determination says more about the sources of change, and the immediate constraints to which it is subject, than about the conditions which will eventually result from the long-term working through of the process of cumulative change.

The purposes of two broad categories of agents are centrally involved in the evolution of the international political economy: the purposes of practitioners in the worlds of government, business and transnational cultural transmission; and the purposes of the varied commentators upon contemporary globalization. Although the purposes of these two sets of actors may often be interrelated and contribute to the complex process of change, they are worth considering as separate phenomena initially.

Governmental purposes

The purposes of myriad practitioners have clearly been implicated in moves towards what would now be termed greater globalization throughout the post-1945 era. The American promoters of the post-war international economic order clearly sought a stable environment for the development of a liberal free trade system, a new global division of labour and enhanced opportunities for overseas investments. Controversy persists as to whether such activities were motivated by altruistic aspirations for a better and less warlike world (Spero, 1985: ch. 1), or to promote a US-led, world-wide capitalist hegemony (Gill, 1991a). Nevertheless, the International Monetary Fund (IMF) and the GATT were the immediate institutional representations of this new order.

The post-war experience demonstrates the complexities and potential contradictions involved in directing, or analysing, central developments in world affairs, for they are rarely perfectly synchronized with one another and may often move in contrary directions for substantial periods of time. Initial aspirations to liberalize the world's trade and currency systems foundered on the twin obstacles of widespread economic destruction and dislocation, together with the apparent political and military threat posed by the Soviet Union. Substantial progress with both trade liberalization and currency convertibility had to wait until the later 1950s, when the recovering industrial economies, other than the USA, had enjoyed sufficient time and opportunity to achieve substantial levels of economic recovery.

The roots of globalization were sown, or substantially fertilized, by a series of significant decisions, mis-decisions and non-decisions by influential governments, particularly that of the USA. For neo-Gramscians, such developments bear witness to the power of the hegemonic bloc of global business interests. Others, however, accept the role of influential economic interests in shaping policy, particularly their 'home' governments, but also admit the effects of multitargeted, and often imprecise, policy-making by clearly limited human agents under conditions of considerable pressure and chronic uncertainty.

By the time in the early 1970s when major advances in global liberalization could be promoted with some confidence, imperfect decision- making had to be undertaken by US governments facing a range of new pressures, including: the politically debilitating debacle of the Vietnam War; the currency crisis of the first two years of the 1970s; and the recovery of America's industrialized competitors, with the consequential growth of competition in markets both abroad and at home. The USA was also faced, along with the rest of the industrialized world, by the steady upward pressure on the demand for and prices of many basic industrial commodities; these pressures were to come to a dramatic head with the oil price rises of 1973/4 and 1979. US administrations that were to do so much to encourage the intensification of globalization processes from the 1970s onwards were thus beset with problems and dilemmas of considerable novelty and complexity.

It was in this atmosphere of dilemma and indecision in the early 1970s that new decisions and mis-decisions were to add their effects to a longer-term drift towards a run-away, and increasingly globalized, international financial system. Susan Strange (1986: 31–8) has charted the critical elements of this process with characteristic vigour and insight. Long-term failings in the management of the international political economy created the background to a set of critical non-decisions from the 1970s onwards. The long-term failings included the failure of all NATO members to contribute proportionately to the costs of western defence from the early 1950s, leaving the USA to shoulder a disproportionate share of the burden and develop a balance of payments deficit; a failure to develop standardized means of dealing with persisting international indebtedness; the spread of export promotion through subsidies and export guarantees; the failure to institutionalize the spread and growing influence of the major, TNCs; and, finally, the decision to reopen the London commodity markets to international trading and, hence, to revive London as a centre for international financial operations.

The five key non-decisions of the 1970s onwards 'occurred' against this background (Strange, 1986: 38–46). The first was the failure to establish effective authority over the foreign exchange markets after 1971 and the failure of the Smithsonian Agreement to re-establish international monetary stability. The second was the failure to establish some new rules for international economic and financial adjustment, possibly through the adoption of a new version of the gold-exchange standard. The third and fourth non-decisions involved the linked failures to establish either a new *modus vivendi* with the major oil producing states or effective support mechanisms for those LDCs that were most adversely affected by the oil price shocks of the 1970s. The final critical 'non-decision' was the failure to create a new 'lender of last resort' within the international economic community.

The combined effect of these later non-decisions and the earlier failures was to reinforce the trend towards the rapid growth of international financial flows and transactions that were increasingly beyond the control of governmental authorities. Levels of international financial flows and the emerging Euro-dollar market both expanded massively: the ratio of financial transactions in the Euro-markets to world trade increased from 6:1 in 1979 to some 25:1 in 1986 (Walter, 1991: 197), with estimates of the ratio now standing at 40:1 or more. The consequences for national and regional economies of these developments were to be discerned in the scale and intensity of the LDC debt crisis from the early 1980s onwards, and in the exchange rate fluctuations that confounded Europe's Exchange Rate Mechanism (ERM) in the late 1980s.

In the face of inherent uncertainty and ignorance about the future consequences of current actions, governmental decision-making frequently falls back upon prevailing doctrines of economic and political conduct. Doctrines, however, change under the influence of circumstances and fashions. They also influence perceptions of current problems, especially their significance, sources and possible resolution. Since the early 1990s, for example, the approach of the Clinton Administration, and of influential voices in Congress and the wider American polity, have reflected a growing concern about America's competitive position within the world economy and with 'unfair competition' from abroad. The NAFTA and the recent adoption of protectionist rhetoric by the Buchanan wing of the Republican Party both provide evidence of the spread of the appeal of 'anti-globalization' sentiments within US politics.

Governments elsewhere have also pursued a variety of purposes in the era of growing apparent globalization, with varying degrees of openness. British governments have generally been in thrall to *laissez faire* doctrines and the hope, at least initially, that Britain might find its economic salvation through the growing contribution of the financial and services sectors. Other European governments have embraced globalizing tendencies with rather more qualified enthusiasm, often deploying the policies of the EU as a cushion against, if not a clear restraint upon, the more severe pressures of growing international economic competition and industrial relocation. This was clear for example in the EU's determined posture during the negotiations for the Uruguay Round of the GATT.

The virtues of unfettered free market processes have failed to impress many of the more successful governments outside Europe and North America. These governments, many of them in South-East Asia, have provided extensive and effective support for industrialization and economic development (Wade, 1990; Weiss and Hobson, 1995: 135–97). Moreover, there is a strong suggestion that those amongst the 'Asian Tigers' which are engaged in growing levels of overseas FDI are doing so with the toleration, if not actual approval, of their home governments. This is especially the case when those overseas investments are part of a strategy of emphasizing greater value-added production at home, with more labour-intensive, lower value-added activity being exported. Home governments are also generally supportive of overseas FDI designed to overcome actual or potential trade barriers created by those countries or blocs within which protectionist sentiments might be rising in the wake of growing imports from these so-called 'Asian Tigers'.

At the same time, the governments of many other regions suffer from relative impotence in the face of the forces of globalization. Much of Africa remains unable to do much more than accept the imperatives of the international economic system or to turn away into a condition of impoverished autarky. Much the same fate confronts many of the economies of the former Soviet bloc.

Non-governmental purposes

The purposes (and practices) of non-governmental actors are often given pride of place in discussions of contemporary globalization. Such non-governmental actors range from increasingly internationalized financial actors and manufacturing enterprises through to internationally organized political movements, interest groups, religious organizations and criminal conspiracies. This range corresponds broadly to the lineage of analytical Marxist and Liberal Institutionalist traditions (Keohane and Nye, 1972). These lineages are portrayed in Figure 10.1.

Globalization thus marks the crystallization of many of the possibilities and potentialities marked out by earlier debates within the field of

Liberal-Institutionalist Tradition	**Marxist tradition**
Liberal Internationalism/Institutionalism ↓ Transnational Relations ↓ Interdependence theory (including Complex Interdependence) ↓ Globalization	Imperialism ↓ Neo-Colonialism and Informal Empire ↓ Globalization and Capitalist Hegemony

Figure 10.1 Lineages of the globalization debate

international political economy. Purpose, however, is no less polymorphous in the non-governmental realm than in the domain of governments. Moreover, such variety of purpose indicates the diverse implications of globalization, when prompted and promoted by non-governmental interests and groupings. The variability of the purposes/practices nexus over time also illustrates their complex interaction, and the difficulty of maintaining a simple empirical distinction between these two facets of human activity.

Financial and commercial interests

Financial and commercial interests are the non-governmental source of globalization most commonly considered, but the enthusiasm of these interests for globalization varies in line with their scale of operation, areas of specialization and the availability of real opportunities for international operation. The internationalization of trade and production has been expanding at an accelerated pace throughout the modern era, frequently under the influence of international trading, extraction or production companies. However, the dramatic development of the past two decades has been the rapid internationalization of the world's financial systems. The liberalization of the financial systems and services of a number of the major industrial/capitalist countries during these decades has permitted or encouraged the opening up and general internationalization of the world's major stock exchanges, banking systems and insurance services, thereby supplementing and reinforcing the long-term role of international currency markets. Although the effects of such financial integration on patterns of production and exchange in the 'real economy' may sometimes be exaggerated, they clearly remain a development of wide-ranging significance (Cerny, 1993). Private acquisition is also the overwhelming motive of this development. The 'public' goods of financial service and stability remain second-order concerns of financiers and tend to surface only at times of instability.

At the same time, those firms which have engaged in extraction, production and shipment have contributed to globalization in more varied ways. Extractive or agricultural industries, for example, may be quite limited in the number of countries in which they operate, and in the range of issues to which they direct their primary attention. Although their end-products often sell within a world market, or are affected by world-wide price movements, the activities in which such firms engage may not directly contribute to any qualitative or quantitative *advance* of globalization.

TNCs, with their highly varied patterns of production, also make an uneven contribution to the growth of globalization. Changing conditions, and even fashions, have influenced enthusiasms for different patterns of international activity. The automobile manufacturer Ford exemplifies such variability over time. Ford's facilities in the UK were initially established to reduce the transport costs involved in 'exporting' Ford's products to Britain and, to a lesser extent, to evade European trade restrictions. Comprehensive kits of parts were initially shipped from the USA to the UK for local assembly. However, the policy of assembling and marketing US model 'kit cars' in Europe was then reversed. European facilities, and particularly the new fully integrated plant in Dagenham, Essex, were turned over to the production of locally designed, locally targeted models constructed primarily from locally produced parts and components. This policy was to be changed again as Ford attempted to design, source and market a 'global' car. This strategy is now under threat due to the disappointing response to the first global car (the Contour/Mondeo) in the US market.

The current arrival of South-East Asian transplant facilities in many European countries resembles Ford's earlier incursion into the UK. Most of the new facilities are essentially plants for the assembly of kits and components imported from factories in the firm's home country, and are designed to overcome actual or potential barriers to imports. The immediate effect of such transplant industries, therefore, is to increase the apparent level of transnationally integrated production, and through this the apparent level of globalization by one of its more critical measures. However, the influence of requirements (particularly those of the EU) for local sourcing of parts and components may reduce the proportion of home–host country shipments within the end-products that are marketed by such enterprises. The home–host country relationship might, in such circumstances, be reduced to home control of design and strategic management, and to host–home transfers of profits. One measure of apparent globalization would have been reduced appreciably by such developments.

Strategic alliances with foreign firms have also become fashionable as an alternative to straightforward FDI (Dunning, 1993a: 190–219). Risks and costs can be shared, particularly in high-tech R&D areas, and the reduction of transaction costs in accessing foreign markets. Asymmetrical benefits from such strategic partnerships may arise, however, as valuable competencies are surrendered in return for the promise of sometimes insubstantial or ephemeral advantages. Moreover, many such strategic partnerships have been focused within regional groupings, such as the EU, or been prompted primarily by political restraints upon direct, solely-owned investments in new markets.

The lack of homogeneous culture and consumer tastes internationally also inhibits the emergence of many truly global products. The disappointing fate of the Contour/Mondeo within the US market evidences such diversity, as have the disparaging reactions in the UK to the styling of Ford's Scorpio. Many internationally operative firms thus feel more confident in accommodating local tastes and preferences in many product areas. Operating transnationally, while focusing design, products and marketing locally, has been given the jarring – but reasonably judicious – title of *glocalization* (Ruigrok and van Tulder, 1995: 178–81 and 277–8) to differentiate it from true globalization. Such *glocalization* marks the maximization of sales and revenue in diverse markets and may also lead to a reduction in transnational shipments of goods and components as improvements in information gathering and processing permit more discriminating responses to local markets.

The major alternative to a *glocalization* strategy may not be true globalization but actually a strategy of imposing consumer tastes and cultural dispositions upon populations and societies that have not traditionally embraced such 'values' and aspirations: a form of westernization (or even of Western cultural imperialism). The primary language of this cultural offensive is of course English, rather than some global Esperanto. Such cultural westernization, however, has been prone to forceful reactions and resistance. An era of the 'clash of civilizations' (Huntington, 1993) would profoundly qualify, if not confound, any simple expectations about globalization (see Chapter 3 in this volume).

Global society[2]

Positive international fellowship, however, may also be facilitated by modern information technology and transport systems. Commonalities of interest and sentiment have some capacity to generate affiliations that may operate on a truly global scale. The emergence of a *global society* is, however, a far more contentious and ambitious matter. For Martin Shaw (1994), common purposes might engender a growing sense of shared human identity and strong mutual regard which could crystallize into a new global *Gemeinschaft.* Alternatively, common problems and pressures might generate a more modest set of common, technical responses on issues of shared concern: a form of global *Gesellschaft.* The emergence of true global *Gemeinschaft,* however, with shared norms and behavioural expectations, confronts the manifest fractiousness of much of humanity and the clear lack of any sense of common global identity beyond the most basic level. Indeed, the many counter-tendencies to globalization demonstrate the strong and persisting influence of established constraints upon (and resistance towards) any advance towards a new global social consciousness (see Chapter 3 in this volume).

At the same time, developing a global *Gesellschaft* is equally problematic. The profusion of common international experiences and problems might encourage the emergence of a sense of common purpose, but such expectations remain unduly rationalistic, if not fatally functionalistic. Past expectations about international interdependence illustrate the problem here. For example, ideas of benign international interdependence flourished at the start of the twentieth century. It was believed that the growth of international trade and a new international division of labour would create such high levels of interdependence and mutual interest that it would be both impossible and undesirable for societies to go to war with one another. The apogee of such views was expressed in *The Great Illusion* (Angell, 1909). Within a few years of its publication, however, these webs of interdependence and mutual interest had been sundered with a speed and brutality that shattered all earlier beliefs and expectations.

Common fate is another supposed source of a new global community. Unfortunately the conditions referenced by popular ideas of common fate vary considerably (Jones, 1995: 75–6). They embrace: (i) transmitted effects; (ii) shared consequences of unilateral actions; (iii) shared consequences of joint actions; and (iv) common exposure to externally generated effects. The first condition, unfortunately, may induce friction rather than a sense of shared community. The consequences of the second condition may be equally fractious unless the generator of the effects perceives a sufficient motive for unilateral action. The third condition may appear to be the most promising for communal responses, but the emergence of such responses will depend upon the development of appropriate mechanisms for co-ordination and cost sharing. In their absence, intersocietal conflict may yet again arise. The fourth condition presumes either that some sort of collective response is possible, or that the world's population will be able to develop a sense of collective togetherness, rather than widespread hysteria, in the face of some potential, and unavoidable, global catastrophe. Widespread perceptions of a common global 'fate' may thus be as divisive in its effects as uniting for a world population that has yet to develop a readiness to accept substantial costs in the interests of others. Even *Gesellschaft* may thus prove to be embarrassingly elusive to achieve in practice, as the immediate purposes of humanity override longer term requirements.

Practices

We have seen that the purposes of myriad actors upon the contemporary international and global stage are so diverse in nature and import that they point to quite different worlds of experience and potentiality. The practices which these individual and collective actors engage in are equally diverse. Moreover, it is these practices which collectively constitute the contemporary global system, its characteristic patterns of behaviour and its prevailing institutions. Although such practices clearly reflect their purposes, through their collective impact they also constitute a major source of pressure for any future change in purposes.

Governmental practices

The role of governmental practices in the contemporary world remains far wider than simple models of a globalized world would suggest. The dominant post-1945 influence of the USA is widely acknowledged. Controversy persists, however, as to whether this use of national hegemonic power was directed towards the promotion of the interests of a transnational capitalist class (Gill, 1991), the interests of a more nationally-specific state-military-industrial complex (Servan-Schreiber, 1968), or for the general benefit of the 'world community' (Gilpin, 1987: 343–45).

Neo-mercantilist practices have been common to virtually all governments at all levels of influence (Jones, 1986; Weiss and Hobson,

1995), irrespective of the range and ingenuity of justificatory arguments and obfuscations. Industry is stimulated and exports are promoted by all but the most dysfunctional of governments. Protectionism, of direct and non-tariff forms, is far more widespread than the rhetoric of a globalized world economy would suggest. Industrial relations are the subject of widespread interest and attention. Education and training is everywhere encouraged, usually with an extensive core of state funding and state direction.

Governments do participate in international fora for global governance. However, the time and energy devoted to the UN, its specialist agencies such as the IMF, or other international institutions such as the Bank for International Settlements (BIS) or the World Radio Conference, pales into relative insignificance in comparison with the attention directed towards 'national' policies or those regional agencies, such as the EU, which both have more immediate implications for economic interests and appear to be more amenable to direct influence. Moreover, when critical issues direct attention beyond national borders, or regional frontiers, governments are far more likely to resort to bilateral negotiations with other involved states (Jones, 1986: 159–62) or to seek resolution of their troubles within such highly selective, elitist international assemblies as the Group of 7 or the Paris Club. Even in such relatively manageable groupings of leading economies, progress on the major issues of global governance remains painfully slow on such central issues as international standards on business accounts, investment and management practices, and trade promotion or on the enduring questions of international economic management, including 'lenders of last resort'.

Non-governmental practices

Much of the strong globalization thesis rests upon the influence and activities of a variety of non-governmental actors. The characteristic practices of these actors, however, remain as diverse if not more so than those of contemporary governments.

Financial and commercial actors

The level of global integration in financial services has proceeded far further than in most other sectors of economic life. International integration has accelerated in the wholesale and retail financial industries in the last two decades (O'Brien, 1992). Although this is not a fully accomplished condition, it has far outpaced the development of government-based regulatory mechanisms. Such developing financial integration has not, however, resulted in a world that behaves in perfect synchronicity in financial matters. Interest rate movements in the major advanced industrial countries were only weakly correlated during the period 1984–93. Similarly, the major stock exchanges were often subject to contrary movements in price levels during the 1986–93 period (Jones, 1995: 105–9). Opposing movements in such financial indicators can sometimes be explained by direct transfers of funds from one country to another. However, there have been periods during which such indicators have moved in sympathy with one another. The relationship thus remains complex and vulnerable to a range of influences which vary in their mutual effect.

The commercial world beyond the frontiers of the financial sector reveals an even more complex and uneven picture. A somewhat simplified picture of globalized industry can be constructed with some ease from a number of indirect indicators of levels of internationalization of a firm's operations. A perfectly globalized industrial corporation would be characterized by:

- industrial ownership and management that reveal an absence of national biases;
- internationally widespread and transnationally integrated production by the major industrial corporations, without marked national or regional biases;
- low and diminishing levels of traditional exports of manufactured goods relative to output from 'local' facilities of the major corporations in host countries or by the local strategic partners of such firms;
- world-wide distributions of sales by major corporations directly proportional to the size of markets, with no home-market bias;
- an increasingly even international spread of the assets owned and operated by the major corporations;
- an even distribution of the world-wide R&D activity of major corporations.

Available evidence suggests a reality at variance with each of these characteristics of advanced globalization. The great majority of all industrial shares continue to be owned within the companies' home countries and the great proportion of the top management of the major transnational companies is still drawn from their home countries. Levels of traditional exports generally remain far greater than levels of internationalized production. Most sales made by the world's major companies are still made within their home countries. Ownership of assets continues to be located preponderantly within the home country of companies; and the great proportion of 'foreign' assets remain within the region of the world economy within which companies' homes are located. The preponderant proportion of the R&D is still undertaken in the home countries of companies. However, a major caveat to such generalizations, and a further qualification to the simple globalization thesis, is that the major corporations of the leading advanced industrial countries exhibit national and regional differences in their practices of asset ownership, production and partnership (Ruigrok and van Tulder, 1995: ch. 7; Hirst and Thompson, 1996: 82–98; *The Economist*, 17 February 1996).

The international practices of major enterprises also continue to be influenced substantially by the existence and practices of governments. Government policies have prompted many strategic partnerships, as evident in the world's airline industry, and restrictions on wholly-owned subsidiaries have stimulated relationships between international operators and 'local' partners. Cultural diversity may reinforce such dispositions. Such factors add their weight to continuing interests in cost reduction and risk sharing.

The fragmentation of sovereignty, legal jurisdiction and accountancy systems within the contemporary world also permits, and even encourages, strategic behaviour by firms, including 'divide and rule' strategies, manipulative secrecy in dealings with local authorities and labour organizations, and most insidiously, transfer pricing (Murray, 1981). Where firms have to deal with separate authorities, all equally jealous of their sovereignty, they are able to manipulate the 'prices' charged for shipments of components and parts between their subsidiaries in various countries. Such price manipulation has the purpose of altering the apparent profitability of the various subsidiaries: profits can be made to appear in the country with the lowest tax rates; capital controls can be evaded by the siphoning of finances through the firm's internal payments; reinvestment abroad can be undertaken relatively invisibly; and, in the extreme, subsidies paid by one government to support continued production within its country can be spirited away to a company's other countries of operation. A transnational mode of operation can thus serve to exploit governments that remain in a low globalized political and regulative condition.

Global society: adherents and advocates

Although the integrated world of business leaders, prominent politicians, civil servants and academics has often been suggestive of a new global society, it has done little to counter the motivational obstacles discussed earlier in this chapter or to reduce the massive differences of culture, language, geographical constraints and disparities of material circumstances that obstruct a global *Gemeinschaft*.

There are many, however, who persist in efforts directed towards greater global homogeneity. The export of Western (and largely American) cultural products is one of the most striking of such ventures. Hollywood may not necessarily wish for a world remade in the image of small-town America, but it would clearly not reduce the acceptability of its products if such were to be the case. Moreover, Hollywood and others in the US cultural/entertainment industry have built upon the earlier world-wide penetration of Western culture and industrial artefacts to achieve a world-wide market of impressive dimensions. Such essentially Western cultural penetration is a major source of the cultural, social, economic and political convergence that has developed to date.

Convergence theses are of course no longer novel, and have well-established 'liberal' and 'Marxist' variants that persist in the face of an uneven historical record. Expectations of convergence towards a prosperous democratic and peace-loving norm have fallen repeatedly in the face of a complex, and more turbulent reality (Fukuyama, 1992). Overall, both the historical record and much contemporary evidence, particularly from South-East Asia, suggest a complex and dynamic pattern of selective absorption of 'Western' influence combined with the re-emphasis of features of 'traditional' social, cultural and even political forms. This suggests a *dialectic of difference* which challenges simplistic notions of convergence. The established state system, for example, has both the characteristic form(s) and problems of globalization as it has emerged thus far. The modern state system developed with the interrelated crystallisation of two pivotal forms of human organization: the system of sovereign states and the system of industrial capitalism (Jones, 1995: 47–54). The persistence of these two definitive institutions conditions the potentialities for global social developments. States continue to maintain distinct currencies, distinct legal and regulative systems, and separate taxation regimes, all of which reflect differing social and cultural conditions. What is likely to emerge under the umbrella of statism and industrial capitalism is thus likely to be a seriously limited and attenuated form of global human association.

The element of functionalism, and even technological determinism, that lurks beyond many convergence theses is also present in the needs-based expectation of the emergence of a global *Gesellschaft*. Problems clearly create needs, but needs do not generate automatic solutions in human affairs. The problems associated with dealing effectively with the issue of the 'global commons' illustrate clearly the path-dependent nature of change, and how difficult it can be to forge new and creative solutions. The Rio Conference on the environment, for example, proved stronger on pious rhetoric than on muscular (and costly) regulation. Where energetic action has been taken on matters of general concern, it has largely been in areas where the interests of major economic and financial interests have been at stake, such as in the debt crisis of the early 1980s or the Mexican financial crisis of the mid-1990s.

The technological imperative

The discussion of globalization, in theory and practice, in terms of purposes and practices, subordinates the issue of technology (see Chapters 8 and 9 in this volume). However, technological determinism, particularly that of information technology, surfaces at various points in any discussion of contemporary globalization (Castells, 1989), suggesting one form of convergence. A path-determined view of change, however, places the role of technology in a clear perspective. Technological innovation is not seen to be exogenous to the system and situation within which it is introduced. Rather, prevailing circumstances determine whether any innovation will find a use and, therefore, be converted from a bright idea into an extensive application. Moreover, the dynamic of innovation is often located within the perceived requirements of industry, or of the wider society. The development of the precision chronometer to meet the requirements of the British Admiralty for an aid to accurate celestial navigation exemplifies such demand-driven innovation. Finally, the precise application of any technological innovation and its wider impact, will be largely determined by prevailing patterns of economic, social and political purposes and practices.

The historical record makes clear that the full impact of any major technological innovation has never been foreseen with any precision. Confident predictions that modern information technology will mark the ultimate victory of hegemonical capitalism or that it will facilitate a new and liberated global society are both likely to be incomplete, or even entirely erroneous. What is clear, however, is that the impact of modern technological innovations upon future developments will be complex, often contradictory, but ultimately conditioned by the circumstances within which they are introduced.

Globalization: complex patterns and contrary trends

Given the diversity of purposes and practices involved in the processes and conditions associated with contemporary globalization, it is unsurprising that the patterns exhibited within the international political economy are complex and sometimes contradictory.

It was noted that even in the highly integrated global financial sector, national developments were not always well synchronized with one another. Such diversity, however, continues to be even more marked in the 'real' economies of the world. Many indices of economic and industrial development within the advanced industrial countries are irregularly interconnected. Correlations for levels of earnings ranged between –0.24 (Germany:UK) and 0.49 (USA:Canada) between 1986 and 1993; correlations of unemployment rates varied between –0.57 (Italy:USA) and 0.7 (UK:USA); correlations of growth rates ranged from –0.24 (UK:Germany) to 0.05 (Germany:France); and correlations of consumer price increases ranged from –0.018 (Canada:Germany) to 0.72 (France:USA: see Jones, 1995: 109–18).

Levels of engagement in international trade also vary considerably. Amongst the advanced industrial countries, exports as a percentage of GDP ranged, in 1991, from 7 per cent for the USA to 60 per cent for Belgium (World Bank, 1993: tables 3 and 14). The combined imports and exports of the advanced industrial countries also vary considerably as a percentage of GDP and have shown only very gradual growth in the post-war era, having yet to reach pre-1913 levels in most cases (World Bank, 1995: tables 13 and 3; Hirst and Thompson, 1996: 27). The consequences of involvement in the contemporary world economy are also highly varied, with problems for some of the older advanced industrial countries, opportunities for the NICs, and often very severe difficulties for the poorer LDCs (Hurrell and Woods, 1995; Hirst and Thompson, 1996: 99–120). Such patterns provide only indirect evidence of some of the dominant characteristics of the contemporary situation, but do suggest much of its complexity and diversity.

Regional patterns also remain strong in the contemporary global political economy. These patterns may often reflect historical interconnections amongst the various regions (Wallerstein, 1979), but remain a strong conditioning influence upon the nature and extent of contemporary globalization. Commodity concentrations and geographical concentrations of exports and imports are far higher for LDCs than for industrialized countries (Jones, 1995: 118–41). Asymmetrical dependencies and uneven experiences, in turn, reflect and underlie regional differences and, in some cases, the growing impact of regionalization within the international political economy (Jones, 1995: 141–53; Gamble and Payne, 1996).

The continued role and relevance of the state, and other local forms of social, economic and political organization, was suggested in the discussion of the purposes and practices of governments. The point of enduring significance here is that governments can, under prevailing conditions, provide their citizens with a range of essential goods, including external security and internal economic and social stability. Other sources of such goods are clearly conceivable, but given the path-dependence of central developments, extremely difficult to orchestrate, peacefully and constructively, within a world fragmented into states and dominated by industrial capitalism. Extant states are therefore likely to be the first point of reference of most populations when faced with major challenges, including those generated by globalization processes and pressures. Localization of responses, and even re-'nationalization' are therefore all too likely as a response to runaway global dynamics.

Conclusion: purposes and the gurus of globalization

The complex relationship between purposes and practices in the contemporary international political economy underlies the polymorphism of the world that we confront: a world that reveals myriad forms and 'realities' upon close inspection. Dominant patterns may differ markedly in differing domains of activity, from 'world cities' down to rural villages in peripheral economies (Knox and Taylor, 1995). In general, financial integration is far more advanced than other areas of activity, while the provision of direct, non-financial services remains the most localized. This complexity and diversity of contemporary 'reality', moreover, draws attention to the diversity of motives underlying those who promote globalization or engage in contemporary debates about the nature and extent of the phenomenon.

A number of major policy-oriented positions are apparent within contemporary globalization debates. Liberal globalists welcome increased globalization as both the fruit of increasing international free trade and as a source of its further advance. Economic realists are deeply sceptical about the benefits and stability of a globalized political economy, advocating instead regional or more local developments that might restrain its further progress or blunt its more damaging effects. Radical globalists are primarily critical of the capitalist character of contemporary globalization, seeking salvation from an ever more exploitative global capitalist hegemony through some form of transnational socialist transformation. Green critics of capitalist globalization fall within the radical camp but tend to emphasize small-scale (neo-anarchistic) solutions to the problems of a run-away global capitalist economy.

Optimists are also opposed to pessimists in the contemporary globalization debate. Liberals are predominantly optimistic, remaining ever sanguine about the capacity of the free market, and associated technological innovations, to resolve all the problems generated by an industrial capitalist world economy. Realists are more ambivalent, seeking redirection through routine political processes, but fearing that the dangers of globalization can be addressed effectively only when the associated strains and stresses have generated uncontainable levels of social, economic and political turbulence. Radicals express the greatest ambivalence in their attitudes towards globalization and its future management. The collapse of radical confidence of the 1980s and early 1990s has deprived many left-leaning analysts of the clear and confident expectations about the future that traditionally gave shape to their analyses and prognostications. A globalizing world seems to lack an emancipatory teleology, with hope resting on the prospects of 'global democracy' (Held, 1995) or new, emancipatory social movements (Shaw, 1994).

A pattern of path-dependent development is characteristic of the contemporary globalization phenomenon. The dominant forces behind contemporary globalization remain those of profit and power. Technological possibilities have been available for exploitation by those who pursue profit or power on a global scale and whose ability to exploit the new opportunities largely reflects prior positions of wealth or power. Those, in contrast, who lack such advantages have been far less successful in shaping a new global landscape more favourable to their purposes, the contribution of the global information highway and 'cheap' international travel notwithstanding. Claims for a new global society and culture thus contrast sharply with a world in which economic dislocation, cultural/religious division and myriad armed conflicts flourish, and even intensify, around the globe.

Moreover, many groups (including, for example, state governments and lower-skilled workers) have found that their capabilities or interests have been challenged, and often reduced, by the progress of globalization. Those who have been thus disadvantaged may well seek the retardation of the progress of globalization, its reversal, and/or the bolstering of alternative patterns of development. Incomplete in its embrace of humanity in all its range and variety, globalization may yet be checked and even sundered by its own antithesis.

Globalization is thus a compelling contemporary issue if only for the way in which it crystallizes the current divisions between celebration and despair, between dispassionate analysis and committed critique and, most importantly, between the 'haves' and the 'have nots' of the global system. The fractious fragmentation of IR and IPE into empiricists, neo-Gramscians and post-modernists exemplifies the potency of such lines of division when confronted by a world of undiminishing complexity and dynamism. The emergence of fissures along many of the contemporary lines of division amongst human beings may be the parallel within the reality of a globalizing world.

Notes

1. I would like to thank participants at the 'Globalization and its Critics' workshop for comments on a previous draft.
2. Arguably, any complete consideration of globalization must include an account of international criminal organizations as the dark underside of internationalized or transnationalized authority and power. Space limitations, however, prevent me from doing more than drawing attention to this particular facet of globalization. See Strange (1996).

References

Abu-Lughod, J. (1989) *Before European Hegemony: The World System A.D. 1250–1350*. New York, Oxford University Press.

Adam, B. (1994) *Timewatch*. Cambridge, Polity.

Agnew, J. (1994) 'Timeless Space and State-Centrism: The Geographical Assumptions of International Relations Theory', in S. Rosow, N. Innyatullah and M. Rupert (eds), *The Global Economy as Political Space*. Boulder, CO, Lynne Rienner: 87–106.

Agnew, J. and S. Corbridge (1995) *Mastering Space: Hegemony, Territory and International Political Economy*. London, Routledge.

Amin, A. (ed.) (1994) *Post-Fordism: A Reader*. Oxford, Basil Blackwell.

Amin, A. and N. Thrift (eds) (1994) *Globalization, Institutions, and Regional Development in Europe*. Oxford, Oxford University Press.

Anderson, K. and H. Norheim (1993) 'History, geography and regional economic integration', in. K. Anderson and R. Blackhurst (eds), *Regional Integration and the Global Trading System*. Hemel Hempstead, Harvester Wheatsheaf: 19–51.

Andrews, D. M. (1994) 'Capital Mobility and State Autonomy: Toward a Structural Theory of International Monetary Relations', *International Studies Quarterly* 38 (2): 193–218.

Angell, N. (1909) *The Great Illusion*. New York, Putnam.

Arase, D. (1994) 'Public-Private Sector Interest Coordination in Japan's ODA', *Pacific Affairs* 67 (2): 171–99.

Archer, M. (1988) *Culture and Agency: The Place of Culture in Social Theory*. Cambridge, Cambridge University Press.

Aron, R. (1962) *Peace and War*. London, Weidenfeld & Nicolson.

Ashley, R. (1981) 'Political Realism and Human Interest', *International Studies Quarterly* 25 (2): 204–36.

Auspitz, J. L. (1976) 'Individuality, Civility, and Theory: The Philosophical Imagination of Michael Oakeshott', *Political Theory* 4 (3): 261–352.

Baily, M. and H. Gersbach (1995). 'Efficiency in manufacturing and the need for global competition', *Brookings Papers on Economic Activity Microeconomics Issue*: 307–58.

Bairoch, P. (1982) 'International Industrialization Levels from 1750 to 1980', *Journal of European Economic History* 11 (2): 269–333.

Bairoch, P. and R. Kozul-Wright (1996) *Globalization Myths: Some Historical Reflections on Integration, Industrialization and Growth in the World Economy*. Geneva, UNCTAD.

Banks, M. (1985) 'The Inter-Paradigm Debate', in M. Light and A. J. Groom (eds), *International Relations: A Handbook of Current Theory*. London, Pinter: 7–26.

Barraclough, G. (1967) *An Introduction to Contemporary History*. Harmondsworth, Penguin.

Barbour, V. (1963) *Capitalism in Amsterdam in the 17th Century*. Ann Arbor, University of Michigan Press.

Baudrillard, J. (1975) *The Mirror of Production*. St Louis, Telos.
Bauman, Z. (1991) *Modernity and Ambivalence*. Cambridge, Polity.
Bauman, Z. (1992a) *Intimations of Postmodernity*. London, Routledge.
Bauman, Z. (1992b) 'Soil, Blood and Identity', *Sociological Review* 40 (4): 675–701.
Bayart, J. F. (1993) *The State in Africa: The Politics of the Belly*. London, Longman.
Baylis, J. and S. Smith (eds) (1997) *The Globalization of World Politics*. Oxford, Oxford University Press.
Beck, U. (1992) *The Risk Society*. London, Sage.
Beck, U., A. Giddens and S. Lash, (1994) *Reflexive Modernization: Politics, Tradition and Aesthetics in the Modern Social Order*. Cambridge, Polity.
Beitz, C. (1979) *Political Theory and International Relations*. Princeton, NJ, Princeton University Press.
Bello, W. and C. S. Cunningham (1994) 'Trade Warfare and Regional Integration in the Pacifics: the USA, Japan and the Asian NICs', *Third World Quarterly* **15** (3): 445–58.
Belton, J., J. Willie, *et al.* (1995) 'International Capital Inflows, Federal Budget Deficits, and Interest Rates, 1971–1984', *Quarterly Journal of Business and Economics* 34 (1): 3–13.
Bernard, M. and J. Ravenhill (1995) 'Beyond Product Cycles and Flying Geese: Regionalization, Hierarchy and the Industrialization of East Asia', *World Politics* 47 (2): 171–209.
Bernstein, P. L. (1996) *Against the Gods: The Remarkable Story of Risk*. New York, Wiley.
Bhaskar, R. (1975) *Realist Theory of Science*. Leeds, Alwa.
Bhaskar, R. (1989) *Reclaiming Reality: A Critical Introduction to Contemporary Philosophy*. London, Verso.
Blainey, G. (1983) *The Tyranny of Distance*. Melbourne, Sun Books (revised edn).
Blomström, M. (1990) *Transnational Corporations and Manufacturing Exports from Developing Countries*. New York, UN.
Blumenthal, R. (1993) 'As the Number of Private Guards Grows, Police Learn to Enlist Their Help', *The New York Times*, 13 July, A16.
Bonturi, M. and K. Fukasaku (1993). 'Globalisation and intra-firm trade', *OECD Economic Studies* (20): 145–59.
Borrus, M. (1995) *Punctuated Equilibria in Electronics: Microsystems, Standards' Competitions, and Asian Production Networks*. The China Circle: Regional Consequences of Evolving Relations among the PRC, Taiwan, and Hong Kong–Macau, Hong Kong.
Boskin, M. J. and L. J. Lau (1992) 'Capital, Technology, and Economic Growth', in N. Rosenberg, R. Landau and D. C. Mowery (eds), *Technology and the Wealth of Nations*. Stanford, CA, Stanford University Press: 17–55.
Botero, G. (1598/1956). *The Reason of State*. London, Routledge.
Bourdieu, P. (1977) *Outline of A Theory of Practice*. Cambridge, Cambridge University Press.
Bourdieu, P. and L. J. D. Wacquant (1992) *An Invitation to Reflexive Sociology*. Chicago, University of Chicago Press.
Boyer, R. and Drache, D. (eds) (1996) *States Against Markets: The Limits of Globalization*. London, Routledge.

Braudel, F. (1973) *Capitalism and Material Life, 1400–1800*, trans. M. Korhan. New York, Harper & Row.

Braudel, F. (1979) *Civilization & Capitalism 15th–18th Century*, Vol. 1, The Structures of Everyday Life, trans. S. Reynolds. New York, Harper & Row.

Braudel, F. (1980) *On History*. Chicago, University of Chicago Press.

Braudel, F. (1982) *Civilization and Capitalism, 15th–18th Century, Vol. 2, The Wheels of Commerce*, trans. S. Reynolds. New York, Harper & Row.

Braudel, F. (1984) *Civilization and Capitalism, 15th–18th Century, Vol. 3, The Perspective of the World*, trans. S. Reynolds. London, Collins/Fontana.

Brown, C. (1992) *International Relations Theory: New Normative Approaches*. Hemel Hempstead, Harvester Wheatshaf.

Brown, C. (1994) 'Critical theory and post-modernism in international relations', in A. J. Groom and M. Light (eds), *Contemporary International Relations: A Guide to Theory*. London, Pinter: 56–68.

Buchanan, J. M. (1985) 'The Moral Dimension of Debt Financing', *Economic Inquiry*, (23): 1–6.

Buchanan, J. M. (1995) 'Clarifying Confusion About the Balanced Budget Amendment', *National Tax Journal* 48 (3): 347–55.

Bull, H. (1966) 'International Theory: The Case for a Classical Approach', *World Politics* 19 (2): 361–78.

Bull, H. (1977) *The Anarchical Society*. London, Macmillan.

Burrell, A. (1990) 'Kant and the Kantian Paradigm in international relations', *Review of International Studies* 16 (3): 183–205.

Burton, J. (1972) *World Society*. Cambridge, Cambridge University Press.

Buzan, B., C. Jones and R. Little, (1993) *The Logic of Anarchy: Neo-Realism to Structural Realism*. New York, Columbia University Press.

Camagni, R. (ed.) (1991) *Innovation Networks: Spatial Perspectives*. London, Belhaven Press.

Camagni, R. (1995) 'The Concept of Innovative Milieu and its Relevance for Public Policies in European Lagging Regions', *Papers in Regional Science* 74 (4): 317–40.

Camilleri, J. and J. Falk. (1992) *The End of Sovereignty? The Politics of a Shrinking and Fragmenting World*. Aldershot: Edward Elgar.

Campbell, D. (1996) 'Political Prosaics, Transversal Politics, and the Anarchical World', in M. Shapiro and H. R. Alker (eds), *Challenging Boundaries: Global Flows, Territorial Identities*. Minneapolis, University of Minnesota Press: 7–32.

Campbell, J., L. Hollingsworth, *et al.* (eds) (1991) *Governance of the American Economy*. New York, Cambridge University Press.

Carlos, A. and S. Nicholas (1988) '"Giants of an earlier capitalism": the chartered trading companies as modern multinationals', *Business History Review* 62: 398–419.

Carlsnaes, W. (1992) 'The Agency-Structure Problem in Foreign Policy Analysis', *International Studies Quarterly* 36 (3): 245–70.

Carr, E. H. (1961) *What is History?* Harmondsworth, Penguin.

Casanova, P. G. (1971) *Socioligia de la exploitacion*. Mexico, Siglo.

Casson, M. (1995) *The Organization of International Business*. Aldershot, Edward Elgar.

Castells, M. (1989) *The Informational City: Information Technology, Economic Restructuring and the Urban-Regional Process*. Oxford, Basil Blackwell.

Castells, M. (1996) *The Rise of the Network Society: The Information Age*. Oxford, Basil Blackwell.

Castles, F. (1971) *Politics and Social Insight*. London, Routledge & Kegan Paul.

Ceglowski, J. (1994) 'The law of one price revisited', *Economic Inquiry* 32: 407–18.

Cerny, P. G. (1990) *The Changing Architecture of Politics: Structure, Agency and the Future of the State*. London, Sage.

Cerny, P. G. (1991) 'The Limits of Deregulation: Transnational Interpenetration and Policy Change', *European Journal of Political Research* 19 (2/3): 173–96.

Cerny, P. G. (1993) *Finance and World Politics: Markets, Regimes and States in the Post-hegemonic Era*. Aldershot, Edward Elgar.

Cerny, P. G. (1994a) 'The Dynamics of Financial Globalization: Technology, Market Structure and Policy Response', *Policy Sciences* 27 (4): 319–42.

Cerny, P. G. (1994b) 'The Infrastructure of the Infrastructure? Toward "Embedded Financial Orthodoxy" in the International Political Economy', in B. Gills and R. Palan (eds), *Transcending the State-Global Divide: The Neostructuralist Agenda in International Relation*. Boulder, CO, Lynne Rienner: 223–49.

Cerny, P. G. (1995) 'Globalization and the changing logic of collective action', *International Organization* 49 (4): 595–626.

Cerny, P. G. (1996a) 'Globalization and Other Stories: The Search for a New Paradigm for International Relations', *International Journal* 51 (4): 617–37.

Cerny, P. G. (1996b) 'International Finance and the Erosion of State Policy Capacity', in P. Gummett (ed.), *Globalization and Public Policy*. Cheltenham and Brookfield, Edward Elgar: 83–104.

Cerny, P. G. (1997) *Embedding Financial Markets*. Annual meeting of the American Political Science Association, Washington, DC.

Cerny, P. G. (1998) 'Globalization, Governance, and Complexity', in A. Prakash and J. A. Hart (eds), *Globalization and Governance* (manuscript submitted to publishers).

Chamberlain, N. W. (1996) 'The Art of Unbalancing the Budget', *The Atlantic Monthly* (January).

Chaudhuri, K. (1985) *Trade and Civilisation in the Indian Ocean*. Cambridge, Cambridge University Press.

Chen, X. (1995) 'The Evolution of Free Economic Zones and the Recent Development of Cross-National Growth Zones', *International Journal of Urban and Regional Research* 19 (4): 593–621.

Child, J., M. Crozier, *et al.* (eds) (1993) *Societal Change between Market and Organization*. Aldershot, Avebury.

Chretien, J. (1996) *Canada Focus* 4 (20): 1.

Christopher, M. (1992) *Logistics and Supply Chain Management*. London, Pitman.

Clapham, C. (1986) *Private Patronage and Public Power: Political Clientalism in the Modern State*. London, Pinter.

Clasters, P. (1977) *Society against State*. Oxford, Basil Blackwell.

Claval, P. (1978) *Espace et Pouvoir*. Paris, Presses universitaires de France.

Clifford, A. J. (1965) *The Independence of the Federal Reserve System*. Philadelphia, University of Pennsylvania Press.

Clulow, R. and P. Teague (1993) 'Governance Structure and Economic Performance', in P. Teague (ed.), *The Economy of Northern Ireland*. London, Lawrence & Wishart: 60–120.

Cohen, B. J. (1996) 'Phoenix Risen: The Resurrection of Global Finance', *World Politics* 48 (2): 268–96.

Collingwood, R. G. (1946) *The Idea of History*. Oxford, Clarendon Press.

Collins, A. F. (1996) 'The Pathological Gambler and the Government at Gambling', *History & the Human Sciences* 9 (3): 69–100.

Conti, S. (1993) 'The Network Perspective in Industrial Geography', *Geografiska Annaler* 75 B (3): 115–30.

Cox, R. W. (1981) 'Social Forces, States and World Order: Beyond International Relations Theory', *Millennium* 10 (2): 126–155.

Cox, R. W. (1983) 'Gramsci, Hegemony and International Relations: an essay in method', *Millennium* 12 (2): 162–75.

Cox, R. W. (1987) *Production, Power, and World Order: Social Forces in the Making of History*. New York, Columbia University Press.

Cox, R. W. (1996) 'Civilisations in World Political Economy', *New Political Economy* 1 (2): 141–56.

Cox, R. W. and T. J. Sinclair (1996) *Approaches to World Order*. Cambridge, Cambridge University Press.

Debray, R. (1981) *Critique of Political Reason*. London, NLB.

De Porte, A. W. (1986) *Europe Between the Super-Powers: The Enduring Balance*. New Haven, Conn.,Yale University Press (2nd edn).

De Roover, R. (1963) *The Rise and Decline of the Medici Bank, 1397–1494*. Cambridge, MA, Harvard University Press.

Devetak, R. (1996) 'Postmodernism', in S. Burchill, A. Linklater, R. Devetak, M. Paterson and J. True (eds), *Theories of International Relations*. London, Macmillan.

Dicken, P. (1992) *Global Shift: The Internationalization of Economic Activity*. London, Paul Chapman (2nd edn).

Diebert, R. (1996) 'Typographica: the medium and the medieval-to-modern transformation', *Review of International Studies* 22 (1): 29–56.

Dietrich, M. (1994) *Transaction Cost Economics and Beyond*. London, Routledge.

Donelan, M. (ed.) (1978) *The Reason of States: A Study in International Political Theory*. London, Allen & Unwin.

Donelan, M. (1990) *Elements of International Political Theory*. Oxford, Clarendon Press.

Dosi, G. (1988) 'The nature of the innovative process', in G. Dosi, C. Freeman, R. Nelson, G. Silverberg and L. Soete (eds), *Technical Change and Economic Theory*. London, Pinter: 221–38.

Dosi, G., C. Freeman, R. Nelson, G. Silverberg and L. Soete (eds) (1988) *Technical Change and Economic Theory*. London, Pinter.

Doty, R. L. (1996) 'Sovereignty and Nation: Constructing the Boundaries of National Identity', in T. Biersteker and C. Weber (eds), *State Sovereignty as Social Construct*. Cambridge, Cambridge University Press: 121–47.

Douglas, R. (1994) *Unfinished Business*. Auckland, Penguin.

Doyle, M. (1986) 'Liberalism and World Politics', *American Political Science Review* 80 (4): 1151–69.

Doyle, M. (1993) 'Liberalism and International Relations', in R. Beiner and W. J. Booth (eds), *Kant and Political Philosophy: The Contemporary Legacy*. London, Routledge.

Dumont, A. (1990) 'Technology, competitiveness and cooperation in Europe', in M. S. Steinberg (ed.), *The Technical Challenges and Opportunities of a United Europe*. London, Pinter: 68–80.

Dunleavy, P. (1994) 'The Globalisation of Public Services Production: Can Government Be "Best in World"?' *Public Policy and Administration* 9 (2): 36–64.

Dunning, J. (1993a) (ed.) *The Globalization of Business*. London and New York, Routledge.

Dunning, J. (1993b) 'Governments, hierarchies and markets: towards a new balance?', in J. Dunning (ed.), *The Globalization of Business*. London, Routledge: 315–29.

Egan, M.-L. and A. Mody (1992) 'Buyer-seller links in export development', *World Development* 20 (3): 321–34.

Ehrenberg, R. (1958) *Capital and Finance in the Age of the Renaissance*. New York, Augustus M. Kelley.

Eisner, R. (1994) *The Misunderstood Economy: What Counts and How to Count It*. Boston, MA, Harvard Business School Press.

Epstein, G. and H. Gintis (1995) 'International Capital Markets and National Economic Policy', *Review of International Political Economy* 2 (4): 693–718.

Evans, M. G. and J. S. Davies (1998) *Beyond Description: Legitimating Policy Transfer Analysis in Political Science*. Conference on Global Policy Transfer, University of Birmingham.

Faini, R., F. Clavijo, *et al.* (1992) 'The fallacy of composition argument: is it relevant for LDCs' manufactures exports?', *European Economic Review* 36 (4): 865–82.

Fairclough, N. (1992) *Discourse and Social Change*. Cambridge, Polity.

Falk, R. A. (1995) *On Humane Governance*. University Park: Penn State Press.

Featherstone, M. (ed.) (1990) *Global Culture: Nationalism, Globalization and Modernity*. London, Sage.

Fédou, R. (1971) *L'état au Moyen Age*. Paris, Presses universitaires de France.

Femia, J. (1981) 'An Historicist Critique of "Revisionist" Methods for Studying the History of Ideas"', *Theory and History* 20 (2): 113–34.

Ferguson, Y. H. and R. W. Mansbach (1991) 'Between Celebration and Despair: Constructive Suggestions for Future International Theory', *International Studies Quarterly* 35 (4): 363–86.

Fichte, J. G. (1981) *Discours à la Nation Allemande*. Paris, Aubier.

Florida, R. (1995) 'Toward the Learning Region', *Futures* 27 (5): 527–36.

Forsyth, M., H. Keens-Soper and P. Savigear, (1970) *The Theory of International Relations*. London, Allen & Unwin.

Foucault, M. (1966) *Les mots et les choses*. Paris, Gallimard.

Foucault, M. (1977) *Discipline and Punish*. London, Allen Lane.

Franko, L. (1990) 'The Impact of global corporate competition and multinational corporate strategy', in M. S. Steinberg (eds), *The Technical Challenges and Opportunities of a United Europe*. London, Pinter: 121–37.

Freeman, C. and C. Perez (1988) 'Structural crises of adjustment, business cycles and investment behaviour', in G. Dosi, C. Freeman, R. Nelson, G. Silverberg and L. Soete (eds), *Technical Change and Economic Theory*. London, Pinter: 38–66.

Frey, B. (1984) 'The public choice view of international political economy', *International Organization* 38 (1): 199–223.

Frieden, J. A. (1991) 'Invested Interests: The Politics of National Economic Policies in a World of Global Finance', *International Organization* 45 (4): 425–51.

Friedman, L. A. (1992) *Covering the World: International Television News Services*. New York, Twentieth Century Fund.

Fukuyama, F. (1992) *The End of History and the Last Man*. London, Hamish Hamilton.

Galbraith, J. K. and W. Darity (1995) 'A Guide to the Deficit', *Challenge* 38 (4): 5–12.

Gallie, W. B. (1978) *Philosphers of Peace and War*. Cambridge, Cambridge University Press.

Gamble, A. and A. Payne (1996) *Regionalism and World Order*. London, Macmillan.

Gereffi, G. and M. Korzeniewicz (eds) (1994) *Commodity Chains and Global Capitalism*. London, Praeger.

Germain, R. D. (1996) 'The Worlds of Finance: A Braudelian Perspective on IPE', *The European Journal of International Relations* 2 (2): 201–30.

Germain, R. D. (1997) *The International Organization of Credit: States and Global Finance in the World-Economy*. Cambridge, Cambridge University Press.

Germino, D. (1974) *Modern Western Political Thought*. New York, HarperCollins.

Ghemawat, P. and A. M. Spence (1986) 'Modelling global competition', in M. Porter (ed.), *Competition in Global Industries*. Cambridge, Mass., Harvard Business School Press: 61–79.

Giddens, A. (1984) *The Constitution of Society: Outline of the Theory of Structuration*. Cambridge, Polity.

Giddens, A. (1990) *The Consequences of Modernity*. Cambridge, Polity.

Giddens, A. (1991) *Modernity and Self-identity: Self and Society in the Late Modern Age*. Cambrigde: Polity Press.

Giddens, A. (1994) *Beyond Left and Right*. Cambridge, Polity.

Giddens, A. (1995) *Politics, Sociology and Social Theory: Encounters with Classical and Contemporary Social Thought*. Cambridge: Polity Press.

Gill, S. (1991a) *American Hegemony and the Trilateral Commission*. Cambridge, Cambridge University Press.

Gill, S. (1991b) 'Reflections on Global Order and Sociohistorical Time', *Alternatives* 16 (2): 275–314.

Gill, S. (1992) 'The Emerging World Order and European Change: The Political Economy of European Union', in R. Miliband and L. Panitch (eds), *New World Order? The Socialist Register 1992*. London, Merlin: 157–96.

Gill, S. (ed.) (1993) *Gramsci, Historical Materialism and International Relations*. Cambridge, Cambridge University Press.

Gill, S. (1994) 'Political Economy and Structural Change: globalizing elites and the emerging world order', in Y. Sakamoto (ed.), *Global Transformation: Challenges to the State System*. Tokyo, United Nations University Press: 169–99.

Gill, S. (1995) 'Globalisation, Market Civilisation, and Disciplinary Neoliberalism', *Millennium* 24 (3): 399–423.

Gill, S. and D. Law (1989) 'Global Hegemony and the Structural Power of Capital', *International Studies Quarterly* 33 (4): 475–99.

Gill, S. and J. Mittelman (eds) (1997) *Innovation and Transformation in International Studies*. Cambridge, Cambridge University Press.

Gills, B. (ed.) (1997) 'The Politics of Globalisation', Special issue of *New Political Economy* 2 (1)

Gills, B. and R. Palan (1994) 'The Neostructuralist Agenda in International Relations', in R. Palan and B. Gills (eds), *Transcending the State-Global Divide: The Neo-Structuralist Agenda in International Relations*. Boulder, CO, Lynne Rienner: 1–14.

Gilpin, R. (1981) *War and Change in World Politics*. Cambridge, Cambridge University Press.

Gilpin, R. (1987) *The Political Economy of International Relations*. Princeton, NJ, Princeton University Press.

Goodman, J. B. and L. W. Pauly (1993) 'The Obsolescence of Capital Controls? Economic Management in an Age of Global Markets', *World Politics* 46 (1): 50–82.

Grabher, G. (1993) *Embedded Firms: On the Socioeconomics of Industrial Networks*. London, Routledge.

Gramlich, E. M. (1995) 'The Politics and Economics of Budget Deficit Control: Policy Questions and Research Questions', in J. S. Banks and E. A. Hanushek (eds), *Modern Political Economy: Old Topics, New Directions*. Cambridge, Cambridge University Press.

Gramsci, A. (1971) *Selections from the Prison Notebooks*. Q. Hoare and G. N. Smith (eds), New York: International Publishers.

Granovetter, M. (1985) 'Economic Action and Social Structure: The Problem of Embeddedness', *American Journal of Sociology* 91 (4): 481–510.

Granovetter, M. (1992) 'Economic Institutions as Social Constructions: A Framework for Analysis', *Acta Sociologica* (35): 3–11.

Gunnell, J. (1979) *Political Theory: Tradition and Interpretation*. Cambridge, Winthrop.

Haas, P. M. (ed.) (1992) 'Knowledge, Power, and International Policy Coordination', Special issue of *International Organization* 46 (1).

Hall, P. A. and R. C. M. Taylor (1996) 'Political Science and the Three New Institutionalisms', *Political Studies* 44 (5): 936–57.

Hamilton, E. J. (1934) 'American Treasure and the Price Revolution in Spain 1501–1650', *Harvard Economic Studies* 42.

Hammer, M. and J. Champy (1993) *Re-engineering the Corporation: a Manifesto for Business Revolution*. London: N. Brealey.

Hannerz, U. (1992) *Cultural Complexity: Studies in the Social Organisation of Meaning*. New York, Columbia University Press.

Harré, R. (1972) *The Philosophies of Science*. Oxford, Oxford University Press.

Hart, J. A. (1992) *Rival Capitalists: International Competitiveness in the United States, Japan, and Western Europe*. Ithaca, NY, Cornell University Press.

Harvey, D. (1989) *The Condition of Postmodernity*. Oxford, Basil Blackwell.

Hayward, K. (1997) 'Technology, Politics and the World Civil Aviation System: The Case of the Global Navigation Satellite System (GNSS)', in M. Talalay, C. Farrands and R. Tooze (eds), *Technology, Culture and Competitiveness: Change and the World Political Economy*. London, Routledge: 196–209.

Hayward, D. and M. Salvaris (1994) 'Rating the States: Credit Rating Agencies and the Australian State Governments', *Journal of Australian Political Economy* (34): 1–26.

Heisler, J. (1994) 'Recent Research in Behavioral Finance', *Financial Markets, Institutions and Instruments* 3 (5): 76–105.

Held, D. (1995) *Global Democracy*. Cambridge, Polity.

Held, D. and A. McGrew (1994) 'Globalization and the Liberal Democratic State', in Y. Sakamoto (ed.), *Global Transformation: Challenges to the State System*. Tokyo, United Nations University Press: 57–84.

Held, D., A. M. McGrew, D. Goldblatt and J. Perraton (1999) *Global Transformation: Politics, Economics, Culture*. Cambridge: Polity Press.

Helleiner, E. N. (1994) *States and Global Finance: From Bretton Woods to the 1990s*. Ithaca, NY, Cornell University Press.

Helleiner, E. N. (1996) 'Post-Globalization: Is the Financial Liberalization Trend Likely to be Reversed?', in R. Boyer and D. Drache (eds), *States Against Markets*. New York, Routledge: 193–210.

Helleiner, E. N. (1997) 'Braudelian Reflections on Globalization: The Historian as Pioneer', in S. Gill and J. Mittelman (eds), *Innovation and Transformation in International Studies*. Cambridge, Cambridge University Press: 90–104.

Henderson, D. (1992) 'International economic integration: progress, prospects and implications', *International Affairs* 68 (4): 634–53.

Higgott, R. and R. Stubbs. (1995) 'Competing conceptions of economic regionalism: APEC versus EAEC in the Asia Pacific', *Review of International Political Economy* 2 (3): 516–35.

Hirst, P. and G. Thompson (1996) *Globalization in Question: The International Economy and the Possibilities of Governance*. Cambridge, Polity.

Hobday, M. (1994) 'Technological Learning in Singapore: A Test Case of Leapfrogging', *Journal of Development Studies* 30 (3): 831–58.

Hobday, M. (1995) *Innovation in East Asia*. Aldershot, Edward Elgar.

Hobsbawm, E. J. (1968) *Industry and Empire*. Harmondsworth, Penguin.

Hodgson, G. (1988) *Economics and Institutions*. Cambridge, Polity.

Hodgson, G. (1993) *Economics and Evolution: Bringing Life Back into Economics*. Cambridge, Polity.

Hoffe, O. (1994) *Immanuel Kant*. New York, State University of New York Press.

Hollis, M. and S. Smith (1991) 'Beware of Gurus: Structure and action in international relations', *Review of International Studies* 17 (4): 393–410.

Hollis, M. and S. Smith (1994) 'Two stories about structure and agency', *Review of International Studies* 20 (3): 241–51.

Hollis, M. and S. Smith (1996) 'A response: why epistemology matters in international theory?', *Review of International Studies* 22 (1): 111–16.

Holloway, J. and S. Picciotto (eds) (1978) *State and Capital: A Marxist Debate*. London, Edward Arnold.

Hoogvelt, A. (1997) *Globalization and the Postcolonial World*. London, Macmillan.

Howard, M. (1976) *War in European History*. Oxford, Oxford University Press.

Howells, J. R. (1995) 'Going Global: The Use of ICT Networks in Research and Development', *Research Policy* 24 (2): 169–84.

Hufbauer, G. (1991) 'World economic integration: the long view', *International Economic Insights* 2 (3): 26–7.

Hughes, T. (1983) *Networks of Power: Electrification in Western Society, 1880–1930*. Baltimore, MD, and London, The Johns Hopkins University Press.

Huntington, S. (1993) 'The Clash of Civilizations?', *Foreign Affairs* 72 (3): 32–49.

Hurrell, A. and N. Woods (1995) 'Globalisation and Inequality', *Millennium* 24 (3): 447–70.

Hutchings, K. (1996) *Kant, Critique and Politics*. London, Routledge.

Irwin, D. (1993) 'Multilateral and bilateral trade liberalization in the world trade system: an historical perspective', in J. de Melo and A. Panagariya (eds), *New Dimensions in Regional Integration*. Cambridge, Cambridge University Press: 90–119.

Jabri, V. and S. Chan (1996) 'The ontologist always rings twice: two more stories about structure and agency in reply to Hollis and Smith', *Review of International Studies* 22 (1): 107–10.

Jackson, J. H. (1989) *The World Trading System*. Cambridge, MA, MIT Press.

Jackson, R. (1990) *Quasi-States: Sovereignty, International Relations and The Third World*. Cambridge, Cambridge University Press.

Jackson, R. and A. James (eds) (1994) *States in a Changing World*. Oxford, Oxford University Press.

Jackson, R. (1996) 'Is there a classical international theory?', in S. Smith, K. Booth and M. Zalewski (eds), *International Theory: Positivism and Beyond*. Cambridge, Cambridge University Press: 203–18.

James, A. (1989) 'The realism of realism: The state and the study of international relations', *Review of International Studies* 15 (3): 215–29.

Jameson, F. (1988) 'Cognitive mapping', in C. Nelson and L. Grossberg (eds), *Marxism and the Interpretation of Culture*. London, Macmillan.

Jameson, F. (1991) *Postmodernism, or The Cultural Logic of Late Capitalism*. London, Verso.

Jarillo, J. C. (1988) 'On Strategic Networks', *Strategic Management Journal* 9: 31–41.

Jessop, B. (1990) *State Theory*. Cambridge, Polity.

Jessop, B. (1993) 'Towards a Schumpeterian Workfare State? Preliminary Remarks on Post-Fordist Political Economy', *Studies in Political Economy* (40): 7–39.

Jessop, B., K. Nielsen, *et al.* (1993) 'Structural Competitiveness and Strategic Capacities: Rethinking the State and International Capital, in S.-E. Sjöstrand (ed.), *Institutional Change: Theory and Empirical Findings*. New York, M. E. Sharpe: 227–62.

Johns, R. A. (1983) *Tax Havens and Offshore Finance: A Study of Transnational Economic Development*. New York, St Martin's Press.

Johnson, C. (1982) *M.I.T.I. and the Japanese Miracle: The Growth of Industrial Policy, 1925–1975*. Stanford, CA, Stanford University Press.

Jones, R. J. B. (1986) *Conflict and Control in the World Economy: Contemporary Economic Realism and Neo-Mercantilism*. Hemel Hempstead, Harvester Wheatsheaf.

Jones, R. J. B. (1994) 'The responsibility to educate', *Review of International Studies* 20 (3): 299–311.

Jones, R. J. B. (1995) *Globalisation and Interdependence in the International Political Economy: Rhetoric and Reality*. London, Pinter.

Kaplan, M. (1957) *System and Process in International Politics*. New York, John Wiley.

Kaplan, M. (1966) 'The new great debate: traditionalism vs. science in international relations', *World Politics* 19 (1): 1–20.

Kapstein, E. B. (1994) *Governing the Global Economy: International Finance and the State*. Cambridge, Harvard University Press.

Keat, R. and J. Urry (1975) *Social Theory as Science*. London, Routledge & Kegan Paul.

Keesing, D. and S. Lall (1992) 'Marketing manufactured exports from developing countries', in G. Helleiner (ed.), *Trade Policy, Industrialization and Development*. Oxford, Oxford University Press: 176–93.

Kegley, C. and E. Wittkopf (1993) *World Politics: Trend and Transformation*. London, Macmillan (4th edn).

Kennedy, P. (1989) *The Rise and Fall of the Great Powers*. London, Fontana.

Keohane, R. (1989) *International Institutions and State Power: Essays in International Relations Theory*. Boulder, CO, Westview Press.

Keohane, R. and H. Milner (eds) (1996) *Internationalization and Domestic Politics*. Cambridge, Cambridge University Press.

Keohane, R. and J. Nye (eds) (1972) *Transnational Relations and World Politics*. Boulder, CO, Westview Press.

Keohane, R. and J. Nye (1977) *Power and Interdependence: World Politics in Transition*. Boston, MA, Little, Brown.

Kettl, D. F. (1992) *Deficit Politics: Public Budgeting in its Institutional and Historical Context*. New York, St Martins Press.

Kidder, T. (1982) *The Soul of a New Machine*. Harmondsworth, Penguin.

Kinser, S. (1991) '*Annaliste* paradigm? The geo-historical structuralism of Fernand Braudel', *American Historical Review* 86 (1): 63–105.

Kirzner, I. (1992) *The Meaning of Market Process*. London, Routledge.

Knox, P. L. and P. J. Taylor (1995) *World Cities in a World-System*. Cambridge, Cambridge University Press.

Kofman, E. and G. Youngs (eds) (1996) *Globalisation: Theory and Practice*. London, Pinter.

Kooiman, J. (ed.) (1993) *Modern Governance: New Government–Society Interactions*. London, Sage.

Kotkin, J. (1992) *Tribes: How Race, Religion and Identity Determine Success in the New Global Economy*. New York, Random House.

Krasner, S. D. (ed.) (1983) *International Regimes*. Ithaca, NY, Cornell University Press.

Krasner, S. D. (1994) 'International Political Economy: abiding discord', *Review of International Political Economy* 1 (1): 13–20.

Krippendorf, E. (1982) *International Relations as a Social Science*. Brighton, Harvester Press.

Krugman, P. (1989) *Exchange-rate Instability*. Cambridge, MA, MIT Press.

Krugman, P. (1994a) 'The Myth of Asia's Miracle', *Foreign Affairs* 73 (6): 63–78.

Krugman, P. (1994b) *Peddling Prosperity: Economic Sense and Nonsense in the Age of Diminished Expectations*. New York, Norton.

Krugman, P. (1995) 'Growing world trade', *Brookings Papers on Economic Activity I*: 327–77.

Kuhn, T. (1962) *The Structure of Scientific Revolutions*. Chicago, University of Chicago Press (2nd edn).

Kwan, C. H. (1994) *Economic Interdependence in the Asia-Pacific Region: Towards a Yen Bloc*. London, Routledge.

Laclau, E. (1980) 'Populist Rupture and Discourse', *Screen Education* 11.

Lapid, J. (1989) 'The Third Debate: On the Prospects of International Theory in a Post-Positivist Era', *International Studies Quarterly* 33 (3): 235–54.

Laurence, H. (1996) 'Regulatory Competition and the Politics of Financial Market Reform in Britain and Japan', *Governance* 9 (3): 311–41.

League of Nations (1942) *The Network of World Trade*. Geneva, League of Nations.

Lever-Tracy, C., D. Ip, *et al.* (1996) *The Chinese Diaspora and Mainland China*. London, Macmillan.

Lévi-Strauss, C. (1953) 'Social Structure', in A. L. Kroeber (ed.), *Anthropology Today: An Encyclopaedic Inventory*. Chicago, The University of Chicago Press.

Levitt, T. (1983) 'The Globalization of Markets', *Harvard Business Review* 61 (3): 92–102.

Lim, H. (1991) 'Japan and the Asian Newly Industrializing Economies', in H. H. Kendall and C. Joewono (eds), *Japan, ASEAN, and the United States*. Berkeley, CA, Institute of East Asian Studies, University of California at Berkeley: 215–21.

Lincoln, B. (1994) *Authority: Construction and Corrosion*. Chicago, University of Chicago Press.

Lindblom, C. E. (1977) *Politics and Markets: The World's Political-Economic Systems*. New York, Basic Books.

Linklater, A. (1986) 'Realism, Marxism and Critical International Theory', *Review of International Studies* 12 (4): 301–12.

Lipietz, A. (1987) *Mirages and Miracles: The Crises of Global Fordism*. London, Verso.

Lipietz, A. (1997) 'The Post-Fordist World: Labour relations, international hierarchy and global ecology', *Review of International Political Economy* 4 (1): 1–41.

Liverani, M. (1990) *Prestige and Interest: International Relations in the Near East. 1600–1100 B.C.* Padova, Sargon Sri.

Lukes, S. (1973) *Individualism*. Oxford, Basil Blackwell.

Lundvall, B. (1992) *National Systems of Innovation*. London, Pinter.

Lury, C. (1996) *Consumer Culture*. New Brunswick, Rutgers University Press.

Machin, H. and V. Wright (eds) (1985) *Economic Policy and Policy-Making Under the Mitterrand Presidency, 1981–84*. London, Pinter.

MacLean, J. (1981a) 'Marxist Epistemology, Explanations of 'Change' and the Study of International Relations', in B. Buzan and R. J. B. Jones (eds), *Change and the Study of International Relations*. London, Pinter: 46–67.

MacLean, J. (1981b) 'Political Theory, International Theory and Problems of Ideology', *Millennium* 10 (2): 102–25.

MacLean, J. (1988a) 'Belief Systems and Ideology in International Relations: A Critical Approach'. *Belief Systems and International Relations*, ed. R. Little and S. Smith. Oxford, Basil Blackwell: 57–82.

MacLean, J. (1988b) 'Marxism and International Relations: A Strange Case of Mutual Neglect', *Millennium* **17** (2): 295–319.

Macpherson, C. (1962) *The Political Theory of Possessive Individualism: Hobbes to Locke*. Oxford, Oxford University Press.

Maddison, A. (1991) *Dynamic Forces in Capitalist Development*. Oxford, Oxford University Press.
Maddison, A. (1995) *Monitoring the World Economy 1820–1992*. Paris, OECD.
Mann, M. (1984) 'The Autonomous Power of the State: its Origins, Mechanisms and Results', *Archives européennes de sociologie* 25 (2): 185–213.
Mann, M. (1986) *The Sources of Social Power. Volume I*. Cambridge, Cambridge University Press.
Mann, M. (1993) *The Sources of Social Power. Volume II*. Cambridge, Cambridge University Press.
Marx, K. (1973) *Grundrisse*. Harmondsworth, Penguin.
Massey, D. (1994) *Time, Place and Gender*. Cambridge, Polity.
Maxfield, S. (1997) *Gatekeepers of Growth: The Politics of Central Banking in Developing Countries*. Princeton, NJ, Princeton University Press.
Mayntz, R., (ed.) (1969) *Theodor Geiger on Social Order and Mass Society: Selected Papers*. Chicago, University of Chicago Press.
Mayntz, R. (1993) 'Modernization and the Logic of Interorganization Networks', in J. Child, M. Crozier and R. Mayntz (eds), *Societal Change Between Market and Organization*. Aldershot, Avebury: 1–17.
McGrew, A. (1992a) 'A global society', in S. Hall, D. Held and A. McGrew (eds) *Modernity and its Futures*. Cambridge, Polity: 61–102.
McGrew, A. (1992b) 'Conceptualizing Global Politics', in A. McGrew and P. Lewis (eds), *Global Politics*. Cambridge, Polity: 1–28.
McGrew, A. (1995) 'World Order and Political Space', in J. Anderson and A. Cochrane (eds), *A Global World? Re-ordering Political Space*. Milton Keynes, The Open University. 11–64.
McGrew, A. and P. Lewis (1992) *Global Politics*. Cambridge, Polity.
McKeown, T. (1991) 'A liberal trade order? The long-run pattern of imports to the advanced capitalist states', *International Studies Quarterly* 35 (2): 151–72.
McNeill, W. H. (1982) *The Pursuit of Power*. Oxford, Basil Blackwell.
McQuaig, L. (1995) *Shooting the Hippo: Death by Deficit and Other Canadian Myths*. Toronto, Viking.
Menon, J. (1995) 'Exchange rate pass-through', *Journal of Economic Surveys* 9 (2): 197–231.
Meszaros, I. (1986) *Philosophy, Ideology and Social Science*. Brighton, Wheatsheaf.
Midford, P. (1993) 'International trade and domestic politics', *International Organization* 47 (4): 535–64.
Milner, H. (1989) *Resisting Protectionism: Global Industries and the Politics of International Trade*. Princeton, NJ, Princeton University Press.
Mittelman, J. (ed.) (1996) *Globalization: Critical Reflections*. Boulder, CO, Lynne Rienner.
Monod, J. (1972) *Chance and Necessity: An Essay on the Natural Philosophy of Modern Biology*. London, Collins.
Morgenthau, H. (1948) *Politics among Nations: The Struggle for Power and Peace*. New York, Knopf.
Morris, C. T. and I. Adelman (1988) *Comparative Patterns of Economic Development, 1850–1914*. Baltimore, MD, Johns Hopkins University Press.
Murphy, C. N. (1994) *International Organization and Industrial Change: Global Governance Since 1850*. New York, Oxford University Press.

Murray, R. (1981) *Multinationals Beyond the Market.* Hemel Hempstead, Harvester Wheatsheaf.

Muscatelli, V., T. Srinivasan, *et al.* (1994) 'The empirical modelling of NIE exports', *Journal of Development Studies* 30 (2): 279–302.

Navari, C. (1991) *The Condition of States.* Milton Keynes, Open University Press.

Neal, L. (1990) *The Rise of Financial Capitalism.* Cambridge, Cambridge University Press.

Nelson, R. (ed.) (1993) *National Systems of Innovation.* Oxford, Oxford University Press.

Nicholson, M. (1970) *Conflict Analysis.* London, English Universities Press.

Nicholson, M. (1989) *Formal Theories in International Relations.* Cambridge, Cambridge University Press.

Nicholson, M. (1992) *Rationality and the Analysis of International Conflict.* Cambridge, Cambridge University Press.

Nicholson, M. (1996) *Causes and Consequences in International Relations.* London, Pinter.

Nierop, T. (1994) *Systems and Regions in Global Politics.* Chichester, John Wiley.

North, D. (1990) *Institutions, Institutional Change and Economic Performance.* Cambridge, Cambridge University Press.

North, D. (1991) 'Institutions, transaction costs, and the rise of merchant empires', in J. Tracy (ed.), *The Political Economy of Merchant Empires.* Cambridge, Cambridge University Press: 22–40.

O'Brien, R. (1992) *Global Financial Integration: The End of Geography.* London, RIIA/Pinter.

O'Connor, J. (1973) *The Fiscal Crisis of the State.* New York, St Martin's Press.

Oakeshott, M. (1962) *Rationalism in Politics and other essays.* London, Methuen.

Oakeshott, M. (1976) 'On Misunderstanding Human Conduct: A Reply to My Critics', *Political Theory* 4 (3): 353–67.

Ohmae, K. (1990) *The Borderless World: Power and Strategy in the Inter-linked Economy.* London, Collins.

Ohmae, K. (1995) *The End of the Nation-state: The Rise of Regional Economies.* London, HarperCollins.

Osborne, D. and T. Gaebler (1992) *Reinventing Government: How the Entrepreneurial Spirit is Transforming the Public Sector, from Schoolhouse to Statehouse, City Hall to the Pentagon.* Reading, MA, Addison-Wesley.

Ostry, S. and R. R. Nelson (1995) *Techno-Nationalism and Techno-Globalism: Conflict and Cooperation.* Washington, DC, The Brookings Institution.

Pacey, A. (1990) *Technology in World Civilization.* Oxford, Basil Blackwell.

Palan, R. (1995) 'Processes of Globalization and Social Classes: the Reluctant Revolutionaries of the Modern World', *Studies in Marxism* 2: 161–78.

Palan, R. (1996) *Having your Cake and Eating It: How and Why the State System has Created Offshore.* Annual Conference of the International Studies Association, San Diego.

Palan, R. and J. Abbott (1996) *State Strategies in the Global Political Economy.* London, Pinter.

Palan, R. and B. Blair (1993) 'On the Idealist Origins of the Realist Theory of International Relations', *Review of International Studies* 19 (4): 385–99.

Parkinson, F. (1977) *The Philosophy of International Relations: A Study in the History of Thought.* London, Sage.

Patel, P. and K. Pavitt (1991) 'Large Firms in the Production of the World's Technology: an Important Case of "Non-globalization"', *Journal of International Business Studies* 22 (1): 1–21.

Patten, C. (1996) 'Queer Peregrinations', in M. Shapiro and H. Alker (eds), *Challenging Boundaries: Global Flows, Territorial Identities*. Minneapolis, University of Minnesota Press.

Pauly, L. W. (1997) *Who Elected the Bankers? Surveillance and Control in the World Economy*. Ithaca, NY, Cornell University Press.

Pauly, L. W. and S. Reich (1997) 'National Structures and Multinational Corporate Behavior: Enduring Differences in the Age of Globalization', *International Organization* 51 (1): 1–30.

Perraton, J. (1994) 'Testing the small country hypothesis for developing countries', *Open University Discussion Papers in Economics* (5).

Perraton, J., D. Goldblatt, D. Held and A. M. McGrew (1997) 'The globalisation of economic activity', *New Political Economy* 2 (2): 257–77.

Peterson, P. G. (1993) 'Facing Up', *The Atlantic Monthly,* October.

Phillips, K. P. (1992) 'US industrial policy: inevitable and ineffective', *Harvard Business Review* 70 (4): 104–12.

Piccioto, S. (1990) 'The Internationalization of the State', *Review of Radical Political Economics* 22 (1): 28–44.

Pierson, P. (1994) *Dismantling the Welfare State? Reagan, Thatcher, and the Politics of Retrenchment*. Cambridge, Cambridge University Press.

Piore, M. and C. Sabel (1984) *The Second Industrial Divide: Possibilities for Prosperity*. New York, Basic Books.

Pocock, J. G. (1962) 'The History of Political Thought: A Methodological Enquiry'. in P. Laslett and W. Runciman (eds), *Philosophy, Politics and Society*. Oxford, Basil Blackwell (2nd edn).

Polanyi, K. (1944) *The Great Transformation: The Political and Economic Origins of Our Time*. New York, Rinehart.

Porter, M. (1990) *The Competitive Advantage of Nations*. London, Macmillan.

Portnoy, B. (1997) *Transnational Networks and Industrial Order*. Annual meeting of the American Political Science Association, Washington, DC.

Poster, M. (1995) *The Second Media Age*. Cambridge, MA, and Oxford, Basil Blackwell and Polity.

Poulantzas, N. (1973) *Political Power and Social Classes*. London, NLB.

Prakash, A. and Hart, J. A. (eds) (1999) *Globalization and Governance*. London, Routledge.

Redwood, J. (1993) *The Global Marketplace*. London, HarperCollins.

Reich, R. (1990) 'Who is Us?', *Harvard Business Review* 90 (1): 53–64.

Reich, R. (1991) *The Work of Nations: Preparing Ourselves for 21st-Century Capitalism*. New York, Knopf.

Renger, N. (1988) 'Serpents and Doves in Classical International Theory', *Millennium* 17 (2): 215–25.

Renger, N. (1995) *Political Theory, Modernity and Postmodernity: Beyond Enlightenment and Critique*. Oxford, Oxford University Press.

Republican National Committee (1994) *Contract with America*. New York, Times Books.

Reynolds, P. (1980) *An Introduction to International Relations*. London, Longman (2nd edn).

Rhoads, S. E. (1985) *The Economist's View of the World: Government, Markets, & Public Policy*. New York, Cambridge University Press.
Richardson, L. F. (1960) *Arms and Insecurity*. Pittsburgh, NJ, Boxwood Press.
Riddle, D. I. (1986) *Service-Led Growth: The Role of Service Sector in World Development*. New York, Praeger.
Rigo Sureda, A. (1973) *The Evolution of the Right of Self-determination: A Study of United Nations Practice*. Leiden, A. Sijthoff.
Ritzer, G. (1992) *The MacDonaldisation of Society*. London, Pine Forge.
Robertson, R. (1992) *Globalization: Social Theory and Global Culture*. London, Sage.
Rodan, G. (1993) 'Reconstructing Division of Labour: Singapore's New Regional Emphasis', in R Higgott, R. Leaver and J. Ravenhill (eds), *Pacific Economic Relations in the 1990s: Cooperation or Conflict?*, St Leonards, Allen & Unwin: 223–49.
Rosenau, J. (1990) *Turbulence in World Politics: A Theory of Change and Continuity*. Princeton, NJ, Princeton University Press.
Rosenberg, N. (1982) *Inside the Black Box: Technology and Economics*. Cambridge, Cambridge University Press.
Rosenberg, N. (1994a) *Exploring the Black Box: Technology, Economics and History*. Cambridge, Cambridge University Press.
Roth, G. and C. Wittich (eds) (1978) *Max Weber: Economy and Society, Vol. II*. Berkeley, University of California Press.
Ruggie, J. (1982) 'International Regimes, Transactions, and Change: Embedded Liberalism in the Postwar Economic Order', in S. D. Krasner (eds), *International Regimes*. Ithaca, NY, Cornell University Press: 195–231.
Ruggie, J. (1995) 'At home abroad, abroad at home: international liberalisation and domestic stability in the new world economy', *Millennium* 24 (3): 507–26.
Ruigrok, W. and R. van Tulder (1995) *The Logic of International Restructuring*. London, Routledge.
Sabine, G. (1973) *A History of Political Theory*. Hinsdal, Drysdale Press (4th edn).
Said, E. (1993) *Culture and Imperialism*. London, Chatto & Windus.
Sassen, S. (1991) *The Global City: New York, London, Tokyo*. Princeton, NY, Princeton University Press.
Sassen, S. (1996a) *Losing Control? Sovereignty in an Age of Globalization*. New York, Columbia University Press.
Sassen, S. (1996b) 'The State and the Global City: Notes towards a Conception of Place-centered Governance', *Competition and Change* 1 (1): 31–50.
Saurin, J. (1995) 'The End of International Relations? The state and international theory in the age of globalization', in J. Macmillan and A. Linklater (eds), *Boundaries in Question: New Directions in International Relations*. London, Pinter: 244–61.
Savage, J. D. (1988) *Balanced Budgets and American Politics*. Ithaca, NY, Cornell University Press.
Savage, J. D. (1994) 'Deficits and the Economy: The Case of the Clinton Administration and Interest Rates', *Public Budgeting and Finance* 14 (1): 96–112.
Saxenian, A.-L. (1994) 'Lessons from Silicon Valley', *Technology Review* 97 (5): 42–51.
Sayer, A. (1992) *Method in Social Science*. London, Routledge (2nd edn).

Schain, M. A. (1980) 'Corporatism and Industrial Relations in France', in P. G. Cerny and M. A. Schain (eds), *French Politics and Public Policy*. New York, Methuen: 191–217.

Schiller, H. (1996) *Information Inequality; The Deepening Social Crisis of America*. London, Routledge.

Schmidt, V. A. (1996) *From State to Market? The Transformation of French Business and Government*. Cambridge, Cambridge University Press.

Scholte, J. A. (1993) *International Relations of Social Change*. Milton Keynes, Open University Press.

Scholte, J. A. (1996) 'Beyond the Buzzword: Towards a Critical Theory of Globalization', in E. Kofman and G. Youngs (eds), *Globalization: Theory and Practice*. London, Pinter: 43–57.

Scholte, J. A. (1997) 'The Globalization of World Politics', in J. Baylis and S. Smith (eds), *The Globalization of World Politics*. Oxford, Oxford University Press: 13–30.

Schubert, E. S. (1988) 'Innovations, debts and bubbles: international integration of financial markets in western Europe, 1688–1720', *Journal of Economic History* 48 (2): 299–306.

Schumpeter, J. (1950) *Capitalism, Socialism and Democracy*. New York, Harper & Row (3rd edn).

Schwartz, H. (1994) *States versus Markets: History, Geography, and the Development of the International Political Economy*. New York, St Martin's Press.

Seagrave, S. (1995) *Lords of the Rim: The Invisible Empire of the Overseas Chinese*. London, Bantam.

Servan-Schreiber, J.-J. (1968) *The American Challenge*. London, Hamish Hamilton.

Shapiro, M. (1996) 'Introduction', in M. Shapiro and H. Alker (eds), *Challenging Boundaries: Global Flows, Territorial Identities*. Minneapolis, University of Minnesota Press: xv–xxiii.

Sharp, M. (1997) 'Technology, Globalization and Industrial Policy', in M. Talalay, C. Farrands and R. Tooze (eds), *Technology, Culture and Competitiveness: Change and the World Political Economy*. London, Routledge: 90–106.

Shaw, M. (1992) 'Global Society and Global Responsiblity: The Theoretical, Analytical and Practical Limits of International Society?', *Millennium* 21 (3): 421–34.

Shaw, M. (1994) *Global Society and International Relations: Sociological Concepts and Political Perspectives*. Cambridge, Polity Press.

Shelley, F. (1993) 'Political Geography, the New World Order and the City', *Urban Geography* 14 (6): 557–67.

Simon, D. F. (1995a) *Corporate Strategies in the Pacific Rim: Global versus Regional Trends*. London, Routledge.

Simon, D. F. (ed.) (1997) *Techno-Security in an Age of Globalization*. Armonk, NY, M.E. Sharpe.

Sinclair, T. J. (1992) 'Competitiveness Strategies and Industrial Governance in the Era of the Global Political Economy', *Problématique: A Journal of Political Studies* 2: 72–94.

Sinclair, T. J. (1994) 'Between State and Market: Hegemony and Institutions of Collective Action Under Conditions of International Capital Mobility', *Policy Sciences* 27 (4): 447–66.

Sinclair, J. T. (1995) 'Guarding the Gates of Capital: Credit Rating Processes and the Global Political Economy', Unpublished doctoral dissertation, Department of Political Science. Toronto, York University.

Sinclair, T. J. (1997) *Global Governance and the International Political Economy of the Commonplace.* Annual Meeting of the International Studies Association, Toronto.

Singer, M. and A. Wildavsky (1993) *The Real World Order: Zones of Peace/Zones of Turmoil.* Chatham, NJ, Chatham House.

Skinner, Q. (1996) *Thomas Hobbes.* Cambridge, Cambridge University Press.

Sklair, L. (1991) *Sociology of the Global System.* Hemel Hempstead, Harvester Wheatsheaf.

Skocpol, T. (1979) *States and Social Revolutions.* Cambridge, Cambridge University Press.

Smith, A. D. (1990) 'Towards a Global Culture?', in M. Featherstone (ed.), *Global Culture: Nationalism, Globalization and Modernity.* London, Sage: 171–91.

Smith, A. D. (1994) 'The problem of national identity: ancient, medieval and modern', *Ethnic and Racial Studies* 17 (3): 375–99.

Smith, A. D. (1995) *Nations and Nationalism in a Global Era.* Cambridge, Polity Press.

Smith, A. K. (1991) *Creating a World Economy: Merchant Capital, Colonialism and World Trade, 1400–1825.* Boulder, CO, Westview Press.

Smith, H. (1996) 'The silence of the academics: international social theory, historical materialism and political values', *Review of International Studies* 22 (2): 191–212.

Smith, M. (1992) 'Modernization, Globalization and the Nation-State', in M. Featherstone (ed.), *Global Politics.* Cambridge, Polity: 253–68.

Smith, S. (1992) 'The Forty Years Detour: The Resurgence of Normative Theory in International Relations', *Millennium* **21** (3): 489–506.

Smith, S. (1996) 'Positivism and beyond', in S. Smith, K. Booth and M. Zalewski (eds), *International Theory: Positivism and Beyond.* Cambridge, Cambridge University Press.

Snyder, R., H. W. Bruck, *et al.* (1962) *Foreign Policy Decision-Making.* New York, Free Press.

So, A. and S. Chiu (1996) *World System and East Asia.* London, Sage.

Solow, R. (1957) 'Technological Change and the Aggregate Production Function', *The Review of Economics and Statistics* 39 (3): 312–20.

Spero, J. E. (1985) *The Politics of International Economic Relations.* London, Allen & Unwin (3rd edn).

Spero, J. E. and J. Hart (1997) *The Politics of International Economic Relations.* London, Routledge (5th edn).

Spike Peterson, V. (1996) 'Shifting Ground(s): Epistemological and Territorial Remapping in the Context of Globalization(s)', in E. Kofman and G. Youngs (eds), *Globalisation: Theory and Practice* London, Pinter: 11–28.

Sprout, H. and M. Sprout (1957) 'Environmental Factors in the study of international politics', *Journal of Conflict Resolution* 1: 309–28.

Sprout, H. and M. Sprout (1965) *The Ecological Perspective on Human Affairs, with Special Reference to International Politics.* Princeton, NY, Princeton University Press.

Stern, J. D. (1964) 'The National Debt and the Peril Point', *The Atlantic Monthly* (January).

Steven, R. (1990) *Japan's New Imperialism*. London, Macmillan.

Stevenson, N. (1995) *Understanding Media Cultures: Social Theory and Mass Communication*. London, Sage.

Stone, D. (1996) *Capturing the Political Imagination: Think Tanks and the Policy Process*. London, Cassell.

Stopford, J. and S. Strange (1991) *Rival States, Rival Firms: Competition for World Market Shares*. Cambridge, Cambridge University Press.

Strange, S. (1986) *Casino Capitalism*. Oxford, Basil Blackwell.

Strange, S. (1988) *States and Markets*. London, Pinter.

Strange, S. (1995) 'The Limits of Politics', *Government and Opposition* 30 (3): 291–311.

Strange, S. (1996) *The Retreat of the State: The Diffusion of Power in the World Economy*. Cambridge, Cambridge University Press.

Sum, N.-L. (1996b) 'Strategies for East Asia Regionalism and the Construction of NIC Identities in the Post-Cold War Era', in A. Gamble and A. Payne (eds), *Regionalism and World Order*. London, Macmillan: 207–46.

Sum, N.-L. (1996a) '"Greater China" and Global-Regional-Local Dynamics in the Post-Cold War Era', in I. Cook, M. Doel and R. Li. (eds), *Fragmented Asia: Regional Integration and National Disintegration in Pacific Asia*. Aldershot, Avebury: 53–74.

Swedberg, R. (1994) 'Markets as Social Structures', in N. J. Smelser and R. Swedberg (eds), *The Handbook of Economic Sociology*. Princeton, NY, Princeton University Press.

Talalay, M. (1996) 'The Coming Energy Revolution and the Transformation of the International Political Economy: Fuel Cell Technology, Public Policy and Global Power Shifts', *Competition and Change* **1** (4): 333–56.

Taylor, P. (1993) *Political Geography: World Economy, Nation State, Locality*. London, Longman (3rd edn).

Taylor, P. J. (1996) *The Way the Modern World Works: World Hegemony to World Impasse*. Chichester, John Wiley.

Thomas, K. P. and T. J. Sinclair (eds) (forthcoming) *Structure and Agency in International Capital Mobility*. London and New York, Macmillan and St Martin's Press.

Thompson, E. P. (1978) *The Poverty of Theory and Other Essays*. London, Monthly Review Press.

Thompson, K. W. (1992) *Traditions and Values in Politics and Diplomacy*. Louisiana, Louisiana State University Press.

Thorndike, T. (1978) 'The revolutionary approach: the Marxist perspective', in T. Taylor (ed.), *Approaches and Theory in International Relations*. London, Longman: 54–99.

Tilly, C. (1992) *Coercion, Capital and European States, A.D. 990–1992*. Oxford, Basil Blackwell.

Tokunaga, S. (ed.) (1992) *Japan's Foreign Investment and Asian Economic Interdependence: Production, Trade and Financial Systems*. Tokyo, University of Tokyo Press.

Tomlinson, J. (1991) *Cultural Imperialism*. London, Pinter.

Tönnies, F. (1887/1957) *Community and Association (*originally published as *Gemeinschaft und Gesellschaft)* East Lansing, Michigan State University Press.
Tool, M. (1994) 'Institutional adjustment and instrumental value', *Review of International Political Economy* 1 (3): 405–44.
Tuchman, B. (1962) *The Guns of August.* New York, Macmillan.
UNCTAD (1995) *World Investment Report 1995.* New York, UN.
Unger, D. (1993) 'Japan's Capital Exports: Molding East Asia', in D. Unger and P. Blackburn (eds), *Japan's Emerging Global Role.* Boulder, CO, Lynne Rienner: 155–70.
van der Pijl, K. (1984) *The Making of an Atlantic Ruling Class.* London, Verso.
van der Pijl, K. (1994) 'The Cadre Class and Public Multilateralism', in Y. Sakamoto (ed.), Tokyo, *Global Transformation: Challenges to the State System.* United Nations University Press.
Vasquez, J. (1983) *The Power of Power Politics.* London, Pinter.
Vasquez, J. (1993) *The War Puzzle.* Cambridge, Cambridge University Press.
Vasquez, J. (1995) 'The Post-Positivist Debate: Reconstructing Scientific Enquiry and International Relations Theory After Enlightenment's Fall', in K. Booth and S. Smith (eds), *International Relations Theory.* Cambridge, Polity Press.
Vico, G. (1968) *The New Science of Giambattista Vico,* trans. T. G. Bergin and M. H. Fisch. Ithaca, NY, Cornell University Press.
Vincent, J. (1981) 'The Hobbesian Tradition in Twentieth Century International Thought', *Millennium* 10 (2): 91–101.
Vogel, D. (1995) *Trading Up: Consumer and Environmental Regulation in a Global Economy.* Cambridge, MA, Harvard University Press.
Vogel, S. K. (1996) *Freer Markets, More Rules: Regulatory Reform in Advanced Industrial Countries.* Ithaca, NY, Cornell University Press.
Vogler, J. (1992) 'Regimes and the Global Commons: Space, Atmosphere and Oceans', in A. McGraw and P. Lewis (eds), *Global Politics.* Cambridge, Polity: 118–37.
Wade, R. (1990) *Governing the Market: Economic Theory and the Role of Government in East Asian Industrialization.* Princeton, NY, Princeton University Press.
Walker, R. B. J. (1988a) *One World; Many Worlds; Struggles for a Just World Peace.* Boulder, CO, Lynne Rienner.
Walker, R. B. J. (1988b) *State Sovereignty, Global Civilization and the Rearticulation of Political Space.* Princeton, NY, Princeton University Center for International Studies.
Walker, R. B. J. (1993) *Inside/Outside: International Relations as Political Theory.* Cambridge, Cambridge University Press.
Wallace, M. and T. Choudhry (1995) 'The gold standard: perfectly integrated world markets or slow adjustment of prices and interest rates?', *Journal of International Money and Finance* 14 (3): 349–71.
Wallerstein, I. (1979) *The Capitalist World-Economy.* Cambridge, Cambridge University Press.
Walsh, E. (1996) 'The Negotiator', *The New Yorker,* 18 March: 86–97.
Walter, A. (1991) *World Power and World Money.* Hemel Hempstead: Harvester Wheatsheaf.
Waltz, K. (1959) *Man, the State and War.* New York, Columbia University Press.

Waltz, K. (1979) *Theory of International Politics*. Reading, MA, Addison-Wesley.

Walzer, M. (1992) *Just and Unjust Wars: A Moral Argument with Historical Illustrations*. New York, Basic Books (2nd edn).

Waters, M. (1995) *Globalization*. London, Routledge.

Weiss, L. and J. M. Hobson (1995) *States and Economic Development: A Comparative Historical Analysis*. Cambridge, Polity Press.

Wendt, A. (1987) 'The Agent-Structure Problem in International Relations Theory', *International Organization* 41 (3): 335–70.

Wendt, A. (1992) 'Anarchy is What States Make of It: The Social Construction of Power Politics', *International Organization* 46 (2): 391–425.

Wendt, A. (1994) 'Collective Identity Formation and the International State', *American Political Science Review* 88 (2): 384–96.

White, J. and A. Wildavsky (1990) *The Deficit and the Public Interest*. Berkeley, University of California Press.

Wight, M. (1946) *Power Politics*. London, RIIA.

Wight, M. (1966) 'Why is there no international theory?', in H. Butterfield and M. Wight (eds), *Diplomatic Investigations: Essays in the Theory of International Politics*. London, Allen & Unwin: 17–34.

Wight, M. (1979) *Power Politics*. Harmondsworth, Penguin.

Wight, M. (1991) *International Theory: The Three Traditions*. Leicester, Leicester University Press.

Wildavsky, A. (1992) *The New Politics of the Budgetary Process*. New York, HarperCollins (2nd edn).

Williams, H. (1992) *International Relations in Political Theory*. Milton Keynes, Open University Press.

Williams, H. (1996) *International Relations and the Limits of Political Theory*. London, Macmillan.

Williams, H., M. Wright and T. Evans (1993) *International Relations and Political Theory*. Milton Keynes, Open University Press.

Williams, M. (1996) 'Rethinking Sovereignty', in E. Kofman and G. Youngs (eds), *Globalisation: Theory and Practice*. London, Pinter: 109–22.

Williamson, O. E. (1975) *Markets and Hierarchies*. New York, Free Press.

Williamson, O. E. (1985) *The Economic Institutions of Capitalism*. New York, Free Press.

Williamson, J. (1994) 'In Search of a Manual for Technopoles', in J. Williamson (ed.), *The Political Economy of Policy Reform*. Washington DC, Institute for International Economics: 11–28.

Winch, D. (1978) *Adam Smith's Politics: An Essay in Historiographic Revision*. Cambridge, Cambridge University Press.

Winch, D. (1996) *Riches and Poverty*. Cambridge, Cambridge University Press.

Wolfers, A. (1956) 'Political Theory and International Relations', in A. Wolfers and L. W. Martin (eds), *The Anglo-American Tradition in Foreign Affairs*. New Haven, Conn., Yale University Press.

Wolfers, A. (1962) *Discord and Collaboration*. Baltimore, MD, Johns Hopkins University Press.

Wolin, S. (1960) *Politics and Vision*. Boston, MA, Little ,Brown.

Womack, J. P., T. J. Daniel, *et al.* (1990) *The Machine that Changed the World*. New York, Macmillan.

Wong, P.-K. (1997) 'The Proliferation of Technology-Based International Strategic Alliances: Contrasting Perspectives', in D. F. Simon (ed.), *Techno-Security in an Age of Globalization*. Armonk, NY, M. E. Sharpe.

Woodward, B. (1994) *The Agenda: Inside the Clinton White House*. New York, Simon & Schuster.

Workman, T. (1996) *Banking on Deception: The Discourse of Fiscal Crisis*. Halifax, Fernwood.

World Bank (1993) *World Development Report 1993*. New York, World Bank/Oxford University Press.

World Bank (1995) *World Development Report 1995*. New York, World Bank/Oxford University Press.

Yeats, A. (1990) 'Do African countries pay more for imports? Yes', *World Bank Economic Review* 4 (1): 1–20.

Zysman, J. (1977) *Political Strategies for Industrial Order: Market, State, and Industry in France*. Berkeley and Los Angeles, University of California Press.

Zysman, J. (1983) *Governments, Markets, and Growth: Financial Systems and the Politics of Industrial Change*. Ithaca, NY, Cornell University Press.

Zysman, J. and L. Tyson (1983) *American Industry in International Competition*. Ithaca, NY, Cornell University Press.

Zysman, J. (1996) 'The Myth of the Global Economy: Enduring National Foundations and Emerging Regional Realities', *New Political Economy* 1 (2): 157–84.

Index